SO-AII-294

THE PRINCETON REVIEW

High School
Math II Review

THE PRINCETON REVIEW

High School Math II Review

BY **DOUG FRENCH**

RANDOM HOUSE, INC.
New York 1998
www.randomhouse.com

Princeton Review Publishing, L.L.C.
2315 Broadway, 3rd Floor
New York, NY 10024
E-mail: info@review.com

Copyright © 1998 by Princeton Review Publishing, L.L.C.

All rights reserved under International and Pan-American Copyright Conventions. Published in the United States by Random House, Inc., New York, and simultaneously in Canada by Random House of Canada Limited, Toronto.

ISBN 0-375-75074-6

Editor: Lesly Atlas
Production Editor: Kristen Azzara
Designer: Illeny Maaza
Production Coordinator: Robert McCormack
Illustrations: The Production Department of The Princeton Review

Manufactured in the United States of America

9 8 7 6 5 4 3 2 1

First Edition

ACKNOWLEDGMENTS

I'm especially grateful to Carl Hostnik and Frank Quinn, two of the best math professors of all time. (When working through really long calculus problems, Mr. Hostnik would routinely write on bulletin boards, walls, and posters when he ran out of space on the blackboard.) They taught me that a math teacher can be completely nuts and still be an outstanding educator.

Thanks to Melanie Sponholz and Evan Schnittman, the powers who got me involved with this project. The rest of The Princeton Review staff, including Lesly Atlas, Amy Zavatto, and Kristen Azzara, all worked very hard in the face of chaos. Thanks also to the PageMakers, Jennifer Arias, Robert "Precious" McCormack, Scott Harris, Adam Hurwitz, Christine Lee, and Iam Williams, who made sure all the diagrams looked good, and to the expert reviewers, Sasha Alcott, Kenneth Butka, Gary King, and Nancy Schneider, who made sure it all made sense.

Thanks to my family (especially Mom, who convinced me that I could sit down long enough to write a book), and to Zsa Zsa, who got me hooked on Tony Packo's pickles.

And most of all, I'd like to thank all the math students I've tutored over the years. There's nothing better than getting a phone call from an ecstatic student who has just aced a final exam.

CONTENTS

INTRODUCTION

In a perfect world, every high school kid would have an older brother or sister around to explain math. Most textbooks are too dull, and let's face it—if you show your dad a graphing calculator, he'll probably try to change channels with it. Many math topics are confusing, and teachers don't always have the time to explain things more thoroughly.

Yep, this is not a perfect world. That's where this book comes in. There are fifteen chapters here, each of which discusses a math subject that just about every high school student has to learn at one point or another. There's also a more hands-on approach to logic (chapter 1) because students usually come in two categories: those who understand logic right away, and those who just don't get it.

No matter how helpful this book may be, though, it can only help you if you're willing to put forth the effort to learn. Here are some helpful hints toward being a better math student.

Learn to use your calculator. Many teachers let you use high-tech graphing calculators. These can be really useful when you have to make complex calculations. If you're uncertain how to make basic calculations, however, you can lose a lot of time during a test. When you first get a new calculator, practice with it and see what it can do.

Use your calculator as a tool, not as a crutch. Problems arise when your first instinct is to reach for your calculator when you have to multiply 3×5. Learn to rely on yourself to calculate the simple stuff. It'll save time, especially because punching in numbers takes time.

Memorize the important formulas. Don't just program them into your calculator. (It takes more time to retrieve them than it would to write them out yourself.) Of course, learning where the formulas came from really helps you remember them.

When a test has answer choices, use Process Of Elimination. One of the best ways to get the right answer is to cross off all the wrong ones. For example, if your answer to a question is $\sqrt{62}$, you should be able to eliminate all the answers that are not between 7 and 8—without having to use your calculator!

Always double-check your algebra. It's easy to make careless mistakes. Therefore, if you solve for a variable, always plug your answer back into the problem and make sure it works (if you have enough time, that is). For example, once you solve for x in the quadratic $x^2 - 5x - 14 = 0$ (the answers are 7 and –2), plug 'em back in:

$$(7)^2 - 5(7) - 14 = 0 \qquad\qquad (-2)^2 - 5(-2) - 14 = 0$$
$$49 - 35 - 14 = 0 \qquad\qquad\qquad 4 + 10 - 14 = 0$$
$$0 = 0. \qquad\qquad\qquad\qquad 0 = 0.$$

Now you know that you're right.

Ask questions. Don't be content simply to sit back and muddle through. Ask for help. Most teachers will accommodate you as best they can. That's why they're there.

If you're still struggling with math, we hope you can use this book as a source of extra help. Do the extra problems, take the sample tests, and check your work. As with most things you try, the work gets easier when you practice.

CHAPTER 1

Logic

Most Course II textbooks start with a unit on logic. It's probably because they want to teach you the challenging stuff early in the year, when your brain is fresh.

This chapter reviews how you can use the basic laws of logic to connect a series of statements to form a logical proof. Once you try a bunch of these, you'll be surprised at how repetitive the process can be.

THE BUILDING BLOCKS

Every proof is a connected series of **statements** that are intended to establish a conclusion. "Pearl Jam sucks" is a statement, but you don't know if it's true or not.

Whether a statement is true or false is the **truth value** of that statement.

In the proofs you write, each statement is represented by a letter (p, for example). The letter can appear in two ways: either as p or $\sim p$. The term $\sim p$ represents the **negation** of the statement p.

Here's the tricky part. A "$\sim$" sign in front of a letter does not mean the term is false. If the original statement p is false, then the statement $\sim p$ is true.

EXAMPLE 1
If R represents the statement "Richard Nixon discovered America," determine the truth value of $\sim R$.

SOLUTION
The statement R is false, because Nixon did not discover America. Therefore, the negation of the statement, $\sim R$, is **true**.

Although this idea might seem a little confusing at first, don't worry. You did most of the work involving truth values in Course I, when you worked with truth tables. (Remember them?) Most of your work with logic in Course II involves putting the statements together, regardless of their truth value.

CONNECTING THE STATEMENTS
When you connect two or more simple statements, the result is a compound statement, or a **connective**. The most common words to use are "and" and "or."

When you connect the statements p and q with "and," the result is the **conjunctive statement** $p \wedge q$. Each of the letters is sometimes referred to as a **conjunct**.

When you connect the statements p and q with "or," the result is the **disjunctive statement** $p \vee q$. Each of the letters is sometimes referred to as a **disjunct**.

If you have trouble remembering which symbol is which, think of this: The "$\wedge$" looks like a capital A, which stands for "and."

EXAMPLE 2
If A represents the statement "Elvis Presley was the American ambassador to Finland" and B represents the statement "Elvis Presley made a bunch of cheesy beach movies," determine the truth value of:

(1) $A \wedge B$; (2) $A \vee B$; and (3) $\sim A \wedge B$.

SOLUTION

Find the truth values of A and B: A is false and B is true. Therefore:

(1) In order for "$A \wedge B$" (which is read "A and B") to be true, both statements have to be true. Since A is false, $A \wedge B$ is also **false**.

(2) In order for "$A \vee B$" to be true, only one of the statements has to be true. Since B is true, $A \vee B$ is also **true**.

(3) Since A is false, the negation of A is true. Therefore, $\sim A \wedge B$ is **true**.

DE MORGAN'S LAWS

Negation of a simple statement is easy: just put a "$\sim$" in front of it. Negating a compound statement is a bit more complicated.

> To negate a conjunction or disjunction, use **De Morgan's Laws:**
>
> $\sim(p \wedge q)$ is logically equivalent to $\sim p \vee \sim q$.
>
> $\sim(p \vee q)$ is logically equivalent to $\sim p \wedge \sim q$.

This basically means than when you negate a parenthetical statement that has a "$\wedge$" or "$\vee$" symbol in it, negate each letter and flip the symbol.

EXAMPLE 3

What statement is logically equivalent to $\sim(A \vee \sim B)$?

SOLUTION

Negate each letter. $\sim(A)$ becomes $\sim A$, and $\sim(\sim B)$ becomes just plain B (this is true because of the Law of Double Negation, which basically states that two wrongs make a right). After you flip the symbol, the resulting statement is $\sim A \wedge B$.

CONDITIONAL STATEMENTS

Another way to connect two simple statements is to say that one statement leads to another. This is called a conditional statement.

> This **conditional** statement is symbolized as $p \rightarrow q$ and is read "if p, then q." The p is the **antecedent** or **hypothesis**, and the q is the **consequent** or **conclusion**.

There's only one situation in which a conditional statement is false: when the first statement is true and the second one is false. Look at this statement:

"If I stay up all night watching infomercials,
then I will win the Boston Marathon."

If it is true that you did stay up all night watching infomercials, yet you did not win the Boston Marathon, the conditional statement must not be true.

> If p leads to q and q leads to p, you can write what is called a **biconditional** statement, which looks like this: $p \leftrightarrow q$. A biconditional statement is true only if the two statements have the same truth value.

There are two other statements that are related to the simple conditional: the converse and the inverse.

> To form the **converse** of a conditional statement, switch the order of the letters. The converse of $p \rightarrow q$ is $q \rightarrow p$.

> To form the **inverse** of a conditional statement, negate both of the letters. The inverse of $p \rightarrow q$ is $\sim p \rightarrow \sim q$.

The truth value of either of these statements does not necessarily have to be the same as the truth value of original statement $p \rightarrow q$.

EXAMPLE 4
If m represents the statement "Maxine lives in Tulsa, Oklahoma," and n represents "Maxine lives in the United States," determine the truth value of $m \rightarrow n$, as well as (1) the converse of $m \rightarrow n$; and (2) the inverse of $m \rightarrow n$.

SOLUTION
The original conditional is **true**, because if Maxine lives in Tulsa, then she does live in the United States. However, look at the other two statements:

(1) The converse of the statement is $n \rightarrow m$, which stands for: "If Maxine lives in the United States, then Maxine lives in Tulsa, Oklahoma." This is **false**.

(2)   The inverse of the statement is $\sim m \rightarrow \sim n$, which stands for: "If Maxine does *not* live in Tulsa, Oklahoma, then Maxine does *not* live in the United States." This is also **false**.

THE CONTRAPOSITIVE

There is one variation of the conditional statement that always has the same truth value as the original. It's a combination of the converse and the inverse.

> To form the **contrapositive** of a conditional statement, reverse the order of the letters and negate each letter. The contrapositive of $p \rightarrow q$ is $\sim q \rightarrow \sim p$.

For example, let C represent "I study hard" and D represent "I will pass the Chem final." The conditional statement certainly makes logical sense:

"If I study hard, then I will pass my Chem final."

The contrapositive of this statement is also true:

"If I *didn't* pass my Chem final, then I *didn't* study hard."

Since each conditional statement and its contrapositive are always logically equivalent, your textbook might refer to the contrapositive as the **Law of Contrapositive Inference**. That's because if $A \rightarrow B$ is true, you can *infer* that $\sim B \rightarrow \sim A$ is also true.

OTHER INFERENCES

Logical proofs take shape when you look at two or more statements, or **premises**, and infer what else must therefore be true. You can *infer* something if you're sure it's true. For example, if your teacher has a number in mind and he or she tells you that the number is not even, you can infer that the number is odd.

In that inference, you just used the **Law of Disjunctive Inference**, which looks like this:

Premise 1: $f \vee g$ (Either f or g is true.)

Premise 2: $\sim f$ (The negation of f is true, or f is false.)

Conclusion: g ($\therefore$ g must be true.)

You can also write the law in the conditional format like this:

$$[(f \vee g) \wedge \sim f] \rightarrow g$$

Note that the first two premises are combined merely by adding an "and" symbol.

Look back at the example above. You know that all numbers are either even or odd. If E represents "The number is even" and O represents "The number is odd," then your first premise is $E \vee O$. The second premise states that the first statement is false: The number is not even, so you can symbolize it as $\sim E$. The conclusion, therefore, is O. The final statement looks like this:

$$[E \vee O) \wedge \sim E] \rightarrow O$$

Many of the following logistic inferences are rather obvious if you use your common sense. The key is memorizing the official names of everything so you can write proofs.

If a conjunctive statement (an "and" statement) is true, then both parts of the statement are true. This is known as the **Law of Conjunctive Simplification**, and it's written like this:

$$(p \wedge q) \rightarrow p; \qquad (p \wedge q) \rightarrow q$$

Another common inference is the **Chain Rule**, which can also be referred to as the **Law of the Syllogism**:

> Premise 1: $f \rightarrow g$
>
> Premise 2: $g \rightarrow h$
>
> Conclusion: $f \rightarrow h$.

Makes sense, doesn't it?

The **Law of Detachment**, or *Modus Ponens*, follows a similarly obvious line of reasoning:

$$[(f \rightarrow g) \wedge f] \rightarrow g$$

If f leads to g, and f is true, then g must be true.

The other *modus* inference is the **Law of *Modus Tollens***:

$$[(f \rightarrow g) \wedge \sim g] \rightarrow \sim f$$

For those of you who may not have studied this rule in school, look at it this way: The Law of *Modus Tollens* is a combination of the Contrapositive and the Law of Detachment.

The contrapositive: $f \rightarrow g$ becomes $\sim g \rightarrow \sim f$.

The Law of Detachment: if $\sim g \rightarrow \sim f$ and $\sim g$, then $\sim f$.

EXERCISES, SET 1A

Those are the laws of logic that you'll use to construct logical proofs in the next part of this chapter. Before you move on to that, though, try these exercises. The answers are in chapter 16.

1. Identify the law of reasoning that can be used to justify each conclusion.
   (a) $[(f \rightarrow g) \wedge \sim g] \rightarrow \sim f$
   (b) $\sim(p \wedge q) \leftrightarrow \sim p \vee \sim q$
   (c) If $p \rightarrow q$, then $\sim q \rightarrow \sim p$.
   (d) $[(f \vee g) \wedge \sim f] \rightarrow g$
   (e) If $a \rightarrow b$ and $b \rightarrow c$, then $a \rightarrow c$.

2. Which of the following is logically equivalent to $\sim(a \wedge \sim b)$? Why?
   (1) $\sim a \wedge b$ (3) $\sim a \vee \sim b$
   (2) $\sim a \vee b$ (4) $a \wedge b$

3. If $d \vee e$ and $\sim d$ is true, what can you infer? Why?
   (1) e (3) $e \rightarrow d$
   (2) $\sim e$ (4) d

4. If $e \rightarrow f$ and $\sim f$ is true, what can you infer? Why?
   (1) e (3) f
   (2) $\sim e$ (4) $f \rightarrow e$

5. "If Garvin gets one more parking ticket, then he'll lose his driver's license" is logically equivalent to which of the following?
   (1) If Garvin didn't lose his driver's license, then he didn't get a parking ticket.
   (2) If Garvin lost his driver's license, then he must have gotten another parking ticket.
   (3) If Garvin does not get one more parking ticket, then he won't lose his driver's license.
   (4) If Garvin loses his driver's license, then he will get another parking ticket.

6. If $\sim m \to \sim n$ and $m \to p$, what can you infer? Why?

   (1) $m \to n$ **(3)** $p \to m$

   (2) $p \to n$ **(4)** $n \to p$

7. Given the statements "Lorraine bought a CD player" and "If Lorraine didn't work last weekend, she did not buy a CD player," what can you infer? Why?

   (1) Lorraine worked last weekend.

   (2) Lorraine did not work last weekend.

   (3) Lorraine did not buy a CD player.

   (4) If Lorraine works weekends, she buys a CD player.

8. Which of the following is logically equivalent to $(r \wedge s) \to \sim t$? Why?

   (1) $t \to (r \wedge s)$

   (2) $t \to (\sim r \wedge \sim s)$

   (3) $t \to (\sim r \vee \sim s)$

   (4) $t \to (r \vee s)$

9. **(a)** If the statement "I will get a haircut only if I get married or I join the Army" is true, which of the following is the proper symbolization of the statement?

   (1) $H \to (M \vee A)$ **(3)** $(M \wedge A) \to H$

   (2) $H \to (M \wedge A)$ **(4)** $(M \vee A) \to H$

   (b) If I didn't get a haircut, what must be true? Why?

   (1) $\sim M \wedge \sim A$ **(3)** $\sim M \vee A$

   (2) $M \wedge \sim A$ **(4)** $M \wedge A$

   (c) Which of the following is the inverse of the statement $M \to A$?

   (1) $A \to M$ **(3)** $\sim M \to \sim A$

   (2) $\sim A \to \sim M$ **(4)** $M \to \sim A$

   (d) Which of the following is the converse of the statement $M \to A$?

   (1) $A \to M$ **(3)** $\sim M \to \sim A$

   (2) $\sim A \to \sim M$ **(4)** $M \to \sim A$

10. If a valid conclusion exists for any of the following, state it and the reason why. Otherwise, write "Nope."

(a) $A \rightarrow B$; ~A

(b) ~$C \lor D$; ~D

(c) ~$E \rightarrow$ ~F; F

(d) $G \land H$; G

(e) $I \rightarrow J$; I

(f) $K \rightarrow$ ~L; ~L

(g) ~$M \lor$ ~N; ~M

(h) $O \rightarrow P$; $Q \rightarrow P$

(i) $R \rightarrow S$; $S \rightarrow T$

(j) ~$(X \land Z)$; Z

CONSTRUCTING TWO-COLUMN PROOFS

Now it's time to put it all together and create more complicated proofs that require more than one or two steps. When you write a proof in standard two-column format, you write each logistic step on the left side (labeled "Statements") and the reason for that step on the right side (labeled "Reasons"). You'll get a feel for the format as we go along.

Here's an example of a more complex proof:

EXAMPLE 5

Given: $c \rightarrow$ ~b Prove: a

$a \lor b$

c

SOLUTION

The place to start is the simple statement c, which asserts that c is true. Now, find another statement that involves c so you can combine them. The only other statement with a c is $c \rightarrow$ ~b. Since c is true and c leads to ~b, you can infer that ~b is true by reason of the Law of Detachment.

Since ~b is true, the truth value of b itself must be false. Combine this thought with the third statement, $a \lor b$, which is presented as true. Thus, either a is true or b is true. We know b is false, so a must be true because of the Law of Disjunctive Inference.

This is the last time you'll see a proof in this boring, text-heavy form. The proof in two-column format looks like this:

Statements	Reasons
1. $c \rightarrow \sim b$; c	1. Given
2. $\sim b$	2. Law of Detachment
3. $a \vee b$	3. Given
4. a	4. Law of Disjunctive Inference (2, 3)*

*Note: If a new statement relies on specific statements in your proof, you should refer to them in parentheses in the Reasons column. In this case, for example, statement 4 used the information in statements 2 and 3.

EXAMPLE 6

Given: $M \rightarrow E$ Prove: P
$M \vee P$
$\sim E$

SOLUTION:

Statements	Reasons
1. $M \rightarrow E$ $\sim E$	1. Given
2. $\sim M$	2. Law of *Modus Tollens*
3. $M \vee P$	3. Given
4. P	4. Law of Disjunctive Inference (2, 3)

Sometimes the proofs are in text form, and you have to do the symbolizing yourself.

EXAMPLE 7

Given: If Gordon sets a new sales record, then he will get a promotion.
If Gordon wins the lottery and gets a promotion, then he will buy a new car.
Gordon sets a new sales record.
Gordon does not buy a new car.

What conclusion can you draw from this information?

(a) Gordon does not get a promotion.

(b) Gordon wins the lottery.

(c) Gordon does not win the lottery.

(d) Gordon buys a new car.

SOLUTION

Symbolize the clues (textbooks usually provide the letters symbols, but you have to connect them):

Let S represent "Gordon sets a new sales record."

Let P represent "Gordon gets a promotion."

Let L represent "Gordon wins the lottery."

Let B represent "Gordon buys a new car."

If Gordon sets a new sales record, then he will get a promotion. $S \rightarrow P$

If Gordon wins the lottery and gets a promotion, then he will buy a new car. $(L \wedge P) \rightarrow B$

Gordon sets a new sales record.　S

Gordon does not buy a new car.　$\sim B$

Statements	Reasons
1. $S \rightarrow P$ S	1. Given
2. P	2. Law of Detachment
3. $(L \wedge P) \rightarrow B$ $\sim B$	3. Given
4. $\sim(L \wedge P)$	4. Law of *Modus Tollens*
5. $\sim L \wedge \sim P$	5. De Morgan's Law
6. $\sim L$	6. Law of Disjunctive Inference (2,5)

The conclusive statement is the negation of L, which means that Gordon does not win the lottery. The correct answer is **(c)**.

EXERCISES, SET 1B

Write a two-column proof for each of the following. The answers are in Chapter 16.

1. Given: $M \vee \sim N$ Prove: M
$L \rightarrow N$
L

2. Given: $E \rightarrow F$ Prove: G
$\sim G \rightarrow \sim F$
E

3. Given: $d \rightarrow \sim e$ Prove: $\sim d$
$c \vee e$
$\sim c$

4. Use the Chain Rule on the following proof.
Given: $A \rightarrow \sim C$ Prove: $\sim D$
$A \vee B$
$D \rightarrow C$
$\sim B$

5. Fill in the missing reasons in the following proof.
Given: $A \vee B$ Prove: A
$B \rightarrow C$
$\sim D \rightarrow \sim C$
$\sim D$

Statements	Reasons
1. $\sim D \rightarrow \sim C;\ \sim D$	1.
2. $\sim C$	2.
3. $B \rightarrow C$	3.
4. $\sim B$	4.
5. $A \vee B$	5.
6. A	6.

6. Fill in the missing statements in the following proof.

Given: $(A \wedge \sim B) \rightarrow C$ Prove: F
A
$B \rightarrow F$
$\sim C$

Statements	Reasons
1.	1. Given
2.	2. Law of Contrapositive Inference (1)
3.	3. Given
4.	4. Law of Detachment (2,3)
5.	5. De Morgan's Law (4)
6.	6. Given
7.	7. Law of Disjunctive Inference (5,6)
8.	8. Given
9.	9. Law of Detachment (7,8)

Note: The Law of Modus Tollens was deliberately not used.

7. **Given:** If Jerome goes to Florida, then he'll get a sunburn.
During his spring break, Jerome will either go to Maine or he will go to Florida.
If Jerome gets a sunburn, he will not enter the back-slapping contest when he gets home.
Jerome entered the back-slapping contest.

Let F represent "Jerome goes to Florida."
Let S represent "Jerome gets a sunburn."
Let M represent "Jerome goes to Maine."
Let B represent "Jerome enters a back-slapping contest."

Prove: Jerome went to Maine.

8. **Given:** It is not true that Evan brushes his teeth and that he flosses.
If Evan doesn't floss, then his teeth will rot.
If Evan's teeth rot, then he won't ever eat corn on the cob again.
Evan brushes his teeth.

Let B represent "Evan brushes his teeth."
Let F represent "Evan flosses."
Let R represent "Evan's teeth will rot."
Let C represent "Evan eats corn on the cob."

Prove: Evan never eats corn on the cob again.

9. **Given:** Either I write my paper, or I don't go see a movie.
If the show is not sold out, then I go see a movie.
If the show is sold out, then Tom Hanks is in it.
Tom Hanks is not in the movie.

Let P represent "I write my paper."
Let M represent "I see a movie."
Let S represent "The show is sold out."
Let T represent "Tom Hanks is in the movie."

Prove: I wrote my paper.

10. **Given:** If the world ends, then I will never buy a Volvo.
If Sonny is president and Cher wins an Academy Award, then the world will end.
Cher wins an Academy Award.
I buy a Volvo.

Let W represent "The world ends."
Let V represent "I buy a Volvo."
Let S represent "Sonny is president."
Let C represent "Cher wins an Academy Award."

Prove: Sonny is not president.

2

Mathematical Systems

Before we move on to the nitty-gritty of this chapter, let's do a little review of numbers and sets.

SETS AND ELEMENTS

A **set** is a bunch of objects, which are called **elements** of that set. A set of elements is usually denoted by {brackets}. If set S consists of all perfect squares less than 50, it looks like this:

$$S = \{1, 4, 9, 16, 25, 36, 49\}$$

If set $T = \{4, 9, 36\}$, then set T is a **subset** of set S because each element in set T is also in set S.

A set with a specific number of elements is **finite**, and a set that goes on forever (such as the set of all integers) is an **infinite** set. An infinite set is usually denoted by an ellipsis (three dots). For example, if set E is the set of all positive even integers, then:

$$\text{Set } E = \{2, 4, 6, 8, 10...\}$$

A number that can be expressed as the quotient of two integers is known as a **rational number**. Other numbers, such as $\sqrt{3}$ and π, that can't be expressed as one integer divided by another are **irrational numbers**. (You may have seen π expressed as $\frac{22}{7}$, but that's only an approximation. In actuality, there are graduate math students who are expanding π to a trillion bazillion decimal points. The reason why is anybody's guess.)

Most of the work in this chapter deals with finite sets of rational numbers (or symbols) and how they react when they undergo an operation.

OPERATIONS

An **operation** occurs when you make a calculation involving two or more numbers. When you calculate $2 + 3$, for example, you're putting 2 and 3 through the operation of addition. Most operations you'll come across will be **binary operations**, because they'll involve only two numbers at a time.

EXAMPLE 1
What is the value of the binary operation 2×3?

SOLUTION
Since you recognize the "$\times$" as the symbol for multiplication, you can multiply 2 and 3 and come up with **6**.

EXAMPLE 2
If the operation $a \oplus b = a^2 - b$, what is the value of $2 \oplus 3$?

SOLUTION
The symbol "$\oplus$" means nothing in standard math, so the operation has to be defined for you. Once you know the process, just plug in $a = 2$ and $b = 3$:

$$\begin{aligned}
2 \oplus 3 &= 2^2 - 3 \\
&= 4 - 3 \\
&= 1
\end{aligned}$$

Making up these weird symbols is a common scare tactic. Students see a symbol they don't recognize and panic. If this happens to you, relax. Any goofy symbol has to be defined in the problem somewhere so you'll know what to do.

OPERATIONS TABLES

The idea of the weird symbol goes a step further in an **operations table**, which shows you what happens when every member of a certain set of numbers undergoes an operation.

Let's look at the operations table that defines the above operation "⊕" for the set of numbers {1, 2, 3}. Notice that we've filled in the answer to Example 2:

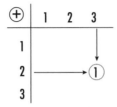

See how that works? You find 2 in the left-hand column and run your finger along that row until you get to the column headed by 3. The result is 1.

Whenever you work with an operations table, always start on the left and work your way to the right.

Here's the rest of the table:

⊕	1	2	3
1	0	−1	−2
2	3	2	1
3	8	7	6

What is the value of 3 ⊕ 3? The table tells you that 3 ⊕ 3 = **6**. Even if you didn't know what the operation means, you still can find the value just by looking at the table.

That's why the operation is almost never defined when you're working with a table. There's no reason to define it.

EXAMPLE 3

Given the table below, find the value of 4 ♪ 6.

♪	3	4	5	6
3	5	2	3	9
4	1	8	5	4
5	3	6	7	1
6	2	4	3	2

SOLUTION

Find the 4 in the left column and see where that row intersects with the 6 column. The value of 4 ♪ 6 is **4**.

♪	3	4	5	6
3	5	2	3	9
4	1	8	5	④
5	3	6	7	1
6	2	4	3	2

See? You have no idea what the " ♪ " means, and it doesn't even matter. You can still get the right answer.

Since the actual operation within a table is unimportant, the numbers in the table don't really matter that much, either. Sometimes, in fact, there aren't any numbers at all; there's only a bunch of letters.

EXAMPLE 4

Given the table below, (1) find the value of $J \oslash H$; and (2) find the value of x if $x \oslash G = F$.

⊘	F	G	H	J
F	G	F	J	H
G	H	G	J	K
H	J	F	H	G
J	F	K	F	G

SOLUTION

(1) The value of $J \oslash H = F$.

(2) The operation of x and G results in F. Look at the column headed by G and see where the F is:

⊘	F	G	H	J
F	G	F	J	H
G	H	G	J	K
H	J	ⓕ	H	G
J	F	K	F	G

As you can see, $H \oslash G = F$, so $x = H$.

Once you learn to read an operations table, the nuts and bolts of the operation aren't worth worrying about that much.

COMPLEX CALCULATIONS

When you see calculations in parentheses, the rules of PEMDAS apply. Do the stuff in the parentheses first.

EXAMPLE 5

Given the table in Example 4, find the value of $F \oslash (G \oslash H)$.

SOLUTION

Work the operation in the parentheses first: $(G \oslash H) = J$. Now, the expression looks like this:

$$F \oslash (G \oslash H) =$$

$$F \oslash J.$$

You can solve this one normally; $F \oslash J = H$. Therefore, the value of $F \oslash (G \oslash H) = \mathbf{H}$.

CLOSURE

If the outcome of any binary operation within a certain set is an element of that set, the operation is **closed**. For example, the set of all integers is closed under addition, because when you add any two integers, you'll get another integer.

The same rule applies to an operations table, only it's a bit easier to figure out.

If there are no new letters or numbers in the grid, the operation is **closed**.

EXAMPLE 6

Is the operation $\ast$ below closed for the set $\{B, A, R, F\}$?

$\ast$	B	A	R	F
B	A	B	R	B
A	B	A	R	F
R	F	F	B	A
F	X	A	F	R

SOLUTION

The operation pertains only to the elements *B*, *A*, *R*, and *F*. Yet, there's an *X* in the grid. Therefore, the operation is **not closed**.

EXERCISES, SET 2A

Before we go any further, use these exercises to lock in what we've discussed so far. The answers are in chapter 16.

1. How many elements does each of the following sets have?
   (a) All even integers between 5 and 17.
   (b) All odd integers between 5 and 17.
   (c) All even integers.
   (d) All even prime integers.
   (e) All fish that have been elected prime minister of Iceland.
   (f) All values of *b* that satisfy the equation $b^2 = 36$.
   (g) All integral values of *b* that satisfy the equation $b^2 < 36$.
   (h) All continental U.S. states that border the Pacific Ocean.
   (i) All U.S. states that begin with "O."
   (j) All U.S. states that begin with "O" and border on the Pacific Ocean.

2. Which of the sets in Question 1 are subsets of other sets in Question 1?

3. If $m \,()\, n = \dfrac{m - 2n}{m^2}$, find the value of the following.
   (a) $1 \,()\, 2$
   (b) $-3 \,()\, 4$
   (c) $\dfrac{1}{2} \,()\, \dfrac{1}{2}$
   (d) $0 \,()\, 500$
   (e) $m \,()\, m$

4.

?	3	4	5	6
3	2	3	5	1
4	6	5	4	2
5	3	1	3	2
6	6	4	2	5

Find the following:

(a) 3 ? 3

(b) 3 ? 4

(c) 4 ? 3

(d) 6 ? 4

(e) 4 ? 5

(f) Is the operation closed for elements {3, 4, 5, 6}?

5.

♠	S	C	R	U	B
S	R	B	U	S	C
C	B	S	S	C	R
R	U	S	B	R	U
U	S	C	R	U	B
B	C	R	U	B	S

Find the following:

(a) $C \spadesuit R$

(b) $U \spadesuit R$

(c) $R \spadesuit U$

(d) $(S \spadesuit R) \spadesuit C$

(e) $S \spadesuit (R \spadesuit C)$

(f) $(B \spadesuit S) \spadesuit (U \spadesuit S)$

(g) Is the operation closed for the elements {S, C, R, U, B}?

THE IDENTITY AND THE INVERSE

There are a few other characteristics of an operation that you should know. The first is how to find the identity element of an operation.

You've probably heard the term "identity element" before when you learned about basic arithmetic. The identity element for addition is 0, because if you add 0 to any number, that number remains the same: $a + 0 = a$, and $0 + a = a$. For the same reason, the identity element for multiplication is 1.

> The **identity element** of an operation is the element that doesn't change any other element that it comes in contact with.

♦	B	O	A	R
B	O	R	O	B
A	R	A	B	O
A	O	B	R	A
R	B	O	A	R

The identity element of the operation ♦ is R because the elements in the column headed by R are the same as those in the left-most column. Similarly, the elements in the row for R are the same as those in the row at the top.

For example, B ♦ $R = B$ and R ♦ $B = B$.

You've probably heard about the **inverse** of an operation as well. In a binary operation, a number and its inverse produce the identity element. Remember that the additive identity is 0? Well, the inverse of a is $-a$, because $a + (-a) = 0$. The multiplicative inverse of a is $\frac{1}{a}$, because $a \times \frac{1}{a} = 1$.

> When an element of an operation is coupled with its **inverse** within that operation, the result is the identity element.

In the operation ◆, we've already determined that the identity element is R. To find the inverse of O, for example, find O in the left-most column and run your finger along that row until you find R. Therefore, the inverse of O is B because O ◆ B = R and B ◆ O = R.

◆	B	O	A	R
B	O	R	O	B
O	R	A	B	O
A	O	B	R	A
R	B	O	A	R

EXAMPLE 7

Using the diagram below, (1) find the identity element of the operation O and (2) find the inverse of W.

O	S	T	E	W
S	E	S	W	T
T	S	T	E	W
E	W	E	T	S
W	T	W	S	E

SOLUTION

(1) The identity element of the operation is T, because the T column is the same as the left column.

(2) To find the inverse of W, set up the equation $W \, O \, x = T$. Find the W in the left column and run along that row until you find T. You'll find it in the S column:

O	S	T	E	W
S	E	S	W	T
T	S	T	E	W
E	W	E	T	S
W	T	W	S	E

From the diagram you can see that $W \, O \, S = T$. Therefore, $x = S$ and the inverse of W is S.

THE COMMUTATIVE PROPERTY

The last property that we'll discuss that pertains to operations tables is commutativity. You've seen the commutative property before.

> A binary operation is **commutative** if you get the same result regardless of the order of the elements.

For example, the operation of addition is commutative because 3 + 4 = 4 + 3. You can switch the order of the elements, but the result is the same (7).

Let's look at an operations table for addition. There's an easy test to determine whether an operation is commutative. It involves drawing a diagonal line from the upper left element to the lower right element of the grid, like this:

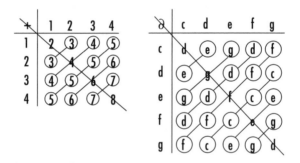

Both the addition table on the left and the unknown operation on the right are commutative, because the elements are symmetrical across that line. You can always double-check your findings by working with a couple of elements. Let's look at the table on the right:

$$e \, \partial \, f = c, \text{ and } f \, \partial \, e = c.$$

OTHER PROPERTIES

There are other properties that your teacher might ask you to study, such as the associative and distributive properties. These properties also have not changed since you first learned them, but there's no cool way to test for them. You have to test the properties by using the elements in the operation and seeing whether they work.

EXERCISES, SET 2B

Here's a review of all the stuff in this chapter. The answers are in chapter 16.

1.

$$
\begin{array}{c|cccc}
+ & -2 & 0 & 2 & 4 \\
\hline
-2 & -4 & -2 & 0 & 2 \\
0 & -2 & 0 & 2 & 4 \\
2 & 0 & 2 & 4 & 6 \\
4 & 2 & 4 & 6 & 8 \\
\end{array}
$$

(a) What is the identity element of the operation +?

(b) What is the inverse of 2 under the operation +?

(c) Is the operation commutative?

(d) Is the operation associative?

(e) Is the system closed for the set {−2, 0, 2, 4}?

2.

$$
\begin{array}{c|cccc}
\& & 1 & 2 & 3 & 4 \\
\hline
1 & 3 & 3 & 4 & 1 \\
2 & 4 & 2 & 1 & 3 \\
3 & 3 & 4 & 2 & 1 \\
4 & 1 & 2 & 3 & 4 \\
\end{array}
$$

(a) Compute (3 & 4).

(b) Compute (4 & 3).

(c) Is the operation commutative?

(d) Compute (1 & 2) & 3.

(e) Compute 1 & (2 & 3).

(f) Is the operation associative?

(g) Is the system closed for the set {1, 2, 3, 4}?

3.

#	a	b	c	d
a	b	d	a	c
b	d	c	b	a
c	a	b	c	d
d	c	a	d	b

(a) Compute $(a \# a) \# (b \# b)$.

(b) Compute $(a \# b) \# (c \# d)$.

(c) What is the identity element of the operation #?

(d) What is the inverse of a under the operation #?

(e) Is the system commutative?

(f) Solve for x: $b \# x = a$.

(g) Solve for x: $x \# x = b$.

4.

Δ	S	P	A	N	K
S	P	S			S
P		A	K	P	
A	N		P	N	A
N	A		N	K	
K		P		N	K

(a) If the operation Δ is commutative for the set $\{S, P, A, N, K\}$, complete the diagram.

(b) What is the identity element of the operation Δ?

(c) What is the inverse of P under the operation Δ?

(d) Compute $S \, \Delta \, (P \, \Delta \, (A \, \Delta \, (N \, \Delta \, K)))$.

5.

∧	3	5	7
3	3	5	7
5	2	7	3
7	4	6	5

∨	3	5	7
3	5	4	3
5	7	1	6
7	3	5	7

(a) What is the identity element of operation ∧?

(b) What is the identity element of operation ∨?

(c) What is the inverse of 5 under ∧?

(d) What is the inverse of 5 under ∨?

(e) Compute 3 ∧ (3 ∨ 3).

(f) Compute (5 ∨ 3) ∧ (3 ∨ 7).

3

Algebra and Polynomials

Throughout much of your time in high school and college, your success in math will depend a great deal on your proficiency with algebra. This chapter is designed to serve as a review of basic algebraic manipulation, some of which you may have learned in your Sequential I course.

WHAT'S A VARIABLE?

Any letter that you see in an algebraic term or equation is a **variable**, because you don't know what its numerical value is. Until you solve an equation, the variable is an unknown quantity. Any single algebraic term is called a **monomial** (because "mono-" means "one," as in monotonous, monopoly, mononucleosis, etc.).

We won't worry about finding the value of variables until the next chapter. For now, we'll look at the basic ways to add, subtract, multiply, and divide monomials.

COEFFICIENTS AND EXPONENTS

A number directly in front of a variable is called a **coefficient**, and it signifies that you should multiply the variable by that number. For example, $3x$ is the same thing as "three times x." You should know how to add and subtract terms that have the same variable in them:

$$3a + 4a = 7a$$

If you have three apples in one hand and four in the other, you have a total of seven apples (as well as a pair of humongous hands). Similarly, you can add three a's and four a's to get a total of seven a's.

A small number in the upper right corner of a term is an **exponent**, and it signifies that you should multiply the variable by itself a certain number of times. For example, x^3 is the same thing as "x times x times x." The 3 is the exponent, and the x is the **base**.

You can only add and subtract terms with exponents if they're **like terms**; that is, each term has the same variables raised to the same exponents.

$$5m^2 - 3m^2 = 2m^2$$

THE RULES FOR EXPONENTS

There are three pairs of basic rules you should know about the multiplication and division of exponential terms. Here's a recap:

1. Terms with the same base.
$$a^x \cdot a^y = a^{x+y}$$
$$\frac{a^x}{a^y} = a^x \div a^y = a^{x-y}$$

Remember MADS: When you **M**ultiply terms, you **A**dd the exponents; when you **D**ivide terms, you **S**ubtract the exponents.

Sometimes you'll see a term with a **negative exponent**, such as x^{-3}. Assuming that $x \neq 0$, you can create a term with a positive exponent by using reciprocal form: $x^{-3} = \dfrac{1}{x^3}$

2. Multiple bases and/or powers. $(a^x)^y = a^{xy}$
$(ab)^x = a^x b^x$

This last rule helps you make the distinction between the terms $3x^2$ and $(3x)^2$. When an exponent appears outside a set of parentheses, it applies to everything in those parentheses:

$$(3x)^2 = (3x)(3x) = (3^2)(x^2) = 9x^2$$

3. Special cases: $x^1 = x$
$x^0 = 1$

Any number to the first power equals itself, and any non-zero number to the zero power equals one.

MULTIPLYING AND DIVIDING

You can multiply any two monomials together, as long as you multiply each base separately.

EXAMPLE 1

Find the product of $-4a^2b^6$ and $3a^3b$.

SOLUTION

Just pair up the like variables and multiply using the rules above:

$$(-4a^2b^6)(3a^3b) =$$
$$(-4 \cdot 3) \cdot (a^2 \cdot a^3) \cdot (b^6 \cdot b) =$$
$$-12 \cdot a^5 \cdot b^7 = -12a^5b^7$$

Dividing works very much the same way.

EXAMPLE 2
Divide $-15x^2y^5z^3$ by $25x^7y^3z^3$.

SOLUTION

$$\frac{-15x^2y^5z^3}{25x^7y^3z^3} =$$

$$-\left(\frac{15}{25}\right) \cdot \left(\frac{x^2}{x^7}\right) \cdot \left(\frac{y^5}{y^3}\right) \cdot \left(\frac{z^3}{z^3}\right) =$$

$$-\frac{3}{5} \cdot \frac{1}{x^5} \cdot y^2 \cdot 1 = -\frac{3y^2}{5x^5}$$

MORE THAN ONE TERM

Each of the concepts we've discussed about monomials also applies to **polynomials**, which have more than one term. You can only add or subtract like terms, and you can multiply or divide virtually anything.

One common error involves subtraction of compound terms. If one polynomial is subtracted from another, remember that the minus sign applies to *everything* within the parentheses.

EXAMPLE 3
Subtract $2m^2 + 4m - 4$ from $5m^2 - 2m + 3$.

SOLUTION
Write the term after the word "from" first:

$$5m^2 - 2m + 3$$

Then, put the term after the word "subtract" in parentheses and put a minus sign in front of it. Be sure to apply the minus sign accordingly:

$5m^2 - 2m + 3 - (2m^2 + 4m - 4) =$

$5m^2 - 2m + 3 - 2m^2 - 4m + 4 = 3m^2 - 6m + 7$

Another common property is the **distributive property**, which you probably first saw when you were learning arithmetic:

$$a(b + c) = ab + ac$$

This is important to note whenever you multiply or divide polynomials by a single algebraic term.

EXAMPLE 4

What is the product of $3b^2$ and $(2b - c^2)$?

SOLUTION

Be sure to multiply the first term by *both* terms in the polynomial.

$$3b^2(2b - c^2) =$$
$$3b^2(2b) - 3b^2(c^2) = 6b^3 - 3b^2c^2$$

FOIL

A polynomial that contains two terms is called a **binomial**, because the prefix "bi-" means "two" (as in bicycle, bifocals, bicentennial, etc.). When you multiply two binomials, you have to use the FOIL method. **FOIL** is an acronym for "Firsts, Outsides, Insides, Lasts."

EXAMPLE 5

Find the product of $(x - 3)$ and $(x + 5)$.

SOLUTION

Each element has a first term and a last term. Multiply the elements by finding these products:

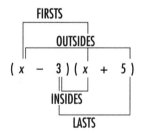

	Firsts	Outsides	Insides	Lasts
$(x - 3)(x + 5)$	$= (x)(x) +$	$(x)(5) +$	$(-3)(x) +$	$(-3)(5)$
	$= x^2 + 5x - 3x - 15$			

After you combine the middle two terms (which are like terms), the product becomes:

$$x^2 + 2x - 15$$

EXERCISES, SET 3A

1. Find the following sums:
   (a) $3a + 5a$
   (b) $3b + b + 5b$
   (c) $4c^2 + 8c + 1 + (2 + 5c^2 + 2c)$
   (d) $d + d^2 + d^3 + d^2 + d$

2. Find the following differences:
   (a) $6a - 2a$
   (b) $5b - 11b$
   (c) $3c - (1 - 2c)$
   (d) $5d^2 - (4d^3 - 2d^2 - 8d) - 5d^3 - d$

3. Find the following products:
   (a) $a \times a^2$
   (b) $b^2 \times (2b^2)^4 \times (5b^3)^2$
   (c) $2c^4(c^2d + 3d^2)$
   (d) $3m^2n^4p \times 2m^5np^3$
   (e) $5x^{-3} \times \dfrac{1}{2x^2}$

4. Find the following quotients:
   (a) $\dfrac{a^8}{a^2}$
   (b) $b^3 \div b^5$
   (c) $\dfrac{-12c^5d^4e^2}{42c^8d^2e^6}$
   (d) $4p^{-4} \div 36p^{-2}$

5. Combine the following:
   (a) $(x - 1)(x - 2)$
   (b) $(x + 3)(x - 7)$
   (c) $(2x + 1)(3x - 4)$
   (d) $(x + 1)(x - 1)(x^2 + 1)$
   (e) $(5x - 2)(5x + 2)$

So far, we've talked a lot about combining terms. Now it's time to reverse the process and turn our attention to breaking them apart.

FACTORING

When you break down a polynomial, the resultant parts are called **factors**. The most basic method of factoring involves finding the greatest common factor of the terms in the polynomial.

EXAMPLE 6

Factor $4x^3 - 16x^2 + 12x$.

SOLUTION

Look at the coefficients first. The greatest number that can be divided evenly into 4, 16, and 12 is **4**. Now look at the variables. The largest power of x that divides evenly into x^3, x^2, and x is x.

Therefore, the greatest common factor of each term in the polynomial is **4x**. Divide each term by $4x$ like this:

$$\frac{4x^3 - 16x^2 + 12x}{4x} =$$

$$\frac{4x^3}{4x} - \frac{16x^2}{4x} + \frac{12x}{4x} =$$

$$x^2 - 4x + 3$$

The factored expression is **4x(x² – 4x + 3)**. Don't forget to put the $4x$ into your final answer.

Whenever you factor an expression, multiply the factors back together to make sure you end up with the original polynomial.

$$4x(x^2 - 4x + 3) =$$
$$4x(x^2) - 4x(4x) + 4x(3) =$$
$$4x^3 - 16x^2 + 12x$$

FACTORING $ax^2 + bx + c$

Everyone comes up against this problem, no matter what math class they take. The challenge is to develop a technique that makes things as easy as possible. The best way to acquire a knack for factoring these **trinomials** (that's right—polynomials with three terms) is to keep practicing until you start seeing the patterns.

Essentially, when you factor a trinomial in the form $ax^2 + bx + c$, you're doing the exact opposite procedure of FOIL.

EXAMPLE 7

Factor $y^2 + 5y + 6$.

SOLUTION

Working backwards, you can start by expressing the term as the product of two binomials:

$$y^2 + 5y + 6 = (y \quad \underline{\quad})(y \quad \underline{\quad})$$

You have to find two numbers to fill in the blanks. Here's a hint: Since there are only plus signs in the trinomial, you know that each factor has a plus sign in it. Therefore, you can add them in:

$$y^2 + 5y + 6 = (y + \underline{\quad})(y + \underline{\quad})$$

Now look at an expanded view of the FOIL diagram from Example 5:

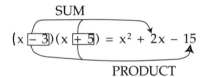

See how the last number, –15, is the product of the two numbers in the binomial factors (5 and –3)? Further, the coefficient of the middle term is 2, which is the sum of 5 and –3.

To fill in the spaces in this example, you have to find two numbers whose product is 6. There are only two sets of possibilities: 1 and 6, or 2 and 3.

From those two sets, which ones can you add to get 5? Only 2 and 3. Therefore, you can place those numbers in the parentheses like this:

$$y^2 + 5y + 6 = (y + 2)(y + 3)$$

Trinomials with two plus signs are the easiest to factor, because there are only plus signs within the two factors. Things get a little trickier when there are minus signs involved.

EXAMPLE 8
Factor $m^2 - 7m - 18$.

SOLUTION
Before you write the trinomial as a product of two binomials, look at the last term, -18. The product of the two numbers in the factors is -18, so one must be positive and the other negative. Therefore, you can write the following:

$$m^2 - 7m - 18 = (m - \underline{})(m + \underline{})$$

The numbers you choose must have a product of -18 and a sum of -7. List the possible pairs of numbers whose product is 18: 1 and 18, 2 and 9, 3 and 6. It looks like there are three possibilities, but there are actually six (because one of the numbers has to be negative). Therefore, the six choices are:

1 and -18	-1 and 18
2 and -9	-2 and 9
3 and -6	-3 and 6

Of these six, only one pair has a sum of -7: 2 and -9. Therefore, the final factorization is $(m + 2)(m - 9)$.

Here's a quick summary of the signs to place in the factors:

Product	Factors
$ax^2 + bx + c$	$(x + \underline{})(x + \underline{})$
$ax^2 - bx + c$	$(x - \underline{})(x - \underline{})$
$ax^2 - bx - c$	$(x + \underline{})(x - \underline{})$

Filling in the right numbers is up to you.

WHEN $a \neq 1$
As you might imagine, this process can get hairy if the coefficient of the first term, a, is not equal to one. Most students get by just with a little trial and error, especially if a is a prime number.

EXAMPLE 9
Factor $3p^2 - 10p - 8$.

SOLUTION
Since the coefficient of the first term is prime, you can write the two factors like this:

$$3p^2 - 10p - 8 = (3p \underline{})(p \underline{})$$

Now you have to list the factors of 8 and try them all until they work. Here's a little trick you can use to make the process a little easier.

If a polynomial is in the form $ax^2 + bx + c$, the sum of the numbers you use in the factors is b, and their product is ac.

In Example 9, $a = 3$, $b = -10$, and $c = -8$. Therefore, the sum of the two missing integers is -10, and their product is $(3)(-8)$, or -24. After a little calculation, you'll find that these numbers are -12 and 2.

Step 1: Replace the middle term $-10p$, using the two new numbers as coefficients: $-12p + 2p$:

$$3p^2 - 10p - 8 = 3p^2 - 12p + 2p - 8$$

Step 2: Pair up the four terms and factor them:

$$(3p - 12p) + (2p - 8) =$$
$$3p(p - 4) + 2(p - 4) =$$

Step 3: Regroup the terms by reversing the distributive property:

$$(3p + 2)(p - 4)$$

Step 4: Check your work by multiplying the factors. Make sure the result is the original trinomial.

$$(3p + 2)(p - 4) = 3p^2 - 12p + 2p - 8$$
$$= 3p^2 - 10p - 8$$

PERFECT SQUARES

If you can recognize that a trinomial is a perfect square, you can save some time. The two formats for perfect squares look like this:

$$(x + y)^2 = (x + y)(x + y) = x^2 + 2xy + y^2$$
$$(x - y)^2 = (x - y)(x - y) = x^2 - 2xy + y^2$$

If you recognize this format, you can save some time when you have to factor.

EXAMPLE 10

Factor $a^2 - 14a + 49$.

SOLUTION

The first term, a^2, is a perfect square. The key is recognizing that the last term is also a perfect square. You can now re-write the problem like this:

$$a^2 - 2(7)a + 7^2$$

The trinomial can therefore be factored down to $(x - 7)(x - 7)$, or $(x - 7)^2$. Whenever you recognize that both the first and last terms of a trinomial are perfect squares, think of the two formulas above.

CONJUGATES

The **conjugate** of the binomial $(x + y)$ is $(x - y)$. To find the conjugate of any binomial, all you do is replace the plus sign with a minus sign, or vice versa.

Let's look at what happens when you use FOIL to multiply a binomial by its conjugate:

$$(x + y)(x - y) = x^2 - xy + xy - y^2$$
$$= x^2 - y^2$$

Notice how the two middle terms always cancel out? This gives us the following formula:

$$(x + y)(x - y) = x^2 - y^2$$

EXAMPLE 11
What is the product of $(c + 4)$ and $(c - 4)$?

SOLUTION
Don't bother with FOIL. Since you're multiplying conjugates, the answer is $c^2 - (4)^2$, or $c^2 - 16$.

The conjugate formula also comes in handy when you're factoring. Just use it in reverse:

$$x^2 - y^2 = (x + y)(x - y)$$

This formula is also known as the **difference of squares**.

EXAMPLE 12
Factor $m^2 - 36$.

SOLUTION
Both m^2 and 36 are perfect squares, so the factors are $(m + 6)$ and $(m - 6)$.

FACTORING COMPLETELY AND SIMPLIFYING

Now it's time to put all this knowledge together and tackle big problems like this one:

$$\frac{2x^3 + x^2 - 6x}{x^2 + 5x} \cdot \frac{x^2 - 2x}{2x^2 - 5x + 3} \div \frac{x^4 - 4x^2}{x^2 + 4x - 5}$$

To simplify this monster, you have to factor each portion of it completely, then cancel out the common factors. Let's look at the numerator of the first term:

$$2x^3 + x^2 - 6x$$

At face value, it doesn't look like anything you've factored before. However, each term has an x in it, so you can factor it out like this:

$$2x^3 + x^2 - 6x = x(2x^2 + x - 6).$$

Now, the trinomial looks like something you can factor. The first coefficient isn't 1, so use the technique we discussed on page 37:

$$a = 2;\ b = 1;\ c = -6$$

The sum of the two numbers you want is 1, and their product is $2(-6)$, or -12. These numbers should be 4 and -3.

$$
\begin{aligned}
2x^2 + x - 6 &= 2x^2 + 4x - 3x - 6 \\
&= 2x(x + 2) - 3(x + 2) \\
&= (2x - 3)(x + 2)
\end{aligned}
$$

The complete factorization looks like this:

$$2x^3 + x^2 - 6x = x(2x - 3)(x + 2)$$

Factor the rest of the polynomials like this:

$$
\begin{aligned}
x^2 + 5x &= x(x + 5) \\
x^2 - 2x &= x(x - 2) \\
2x^2 - 5x + 3 &= (2x - 3)(x - 1) \\
x^4 - 4x^2 &= x^2(x^2 - 4) = x^2(x + 2)(x - 2) \\
x^2 + 4x - 5 &= (x + 5)(x - 1)
\end{aligned}
$$

The expression now looks like this:

$$\frac{x(2x - 3)(x + 2)}{x(x + 5)} \cdot \frac{x(x - 2)}{(2x - 3)(x - 1)} \div \frac{x^2(x + 2)(x - 2)}{(x + 5)(x - 1)}$$

Before you simplify, there's the little matter of the division sign. It's easiest to cancel out like terms when the expression only involves multiplication, so remember the rule:

"When dividing fractions, don't ask why. Just flip the second and multiply."

In this case, flip the last term and add a multiplication sign:

$$\frac{x(2x-3)(x+2)}{x(x+5)} \cdot \frac{x(x-2)}{(2x-3)(x-1)} \cdot \frac{(x+5)(x-1)}{x^2(x+2)(x-2)}$$

Now you can cancel everything that appears both on the top and the bottom:

$$\frac{x(2x-3)(x+2)}{x(x+5)} \cdot \frac{x(x-2)}{(2x-3)(x-1)} \cdot \frac{(x+5)(x-1)}{x^2(x+2)(x-2)} = \frac{1}{x}$$

Simple, right?

As this example illustrates, it's possible for a huge problem to boil down to a simple fraction. The final result won't always be as basic as $\frac{1}{x}$, but you can bet that any problem you see in your textbook will have many common factors that will ultimately disappear. This example is about as complicated as any you'll experience in Course II.

There's one more bit of business to attend to before you try some examples on your own.

ADDING AND SUBTRACTING ALGEBRAIC FRACTIONS

What would you do if you saw this problem? $\frac{1}{4} + \frac{2}{3} =$

As you probably learned before, you can't do anything with this addition problem until the two fractions have the same denominator. The same is true for an algebraic expression like this:

$$\frac{2}{x+3} + \frac{x}{x+2} =$$

The fastest way to simplify this is to multiply both the numerator and denominator of each fraction by the other denominator:

$$\frac{2}{x+3} \cdot \frac{(x+2)}{(x+2)} + \frac{x}{x+2} \cdot \frac{(x+3)}{(x+3)} =$$

$$\frac{2(x+2)}{(x+3)(x+2)} + \frac{x(x+3)}{(x+2)(x+3)} =$$

$$\frac{(2x+4) + x^2 + 3x}{(x+3)(x+2)} = \frac{x^2 + 5x + 4}{(x+3)(x+2)}$$

Notice that it's rarely worth it to use FOIL on the new denominator. Since most problems want you to indicate your response in its most simplified form, it's best to keep the factors separate—especially if you have to cancel some stuff later on.

Once you factor the numerator, the fraction looks like this:

$$\frac{(x+1)(x+4)}{(x+3)(x+2)}$$

Since you can't cancel anything, this is your final answer.

When a problem involves three or more terms, it's a good idea to find the lowest common denominator.

EXAMPLE 13

Simplify the following: $\dfrac{x}{9} - \dfrac{2x+1}{18} + \dfrac{5}{12x}$.

SOLUTION

Find the lowest common denominator of the coefficients in the denominators first: the LCD of 9, 18, and 12 is 36. Since there's only one x involved, the LCD of the expression is $36x$.

In order for the first denominator to equal $36x$, you have to multiply it by $4x$. Whenever you multiply anything by the denominator, you have to do the same to the numerator:

$$\frac{x}{9} \cdot \frac{(4x)}{(4x)} = \frac{4x^2}{36x}.$$

Follow similar instructions on the other two terms:

$$\left[\frac{x}{9} \cdot \frac{(4x)}{(4x)} \right] - \left[\frac{2x+1}{18} \cdot \frac{(2x)}{(2x)} \right] + \left[\frac{5}{12x} \cdot \frac{(3)}{(3)} \right] =$$

$$\frac{4x^2}{36x} - \frac{4x^2 + 2x}{36x} + \frac{15}{36x}$$

Now that all three fractions have the same denominator, you can add or subtract them as you normally would:

$$\frac{4x^2 - (4x^2 + 2x) + 15}{36x}$$

$$= \frac{4x^2 - 4x^2 - 2x + 15}{36x}$$

$$= \frac{-2x + 15}{36x}$$

EXERCISES, SET 3B

Here's some more practice work involving basic algebra. The answers are in chapter 16.

1. Factor the following completely.
   (a) $2x^2 - 8$
   (b) $12y + 2y^2 - 8y^4$
   (c) $x^2 + 2x - 35$
   (d) $2x^2 + 5x + 3$
   (e) $3m^2n^3 - 75m^2n$
   (f) $3x^2y^3 + 12xy^3 + 12y^3$
   (g) $18p^2 - 50q^2$

2. Square the following:
   (a) $n - 2$
   (b) $p + \dfrac{1}{2}$
   (c) $3y - 2z$
   (d) $0.7s + 1.5t$
   (e) $2d^3 - 3e^4$

3. Which of the following is the conjugate of $(2x + 3)$?
   (1) $3 + 2x$
   (2) $2x - 3$
   (3) $3 - 2x$
   (4) $6x$

4. Multiply each of the following by its conjugate.
   (a) $x + 1$
   (b) $3x - 4y$
   (c) $0.5m + 0.2n$
   (d) $\dfrac{d}{3} - \dfrac{1}{e}$
   (e) $3h^2 - 7k^5$

Simplify each of the following.

5. $\dfrac{x^2 + 2x}{x^2 - 2x - 3} \cdot \dfrac{x^2 - 16}{x + 2} \cdot \dfrac{x - 3}{2x^2 - 8x}$

6. $\dfrac{m^2 - 5m + 6}{m^3 + 5m^2} \cdot \dfrac{m^2 + 3m}{m - 2} \div \dfrac{9 - m^2}{m^2 + 5m}$

7. $\dfrac{2y^3 + 6y}{y^2 - 3y - 4} \cdot \dfrac{y^2 - 7y + 12}{y^2 - 9} \cdot \dfrac{y^3 + 2y^2 + y}{y^2 + 3}$

8. $\dfrac{b}{b^3 - 3b^2c} \cdot \dfrac{b^2 - 3bc + 2c^2}{b - c} \div \dfrac{b^2 - 4c^2}{2b^2 - 5bc - 3c^2}$

9. Which of the following is a perfect square?
   (a) $x^2 - 6x + 9$
   (b) $4b^2 + 4b + 4$
   (c) $81z^2 - 18z + 1$
   (d) $25c^4 + 20c^2d + 4d^2$
   (e) $16x^2 + 16xy - 4y^2$
   (f) $m^2n^2 + 2mnpq + p^2q^2$

10. Combine the following.
   (a) $\dfrac{1}{3a} + \dfrac{3}{2a^2}$

   (b) $\dfrac{2c}{7} + \dfrac{c + 1}{c} + \dfrac{4}{c^2}$

   (c) $\dfrac{d + 3}{2d} - \dfrac{4}{d + 1}$

   (d) $\dfrac{m - 2n}{2} + \dfrac{m + n}{m^2} - \dfrac{1}{4m}$

   (e) $2 - \left(\dfrac{v + 2}{5} - \dfrac{v}{v - 3} \right)$

4

Algebraic Equations

The last chapter was an exhaustive review of how to manipulate variables. In this chapter, our chief goal will be to determine the value of those variables. This process is also known as **solving an equation**.

LINEAR EQUATIONS

The most basic equation to solve is a **linear equation**, because these equations contain no exponents. Here's an example:

$$4a + 7 = 15$$

In English, this equation reads, "If you multiply a certain number by 4 and then add 7 to the result, you get 15." To solve for a, you have to undo each step separately and in reverse order. The reverse of "multiply by 4 and then add 7" is "subtract 7, then divide by 4." Don't forget the paramount rule of solving for a variable:

Whatever you do to one side of an equation, you have to do to the other side as well.

$$4a + 7 = 15$$
$$\underline{-7 -7}$$
$$4a = 15$$
$$\frac{4a}{4} = \frac{8}{4}$$
$$a = 2$$

Whenever you solve for a variable, plug that variable back into the original equation to make sure it works:

$$4(\mathbf{2}) + 7 = 15$$
$$8 + 7 = 15$$
$$15 = 15$$

No matter how complicated an equation is, the goal remains the same: put all the variables on one side of the equal sign and all the numerical values on the other.

EXAMPLE 1
Solve for b: $2(b + 5) - 6 = 5(b - 1)$.

SOLUTION
Before you start moving things around, you have to simplify both sides of the equation. Whenever you simplify, remember that the rules of PEMDAS apply—parentheses first:

$$2(b + 5) - 6 = 5(b - 1)$$
$$2b + 10 - 6 = 5b - 5$$
$$2b + 4 = 5b - 5$$
$$2b + 4 - \mathbf{2b} = 5b - 5 - \mathbf{2b}$$
$$4 + \mathbf{5} = 3b - 5 + \mathbf{5}$$
$$9 = 3b$$
$$\frac{9}{3} = \frac{3b}{3}$$
$$\mathbf{3 = b}$$

Now check it:

$$2(3 + 5) - 6 = 5(3 - 1)$$
$$2(8) - 6 = 5(2)$$
$$16 - 6 = 10$$
$$10 = 10$$

FRACTIONAL EQUATIONS

The simplest fractional equations are those in which one fraction equals another. All you have to do is cross-multiply and check.

EXAMPLE 2

Solve for c: $\dfrac{c+4}{6} = \dfrac{c}{4}$.

SOLUTION

To review: If $\dfrac{a}{b} = \dfrac{c}{d}$, then $ad = bc$. This is known as **cross-multiplication**.

$$4(c + 4) = 6c$$
$$4c + 16 = 6c$$
$$16 = 2c$$
$$8 = c$$

It gets a little harder if there are more than two fractions in the equation. If that's the case, you have to find the lowest common denominator of the fractions and multiply.

EXAMPLE 3

Solve for d: $\dfrac{d}{4} + \dfrac{d+2}{6} = \dfrac{d}{3}$.

SOLUTION

The LCD of 4, 6, and 3 is 12. Therefore, you should multiply every term in the equation by 12, like this:

$$(12)\frac{d}{4}+(12)\frac{d+2}{6}=(12)\frac{d}{3}$$
$$3d+2(d+2)=4d$$
$$3d+2d+4=4d$$
$$5d+4=4d$$
$$4=-d$$
$$-4=d$$

This problem worked out rather easily, because the variable was always to the first power. Your calculations can get tougher if the fractions look like this: $\dfrac{e}{6}+\dfrac{e+1}{e}=\dfrac{-1}{2e}$

The LCD of 6, e, and $2e$ is $6e$. When you multiply everything by $6e$, the equation looks like this:

$$(6e)\frac{e}{6}+(6e)\frac{e+1}{e}=(6e)\frac{-1}{2e}$$
$$e^2+6(e+1)=-3$$
$$e^2+6e+6=-3$$
$$e^2+6e+9=0$$

Now, the calculations aren't as simple. You'll see how to solve this in the next portion of this chapter.

EXERCISES, SET 4A

Solve for the variable in each of these problems. The answers are in chapter 16.

1.   **(a)** $2a - 3 = 11$
    (b) $5a - 2 = -22$
    (c) $3 - 4a = 15$
    (d) $38 = 3a + 14$

2.   **(a)** $2(b + 2) = 2$
    (b) $5 - 3(1 + b) = -4$
    (c) $14 + b = 3(b - 2)$
    (d) $7(b + 1) - 2b = 17$

3.   **(a)** $c + 11 = 3c + 1$
    (b) $4(c - 3) - 2(c + 1) = c - 6$
    (c) $-33 = 3(2c - 4) + c$
    (d) $10(c - 3) + 2c = 10(c - 1)$

4.   **(a)** $\dfrac{d-1}{3} = \dfrac{3d}{12}$

    (b) $\dfrac{2d+5}{5d+7} = \dfrac{1}{2}$

    (c) $\dfrac{d-5}{8} = \dfrac{d+4}{3}$

    (d) $\dfrac{5}{2(3d-7)} = -\dfrac{3}{2d}$

5.   **(a)** $3 - \dfrac{e}{4} = 1$

    (b) $\dfrac{e+6}{12} + \dfrac{e}{12} = 1$

    (c) $e + \dfrac{e}{2} = 2e - 3$

    (d) $\dfrac{2(e+1)}{3} - 2 = e - 3$

    (e) $\dfrac{3(e+2) - 2e}{2} = -1 - \dfrac{e+3}{8}$

    (f) $\dfrac{2e}{5} + \dfrac{3e}{4} = e - 1$

QUADRATIC EQUATIONS

An equation in which a variable is squared is called **a quadratic equation**, and the **standard format** of a quadratic equation is $ax^2 + bx + c$ (in which $a \neq 0$). Most of the exercises in this chapter involve equations in standard format. When you solve for a variable, those values are called the **roots** of the equation.

As we discussed in chapter 3, many trinomials in quadratic form are products of two binomials. If a quadratic is factorable, you can solve for the variable by setting each factor equal to zero.

EXAMPLE 4
Solve for g: $g^2 - 4g - 12 = 0$.

SOLUTION
This equation is factorable like this:

$$(g - 6)(g + 2) = 0$$

If the product of two numbers is zero, then at least one of them must be equal to zero. Set each factor equal to zero and solve for each one:

$$
\begin{array}{ll}
g - 6 = 0 & \quad g + 2 = 0 \\
g = 6 & \quad g = -2
\end{array}
$$

As always, you should check your work by plugging your answers back into the equation:

$$
\begin{array}{ll}
(6)^2 - 4(6) - 12 = 0 & \quad (-2)^2 - 4(-2) - 12 = 0 \\
36 - 24 - 12 = 0 & \quad 4 + 8 - 12 = 0 \\
0 = 0 & \quad 0 = 0
\end{array}
$$

Both answers work, so the roots of the equation are **6 and –2**.

There are several variations on this technique.

Variation No. 1: When $b = 0$ and $c < 0$.

EXAMPLE 5
Solve for h: $h^2 - 49 = 0$.

SOLUTION
This is an example of the difference of squares we discussed in chapter 3. You might remember, then, that the expression factors like this:

$$h^2 - (7)^2 = (h + 7)(h - 7)$$
$$h = \{7, -7\} \text{ or } h = \pm 7$$

Variation No. 2: When $c = 0$.

EXAMPLE 6
Solve for k: $k^2 + 3k = 0$.

SOLUTION
There's no number on the end, so you have to work a different way by factoring k out of each term.

$$k^2 + 3k = 0$$
$$k(k + 3) = 0$$
$$k = \{0, -3\}$$

Variation No. 3: When $a \neq 1$, and all three terms have a common factor.

EXAMPLE 7
Solve for k: $3k^2 + 21k - 54 = 0$.

SOLUTION
Sometimes a quadratic looks tougher than it is. Each coefficient in the equation is divisible by 3, so you can simplify the equation before you factor it:

$$\frac{3k^2}{3} + \frac{21k}{3} - \frac{54}{3} = 0$$
$$k^2 + 7k - 18 = 0.$$

Now, you can factor it normally:

$$(k - 9)(k + 2) = 0$$
$$k = \{9, -2\}$$

Variation No. 4: When $a \neq 1$, and you can't simplify the equation.

EXAMPLE 8

Solve for m: $2m^2 + 3m - 9 = 0$.

SOLUTION

If you're sure you can't simplify the equation until the first coefficient is 1, you can still factor the way you learned in chapter 3. Chances are, one of your answers won't be an integer.

$$2m^2 + 3m - 9 = 0$$

$$(2m - 3)(m + 3) = 0$$

$$2m - 3 = 0$$
$$2m = 3$$
$$m = \frac{3}{2}$$

$$m + 3 = 0$$
$$m = -3$$

The check is also a bit more complicated, but it's worth it:

$$2\left(\frac{3}{2}\right)^2 + 3\left(\frac{3}{2}\right) - 9 = 0$$

$$2\left(\frac{9}{4}\right) + \frac{9}{2} - 9 = 0$$

$$\frac{9}{2} + \frac{9}{2} - 9 = 0$$

$$9 - 9 = 0$$

$$2(-3)^2 + 3(-3) - 9 = 0$$

$$2(9) - 9 - 9 = 0$$

$$18 - 9 - 9 = 0$$

$$9 - 9 = 0$$

The solution set is: $m = \left\{\frac{3}{2}, -3\right\}$.

WORD PROBLEMS

The challenge of word problems is to construct the algebraic equation properly. It's usually best to draw a diagram representing the situation in the problem.

EXAMPLE 9

A rectangular picture measures 8 inches by 11 inches before it is framed. The frame has a uniform width, and the total area of the picture and the frame is 238 square inches. What is the width of the frame?

SOLUTION

Draw the diagram first. The picture is 8 × 11, and the frame has a uniform width, n:

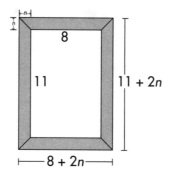

The dimensions of the framed picture are $(8 + 2n)$ and $(11 + 2n)$, and the area is 238. Since the formula for the area of a rectangle is length × width, the equation looks like this:

$$(8 + 2n)(11 + 2n) = 238$$

Use FOIL to combine the factors, then rearrange the terms until the resultant quadratic is in standard form.

$$88 + 16n + 22n + 4n^2 = 238$$

$$4n^2 + 38n + 88 = 238$$

$$4n^2 + 38n - 150 = 0$$

Each coefficient is divisible by 2, so you can factor it out. Then factor the trinomial and solve.

$$2n^2 + 19n - 75 = 0$$

$$(2n + 25)(n - 3) = 0$$

$$n = \left\{-\frac{25}{2}, 3\right\}$$

The answer you're looking for represents a distance, and distances can't be negative. Therefore, you can throw out the first root. The width of the frame is **3 inches**.

EXERCISES, SET 4B

Here's an opportunity to practice solving quadratic equations. The answers are in chapter 16.

1. Solve for a.
   (a) $a^2 - 4 = 0$
   (b) $4a^2 - 9 = 0$

   (c) $\dfrac{a^2}{25} - 7 = -3$

   (d) $a^2 - \dfrac{25}{144} = 0$

   (e) $(2a)^2 - 5 = 0$

2. Solve for b.
   (a) $b^2 + 5b = 0$
   (b) $3b^2 - 21b = 0$
   (c) $(4b)^2 - 48b = 0$
   (d) $b^2 - x^2 = 0$

3. Solve for c.
   (a) $2c^2 + 4c + 2 = 0$
   (b) $4c^2 + 12c - 40 = 0$
   (c) $-3c^2 + 3c + 90 = 0$

   (d) $\dfrac{1}{2}c^2 + 2c - 6 = 0$

   (e) $-10c^2 + 180c = 770$

4. Solve for d.
   (a) $2d^2 + 3d - 5 = 0$
   (b) $3d^2 + 2d - 8 = 0$
   (c) $6d^2 + 13d + 5 = 0$
   (d) $10d^2 + d = 21$
   (e) $12d^3 - 16d^2 - 3d = 0$

5. **(a)** The length of a rectangular parking lot is seven meters longer than its width. If the area of the parking lot is 198 square meters, what are the parking lot's dimensions?

(b) One positive number is 3 more than another positive number. If the sum of their squares is 89, what are the numbers?

(c) Grammy Wedul had knitted a rectangular baby blanket that measured six feet by four feet before she realized her daughter was having twins. If she increases each dimension by the same amount, she will double the size of the blanket. By how much should she increase each dimension?

(d) The area of a rectangle is 20 square inches. If the sides are in a ratio of 5:16, what is the length of each side?

(e) A rectangular plot of land measures 24 meters by 40 meters. If the Department of Public Works covers the perimeter of this land with a sidewalk of uniform width, the area of exposed land shrinks to 665 square meters. How wide is the sidewalk?

THE QUADRATIC FORMULA

Factoring is always an appealing shortcut, but it doesn't always work. If a trinomial is unfactorable, the roots are **irrational** and there will probably be a square root involved in your answer.

For example, if $x^2 - 17 = 0$, then the roots of the equation are $\sqrt{17}$ and $-\sqrt{17}$.

If you can't factor a trinomial, you have to use the **Quadratic Formula**, which will always work if the equation is in the standard form $ax^2 + bx + c = 0$.

$$x = \frac{-b \pm \sqrt{b^2 - 4ac}}{2a}$$

Your math textbook probably goes to great pains to show how this theorem was derived. (We're not gonna bother.)

Important: Do *whatever it takes* to commit this formula to memory. Say it over and over to yourself 100 times. Tattoo the formula on your forearm if you have to. You'll use this formula a lot in Course II math.

EXAMPLE 10
Solve for x: $x^2 - 4x - 9 = 0$.

SOLUTION
Since you can't factor the equation, you have to use the Quadratic Formula. The equation is in standard format, so $a = 1$, $b = -4$, and $c = -9$:

$$x = \frac{-(-4) \pm \sqrt{(-4)^2 - 4(1)(-9)}}{2(1)}$$

$$= \frac{4 \pm \sqrt{16 - (-36)}}{2}$$

$$= \frac{4 \pm \sqrt{52}}{2}$$

$$= \frac{4 \pm 2\sqrt{13}}{2}$$

$$= 2 \pm \sqrt{13}$$

The "$\pm$" symbol tells you that there are two roots: $2 + \sqrt{13}$ and $2 - \sqrt{13}$.

Some teachers will let you leave your answer in radical form. Others will want you to turn your answer into a decimal. For a numerical value, use your calculator to find that $\sqrt{13} = 3.6$. Then substitute:

$$2 + 3.6 = 5.6$$
$$2 - 3.6 = -1.6$$

The two roots are {**5.6, –1.6**}.

Here's another important point: The Quadratic Formula *always* works when you want to solve a quadratic equation. Factoring is only a shortcut.

EXAMPLE 11

Find the roots of the equation $x^2 + 9x - 22 = 0$.

SOLUTION

If you use the Quadratic Formula, the math looks like this:

$$x = \frac{-9 \pm \sqrt{(9)^2 - 4(1)(-22)}}{2(1)}$$

$$= \frac{-9 \pm \sqrt{81 - (-88)}}{2}$$

$$= \frac{-9 \pm \sqrt{169}}{2}$$

$$= \frac{-9 + 13}{2}, \frac{-9 - 13}{2}$$

$$= \frac{4}{2}, \frac{-22}{2}$$

$$= \{2, -11\}$$

If you factor the equation, you get this:

$$x^2 + 9x - 22 = 0$$
$$(x - 2)(x + 11) = 0$$

$x - 2 = 0$ $\qquad\qquad$ $x + 11 = 0$

$x = 2$ $\qquad\qquad\qquad$ $x = -11$

Easier, isn't it?

COMPLETING THE SQUARE

A third, less common method for finding the roots of a quadratic equation is called completing the square. As if memorizing the Quadratic Formula wasn't enough, many teachers will teach you this method as a more complicated algebraic exercise. Let's look at Example 10 once again:

EXAMPLE 10 (AGAIN)

Solve for x in the equation $x^2 - 4x - 9 = 0$ by completing the square.

SOLUTION

Throughout this example, we'll refer to the a, b, and c terms (since the equation is still in standard form). The first thing to do is to put the c term on the other side of the equal sign. In this case, add 9 to both sides:

$$x^2 - 4x = 9$$

Now comes the tricky part. You have to turn the expression on the left into a perfect square by adding a certain constant. (**Note:** For this to be legal, you have to add that same constant to the other side.)

To find that constant, divide b by 2, then square the result:

$$\frac{-4}{2} = -2 \qquad (-2)^2 = 4.$$

Now add 4 to both sides:

$$x^2 - 4x + 4 = 9 + 4$$

Using your factoring skills from chapter 3, you can determine that you've created a perfect square on the left side:

$$x^2 - 4x - 4 = (x - 2)^2$$
$$(x - 2)^2 = 13$$

Take the square root of both sides:

$$\sqrt{(x-2)^2} = \sqrt{13}$$
$$x - 2 = \pm\sqrt{13}$$

Add 2 to both sides, and you're finished: $x = 2 \pm \sqrt{13}$

(Note that the answer matches the previous one in Example 10.)

SIMPLIFYING SQUARE ROOTS

There's one more thing to note about Example 10. Did you see how $\sqrt{52}$ was simplified to $2\sqrt{13}$? That's an important step. If a problem asks you to provide an answer in its *simplest* form, you're usually penalized if you forget to reduce the radical.

WRONG	RIGHT
$\dfrac{4 \pm \sqrt{52}}{2}$	$2 \pm \sqrt{13}$

A square root can be reduced if one of the factors of the **radicand** (the number under the square root sign) is a perfect square. Since 4 is a factor of 52, you can do this: $\sqrt{52} = \sqrt{4 \times 13} = \sqrt{4} \times \sqrt{13} = 2\sqrt{13}$

Your answer now looks like this:

$$\frac{4 + 2\sqrt{13}}{2} = \frac{2(2 + \sqrt{13})}{2} = 2 + \sqrt{13}$$

THE DISCRIMINANT

The rest of this chapter is devoted to figuring things out about the roots of an equation using its coefficients. For instance, you can tell how many roots an equation has (as well as whether they're rational) by analyzing the **discriminant**, which is the $b^2 - 4ac$ term beneath the square root sign in the Quadratic Formula.

You can't take the square root of a negative number. Therefore, if the discriminant is negative, the roots are **imaginary**.

If the discriminant is equal to zero, then the entire square root term drops out. Therefore, the roots are **rational** and **real**. Since there's no more "±" sign, there's only one root. (Actually there are two roots, but they're equal. Same difference.)

If the discriminant is positive, there are **two real roots**. The only question is whether the roots are rational. If $b^2 - 4ac$ is a perfect square, then there's no more square root sign and the roots are **rational**. If it's not a perfect square, the roots are **irrational**.

These rules are summarized below:

Value of Discriminant		Two Roots
b2 – 4ac < 0		imaginary
b2 – 4ac = 0		real, rational, equal
b2 – 4ac > 0	perfect square	real, rational, unequal
	not a perfect square	real, irrational, unequal

EXAMPLE 12
Analyze the roots of the equation $3s^2 - 2s - 2 = 0$.

SOLUTION
In this equation, $a = 3$, $b = -2$, and $c = -2$.

$$b^2 - 4ac = (-2)^2 - 4(3)(-2)$$
$$= 4 - (-24)$$
$$= 28$$

There are **two real, irrational roots**.

THE SUM AND PRODUCT OF ROOTS

When a trinomial is in standard form, the **sum of the roots** is equal to $-\dfrac{b}{a}$, and the **product of the roots** is $\dfrac{c}{a}$.

EXAMPLE 13

Find the sum and product of the roots of the equation $2t^2 - 7t - 4 = 0$.

SOLUTION

In this equation, $a = 2$, $b = -7$, and $c = -4$:

$$\text{sum: } -\frac{b}{a} = -\frac{(-7)}{2} = \frac{7}{2} \qquad\qquad \text{product: } \frac{c}{a} = \frac{-4}{2} = -2$$

For the record, you can factor the equation like this:

$$(2t + 1)(t - 4) = 0 \, t = \left\{-\frac{1}{2}, 4\right\}$$

The sum of the roots is $4 + \left(-\dfrac{1}{2}\right)$, or $\dfrac{7}{2}$. The product is $4 \times \left(-\dfrac{1}{2}\right)$, or -2.

WRITING THE EQUATION

If you know the roots of an equation, you can work backwards and find the equation by using FOIL.

EXAMPLE 1

Find the equation whose roots are 4 and –5.

SOLUTION

If 4 and –5 are the roots of an equation, then each must have been subtracted from x at some point and the result was zero:

$$x - 4 = 0 \qquad\qquad\qquad x - (-5) = 0$$
$$x + 5 = 0$$

From this point, multiply the two terms together using FOIL:

$$(x - 4)(x + 5) = x^2 + 5x - 4x - 20$$
$$= x^2 + x - 20$$

The equation with roots $\{4, -5\}$ is $x^2 + x - 20 = 0$.

EXERCISES, SET 4C

The answers are in chapter 16.

1. Write out the Quadratic Formula.

2. Write it out 10,000 times, or until you memorize it.

3. Simplify the following square roots.

   (a) $\sqrt{12}$ (b) $\sqrt{45}$ (c) $\sqrt{60}$ (d) $\sqrt{75}$ (e) $\sqrt{243}$

   (f) $\sqrt{450}$ (g) $\sqrt{1,024}$ (h) $\sqrt{4,000}$

4. In each of the following, solve for x using the Quadratic Formula. Leave your answer in reduced radical form.

   (a) $x^2 - 2x - 2 = 0$
   (b) $x^2 + 5x + 5 = 0$
   (c) $2x^2 - 3x - 4 = 0$
   (d) $2x^2 - 6x + 1 = 0$
   (e) $2x^2 - 20x + 50 = 0$
   (f) $3x^2 - 6x = 1$

5. Using the Quadratic Formula, solve for x to the nearest tenth.

   (a) $x^2 + x - 3 = 0$
   (b) $x^2 - 5x - 7 = 0$
   (c) $2x^2 - x - 14 = 0$
   (d) $3x^2 - 7x = 20$
   (e) $3x^2 + 8x - 24 = 0$
   (f) $6x^2 - 3x - 4 = 0$
   (g) Which one of the previous problems was factorable?

6. Using the discriminant, analyze the roots of each of the following:

   (a) $x^2 - 2x + 4 = 0$
   (b) $x^2 + 3x - 9 = 0$
   (c) $x^2 - 8x + 16 = 0$
   (d) $x^2 - 5x + 7 = 0$
   (e) $2x^2 + 5x + 3 = 0$
   (f) $3x^2 - 2x = -7$
   (g) $2x^2 = 3 - 4x$

7. Find the sum and product of each of the following.
   (a) $x^2 - 2x - 15 = 0$
   (b) $x^2 + 6x + 9 = 0$
   (c) $2x^2 + 7x - 4 = 0$
   (d) $3x^2 - mx - n = 0$

8. Write the quadratic equation for each of the following sets of roots.
   (a) $x = \{2, -3\}$
   (b) $x = \{-4, 4\}$
   (c) $x = \{5\}$
   (d) $x = \left\{\dfrac{5}{2}, -5\right\}$
   (e) $x = \left\{-\dfrac{5}{4}, -\dfrac{4}{3}\right\}$

9. What would you add to each of the following to make it a perfect square?
   (a) $x^2 + 6x +$ ___
   (b) $x^2 - 8x +$ ___
   (c) $x^2 + 5x +$ ___
   (d) $x^2 - x +$ ___

5

Graphing and Graphic Solutions

The next three chapters are devoted to using the coordinate axes (that's the plural of "axis," not "axe," although some might think it would be really cool if graphing involved hatchets).

THE COORDINATE PLANE

The next three chapters center on the **coordinate plane**, which is nothing more than a two-dimensional number line. The x-**axis** (the horizontal line) and the y-**axis** (the vertical line) meet at the **origin**, which has the coordinates (0, 0).

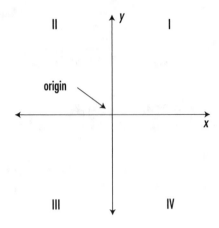

The coordinate system divides two-dimensional space into the four **quadrants** shown above.

Each point in a graph is identified by its **coordinate pair**, which is denoted by its **x-coordinate**, then its **y-coordinate**; this is written more simply as **(x, y)**. (Note: Teachers sometimes refer to the x-coordinate as the **abscissa** and the y-coordinate as the **ordinate**.)

EXAMPLE 1

Graph and label the following points: $A(2, 5)$, $B(-4, 1)$, $C(5, -2)$, $D(-3, -3)$, $E(0, 4)$, $F(-2, 0)$.

SOLUTION

When you graph a coordinate pair, the x always comes first. To graph point $A(2, 5)$, start at the origin, move two units to the right and five units up, like this:

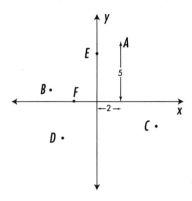

The other points are graphed as well. If you keep getting your coordinates mixed up, remember this:

"X before Y, run before you fly."

That means that all graphing is horizontal first, followed by vertical.

Any equation involving x and y represents a steady relationship between those two coordinates. A graph of the equation is a composite of all the points (x, y) that satisfy the equation.

LINES

The most basic equation to graph is a **linear equation**, because its graph is a line. You can recognize a linear equation right away, because neither x nor y is squared.

EXAMPLE 2
Graph the equation $y = 2x + 1$.

SOLUTION
Select a few values of x to plug into the equation: $x = \{-2, -1, 0, 1, 2\}$. Try -2 first:

x	$2x + 1$	y
-2	$2(-2) + 1$	-3

Your first ordered pair is $(-2, -3)$.

The rest of the ordered pairs and the graph of the equation are below:

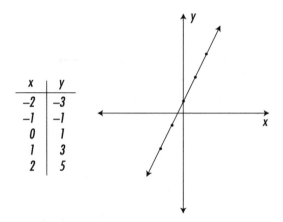

x	y
−2	−3
−1	−1
0	1
1	3
2	5

As you can see, all the points are lined up in a row.

Note: For more detailed work with the slope of the line, turn to chapter 8.

PARABOLAS

The graph of a quadratic equation is a **parabola**, which is a smooth, symmetric arc. Most parabolas that you'll work with will appear in standard form $y = ax^2 + bx + c$. The graphing process is the same as before.

EXAMPLE 3

Graph the equation $y = x^2 - 2x - 3$, including all values of x in the interval $-2 \leq x \leq 4$.

SOLUTION

Plug in all the x-coordinates one at a time.

x	$x^2 - 2x - 3$	y	(x, y)
-2	$(-2)^2 - 2(-2) - 3$	5	$(-2, 5)$
-1	$(-1)^2 - 2(-1) - 3$	0	$(-1, 0)$
0	$(0)^2 - 2(0) - 3$	-3	$(0, -3)$
1	$(1)^2 - 2(1) - 3$	-4	$(1, -4)$
2	$(2)^2 - 2(2) - 3$	-3	$(2, -3)$
3	$(3)^2 - 2(3) - 3$	0	$(3, 0)$
4	$(4)^2 - 2(4) - 3$	5	$(4, 5)$

Do you see a pattern within the set of y-coordinates? Look at the points at either end of the list: $(-2, 5)$ and $(4, 5)$. Two separate x-values yield the same y-value, a phenomenon that suggests symmetry. The parabola looks like this:

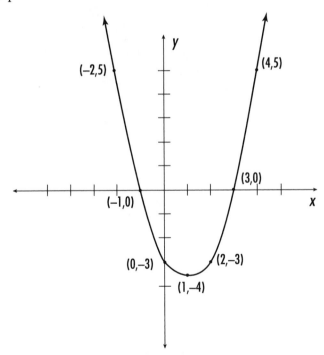

In the last chapter, you solved quadratic equations that were equal to zero. You can also find the roots of an equation by analyzing its graph.

ROOTS AND X-INTERCEPTS

The roots of a quadratic equation are the points at which the graph of the equation (a parabola) intersects the x-axis. Look at the equation in Example 3 again:

$$y = x^2 - 2x - 3$$

It crosses the x-axis at two points: $(-1, 0)$ and $(3, 0)$. That means the roots of the equation are -1 and 3.

When the graph of this equation hits the x-axis, the value of y is zero. At that point, you can re-write the equation like this:

$$0 = x^2 - 2x - 3$$

Now factor it:

$$0 = (x + 1)(x - 3)$$
$$x = \{-1, 3\}$$

If the equation of a parabola is in standard form, you can determine whether the graph opens up or opens down by looking at a, the coefficient of the x^2 term.

> If $a > 0$, the parabola **opens up**. If $a < 0$, it **opens down**. Think about it like this: If a is **positive**, the parabola **smiles**. If a is **negative**, it **frowns**.

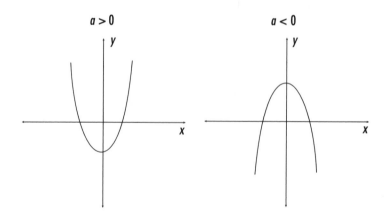

Usually, a problem will give you the values of x to plug into the equation. There are usually seven of them, and the middle one is the **turning point**, the point at which the parabola bends and changes direction. If there are no values of x given, figure out the best ones to try by determining the parabola's location on the coordinate plane.

AXIS OF SYMMETRY AND TURNING POINT
Since every parabola is symmetrical, there's a line that cuts each parabola right down the middle. This line is called the **axis of symmetry,** and here's the formula to find it: $x = -\dfrac{b}{2a}$

Again, the parabola has to be in standard form.

EXAMPLE 4
Solve the equation $x^2 - 2x - 8 = 0$ graphically.

SOLUTION

Find the axis of symmetry first; $a = 1$, and $b = -2$: $x = -\dfrac{b}{2a} = -\dfrac{(-2)}{2(1)} = 1$.

The line $x = 1$ is the axis of symmetry, so 1 should be the middle point that you plug in. Pick three numbers to the left (–2, –1, and 0) and three to the right (2, 3, and 4) and find the points on the parabola:

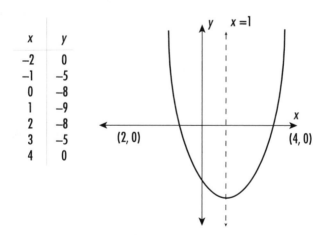

x	y
–2	0
–1	–5
0	–8
1	–9
2	–8
3	–5
4	0

The graph intersects the x-axis at points (–2, 0) and (4, 0). Therefore, the roots of the equation are **–2** and **4**.

As always, you can plug these values back into the equation to make sure they work.

Once you know the axis of symmetry of a parabola, you can determine the coordinates of the **turning point** (which is sometimes referred to as the vertex). Since the axis of symmetry cuts a parabola in half, the turning point is on that axis.

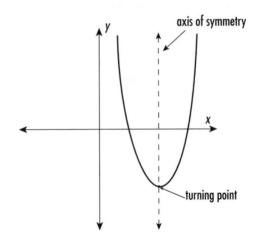

Therefore, the value of x that represents the axis of symmetry is the x-coordinate of the vertex. To find the turning point, plug the value of x into the original equation and solve for the y-coordinate.

EXAMPLE 5
Find the turning point of the parabola in Example 4.

SOLUTION
From the example, you know that the axis of symmetry of the parabola $y = x^2 - 2x - 8$ is $x = 1$. Plug 1 into the equation like this:

$$y = (1)^2 - 2(1) - 8$$
$$= 1 - 2 - 8$$
$$= -9$$

The coordinates of the turning point are **(1, –9)**.

EXERCISES, SET 5A

Just how graphic is your imagination? Find out by trying these exercises. The answers are in chapter 16.

1. Which of the following is the equation for the y-axis?
   (1) $x + y = 0$
   (2) $x = 0$
   (3) $y = 0$
   (4) $y = x$

2. Graph the following on the coordinate axes.
   (a) $(3, -4)$
   (b) $(-5, 1)$
   (c) $(0, 6)$
   (d) $(-4, -7)$
   (e) $(5, 4)$
   (f) $(7, 0)$

3. Which quadrant contains each of the following points?
   (a) $(-4, 2)$
   (b) $(5, -1)$
   (c) $(-3, -3)$
   (d) $(0, 8)$
   (e) $(2, 3)$

4. Graph the following linear equations.
   (a) $y = x + 2$
   (b) $y = 3x + 5$
   (c) $y - 2 = -\dfrac{3}{2}x$
   (d) $x - 3y = 6$
   (e) $\dfrac{3x + y}{2} = -2$

5. Graph the following parabolas.
   (a) $y = x^2 + 2$
   (b) $y = (x + 2)^2$
   (c) $y = x^2 - 3x - 10$
   (d) $y = -x^2 - 4x + 8$
   (e) $y = (x - 2)(3 - x)$
   (f) $y = x^2 + 2x + 6$
   (g) $2y - 2 = 3x^2 + 4x$

6. Identify the axis of symmetry of each of the following.
   (a) $y = x^2$
   (b) $y = x^2 - 4x + 6$
   (c) $y = 2x^2 + 5x + 3$
   (d) $y - 3 = 4(x - 1)^2$
   (e) $\dfrac{y+1}{4} = x^2 + x$

7. Identify the turning point of each of the following.
   (a) $y = x^2$
   (b) $y = x^2 - 6x + 5$
   (c) $y = -x^2 + 3x - 6$
   (d) $y = 3x^2 + 4x - 4$
   (e) $y = 4x^2 + 8x - 21$

8. Identify the roots of each of these by graphing. (If the result is not an integer, estimate the roots by identifying the two nearest integers. For example, 1.6 is between 1 and 2.)
   (a) $y = x^2 + 5x - 14$
   (b) $y = x^2 - 2x - 5$
   (c) $y = -x^2 + 5x + 3$
   (d) $y = x^2 + 3x + 5$
   (e) $y = 2x^2 - x - 10$
   (f) $y + 90 = 6x^2 - 7x$

MORE THAN ONE GRAPH

You can also find out the points at which two graphs intersect using this graphing method. This is often called **solving a system of equations**.

EXAMPLE 6

Solve graphically:
$$y = -x^2 + 6x - 2$$
$$y = x + 2$$

SOLUTION

By now, you should recognize the first equation as a parabola and the second one as a line. Find the axis of symmetry first:

$$x = -\frac{b}{2a} = -\frac{6}{2(-1)} = 3.$$

Pick three values to the left (0, 1, and 2) and three values to the right (4, 5, and 6). Then find the coordinates like this:

x	$-x^2 + 6x - 2$	y	(x, y)
0	$-(0)^2 + 6(0) - 2$	-2	$(0, -2)$
1	$-(1)^2 + 6(1) - 2$	3	$(1, 3)$
2	$-(2)^2 + 6(2) - 2$	6	$(2, 6)$
3	$-(3)^2 + 6(3) - 2$	7	$(3, 7)$
4	$-(4)^2 + 6(4) - 2$	6	$(4, 6)$
5	$-(5)^2 + 6(5) - 2$	3	$(5, 3)$
6	$-(6)^2 + 6(6) - 2$	-2	$(6, -2)$

Since two points determine a line, you only need two values of x to graph the second equation.

The two graphs look like this:

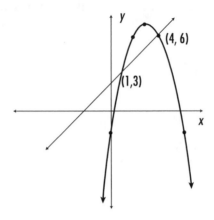

Your ability to find the two points of intersection relies on how accurately you drew this diagram. The graphs appear to intersect at two points: (1, 3) and (4, 6). Always double-check your work by plugging the values into each equation:

$$y = -x^2 + 6x - 2 \qquad\qquad y = x + 2$$

$$3 = -(1)^2 + 6(1) - 2 \qquad\qquad 3 = 1 + 2$$
$$3 = -1 + 6 - 2 \qquad\qquad\qquad 3 = 3$$
$$3 = 3$$

$$6 = -(4)^2 + 6(4) - 2 \qquad\qquad 6 = 4 + 2$$
$$6 = -16 + 24 - 2 \qquad\qquad\quad 6 = 6$$
$$6 = 6$$

The points of intersection are **(1, 3)** and **(4, 6)**.

SOLVING ALGEBRAICALLY
Graphing isn't the only method for solving a system of equations. You can solve them algebraically as well, and it doesn't require any outstanding artistic talent.

EXAMPLE 7

Solve the system of equations in Example 6 algebraically.

SOLUTION

You have two equations that express y in terms of x. Since each expression is equal to y, then they're equal to each other.

$$-x^2 + 6x - 2 = x + 2$$
$$-x^2 + 5x - 4 = 0$$

Once you multiply everything by –1, you'll have another quadratic equation suitable for factoring:

$$x^2 - 5x + 4 = 0$$
$$(x - 1)(x - 4) = 0$$
$$x = \{1, \ 4\}$$

Those are the x-coordinates of the two points of intersection. Plug each one into one of the original equations to find its corresponding y-coordinate:

$x = 1$	$x = 4$
$y = -(1)^2 + 6(1) - 2$	$y = -(4)^2 + 6(4) - 2$
$= -1 + 6 - 2$	$= -16 + 24 - 2$
$= 3$	$= 6$

The solution to this system of equations is **(1, 3)** and **(4, 6)**.

As we mentioned before, there's a lot more work on graphing and coordinate geometry in the next two chapters. This chapter is here to show you the parallels between algebraic and graphic solutions.

EXERCISES, SET 5B

Find the intersection between each of the following pairs of systems. The answers are in chapter 16.

Solve the following pairs of systems graphically and algebraically.

1. $y = x^2 + 1$
   $y = 5$

2. $y = x^2 - 3$
   $y = 2x + 5$

3. $y = x^2 + 2x + 7$
   $y = 3x - 1$

4. $y = x^2 - 6x + 2$
   $y = x - 4$

5. $y = x^2 + 2x - 1$
   $y = -2x - 4$

6. $y = 2x^2 - 2x + 5$
   $y = 3x + 3$

7. $y = -\frac{1}{2}x^2 + 2x - 3$
   $x + y = 1$

6

Transformations

In the coordinate plane, a **transformation** maps one point A onto its image A' (pronounced "A prime").

Warning: This chapter contains a lot of similar-sounding formulas for reflecting, sliding, and dilating points on the coordinate axes. The best way to memorize them is to keep practicing and to use diagrams.

REFLECTIONS IN A LINE

The reflection of a point in a line is the "mirror image" of that point in that line. If A' is the image of A in line l, then line l is the perpendicular bisector of segment $\overline{AA'}$. (**Note:** For more information about perpendicular bisectors, see chapter 12 on locus and constructions.)

Most reflection questions involve three lines: the x-axis, the y-axis, and the line $y = x$.

After a reflection in the x-axis, the x-coordinate remains the same and the y-coordinate is negated:

$$r_{x\text{-axis}}\ (x,\ y)\ \rightarrow\ (x,\ -y)$$

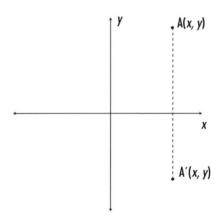

After a reflection in the y-axis, the y-coordinate remains the same and the x-coordinate is negated:

$$r_{y\text{-axis}}\ (x,\ y)\ \rightarrow\ (-x,\ y)$$

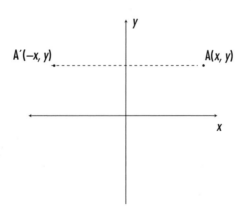

Basically, these two formulas boil down to this: Whenever you reflect a point in an axis, negate the other coordinate. When you reflect in the *x*-axis, negate the *y*; when you reflect in the *y*-axis, negate the *x*.

After a reflection in the line $y = x$, the *x*- and *y*-coordinates are interchanged: $r_{y=x} (x, y) \rightarrow (y, x)$

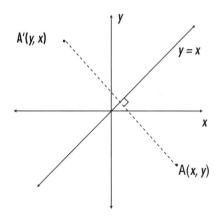

EXAMPLE 1
Given the coordinates $A(3, 5)$, $B(5, -1)$, and $C(0, 4)$, find (1) the coordinates of $\triangle A'B'C'$ after a reflection in the *x*-axis; and (2) the coordinates of $\triangle A''B''C''$ after $\triangle A'B'C'$ is reflected in the *y*-axis.

SOLUTION
(1) Put the three points through the formula for a reflection in the *x*-axis by negating each *y*-coordinate:

$$r_{x\text{-axis}} \; A(3, 5) \rightarrow A'(3, -5)$$
$$r_{x\text{-axis}} \; B(5, -1) \rightarrow B'(5, 1)$$
$$r_{x\text{-axis}} \; C(0, 4) \rightarrow C'(0, -4)$$

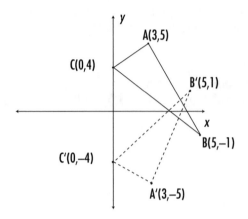

The coordinates of $\triangle A'B'C'$ are $A'(3, -5)$, $B'(5, 1)$, and $C'(0, -4)$.

(2) Now find the reflections of A', B', and C' in the y-axis:

$$r_{y\text{-axis}} \ (3, -5) \rightarrow (-3, -5)$$
$$r_{y\text{-axis}} \ (5, 1) \rightarrow (-5, 1)$$
$$r_{y\text{-axis}} \ (0, -4) \rightarrow (0, -4)$$

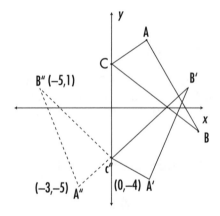

The coordinates of $\triangle A''B''C''$ are $A''(-3, -5)$, $B''(-5, 1)$, and $C''(0, -4)$.

REFLECTIONS IN A POINT

As it turns out, if you reflect a point consecutively in both axes (it doesn't matter which one's first), it has the same effect as a reflection in the origin.

> After a reflection in the origin, both the x- and y-coordinates are negated:
>
> $r_{(0, 0)} \; (x, y) \rightarrow (-x, -y)$

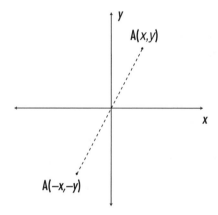

If you reflect a point in another point that is *not* the origin, the rule is this:

> If the point P' is the image of point P after a reflection in point Q, then Q is the midpoint of line segment $\overline{PP'}$.

Here's a sneak preview of the formula for the midpoint of a segment. There's a lot more work with midpoints in the next chapter.

> Given the points $A(x_1, y_1)$ and $B(x_2, y_2)$, the coordinates of the midpoint $(\bar{x}, \bar{y})$ of segment $\overline{AB}$ are: $(\bar{x}, \bar{y}) = \left(\dfrac{x_1 + x_2}{2}, \dfrac{y_1 + y_2}{2} \right)$

EXAMPLE 2

Find the image A' of the point $A(3, -5)$ after a reflection in the point $(-1, -2)$.

SOLUTION

The reflection point $(-1, -2)$ is the midpoint of $\overline{AA'}$. Use the midpoint formula a little differently by solving for each coordinate individually.

Let $(\overline{x}, \overline{y}) = (-1, -2)$, $(x_1, y_1) = A(3, -5)$ and $(x_2, y_2) = A'(x, y)$:

$$\overline{x} = \frac{x_1 + x_2}{2} \qquad\qquad \overline{y} = \frac{y_1 + y_2}{2}$$

$$-1 = \frac{3 + x}{2} \qquad\qquad -2 = \frac{-5 + y}{2}$$

$$-2 = 3 + x \qquad\qquad -4 = -5 + y$$

$$-5 = x \qquad\qquad 1 = y$$

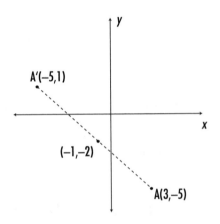

The coordinates of point A' are **(−5, 1)**.

TRANSLATIONS

A transformation that "slides" a point along the coordinate plane is called a **translation**, and its formula looks like this:

$$T_{h, k} (x, y) \rightarrow (x + h, y + k)$$

The translations break down like this:

If this is true   The point moves

If this is true:	The point moves:
$h > 0$	to the right
$h < 0$	to the left
$k > 0$	up
$k < 0$	down

EXAMPLE 3

Find the image of the point (1, −4) under a translation $T_{-5, 3}$.

SOLUTION

Since $h = -5$ and $k = 3$, you know that the point will slide (a) to the left and (b) up. In order to find the image of a point (x, y) after a translation that maps it onto its image $(x - 5, y + 3)$, subtract 5 from the x-coordinate and add 1 to the y-coordinate.

Under this translation, the point (1, −4) is mapped onto point (1 − 5, −4 + 3), or **(−4, −1)**.

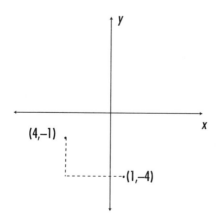

Sometimes, you have to figure out the values of h and k first.

EXAMPLE 4

If a translation maps the point $P(-1, 4)$ onto $P'(5, 2)$, what is the image of point $Q(-4, -2)$ under the same translation?

SOLUTION

The easiest way to figure out a translation is to subtract the coordinates of the original point P from those of its image P'. Look at the x-coordinates of $P(-1, 4)$ and $A'(5, 2)$ first. Since $5 - (-1) = 6$, the translation adds 6 to each x-coordinate. The difference of the y-coordinates $(2 - 4 = -2)$ tells you that this same translation subtracts 2 from each y-coordinate.

The formula looks like this:

$$T(x, y) \rightarrow (x + 6, y - 2)$$

Now, plug the point $Q(4, 0)$ into the formula:

$$Q' = (-4 + 6, -2 - 2) = (2, -4)$$

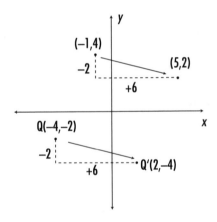

So far, we've dealt only with **isometries**, which are translations in which the image of any line or polygon is the same size as the preimage. There's one more transformation that figures prominently in Course II, and this one changes the image's shape.

DILATIONS

Under a **dilation**, the image of a polygon is similar to its pre-image, but the two are not the same size. (The only exception, of course, is if the figure undergoes a dilation of 1, which is the same as doing nothing at all.)

Have you ever gone to the eye doctor and had your pupils dilated? Well, this is sort of the same thing.

When a point undergoes a dilation, each coordinate of that point is multiplied by a constant k. The formula looks like this:

$$D_k \ (x, \ y) \ \rightarrow (kx, \ ky)$$

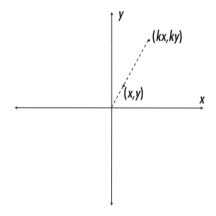

Most dilations center on the origin, so if $k > 1$, the image is further from the origin than the pre-image is; if k is between 0 and 1, the image is nearer. Similarly, if a line segment undergoes a dilation in which $k > 1$, the image is larger than its pre-image; if $0 < k < 1$, the image is smaller.

EXAMPLE 5

If a dilation with respect to the origin maps the point (1, –4) onto the point (3, –12), what is the image of M(–2, 2) under the same dilation?

SOLUTION

Since $1 \times 3 = 3$ and $-4 \times 3 = -12$, the dilation constant k must equal 3. Now, plug the point (–2, 2) into the equation:

$$D_3 \, (-2,\, 2) \rightarrow (3 \times -2,\, 3 \times 2) = M'(-6,\, 6)$$

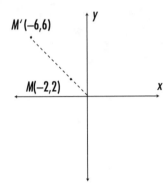

EXERCISES, SET 6A

For expanded work in coordinate geometry, including work with slopes, midpoints, and distances, refer to chapter 7. In the meantime, try these exercises. The answers are in chapter 16.

1. What is the image of point (4, –2) after a reflection in
    (a) the x-axis?
    (b) the y-axis?
    (c) the line $y = x$?
    (d) the origin?
    (e) the point (–3, 2)?

2. If you reflect the point (–3, –4) in the x-axis, the line $y = x$, the x-axis (again), and the y-axis, what are the coordinates of the image?

3. What is the equation of the line that is a reflection of the line $y = x$ in the x-axis?

4. What is the image of the point (2, –5) after
    (a) a translation $(x - 3, y + 2)$?
    (b) a dilation of 3?
    (c) a reflection in the point (–4, 8)?
    (d) If the point undergoes parts (a), (b), and (c) in that order, what is the final image?

5. Graph the following:
    (a) $\triangle LBJ$ with vertices L(–2, 2), B(3, 0), and J(1, 5).
    (b) the image of $\triangle LBJ$ after a reflection in the x-axis. (Label it $\triangle L'B'J'$)
    (c) the image of $\triangle L'B'J'$ after a translation $(x + 1, y - 2)$. (Label it $\triangle L''B''J''$)
    (d) the image of $\triangle L''B''J''$ after a dilation of 2.

6. A translation maps the point E(4, 2) onto its image E'(–1, –2). What is the image of the point F(5, –6) under the same translation?

7. A dilation maps the point $G(-3, 2)$ onto its image $G'(-9, 6)$. What is the image of the point $H(1, -4)$ under the same dilation?

8. What are the final coordinates of $(3, 5)$ after (1) a reflection in the point $(2, 1)$; (2) a reflection in the x-axis; (3) a dilation of 2; and (4) a translation of $(x + 1, y - 1)$?

9. Under which transformation of each of the following is B the image of A?
   (a) $A(1, 4)$; $B(-1, 4)$
   (b) $A(-3, 7)$; $B(7, -3)$
   (c) $A(-2, 6)$; $B(0, 0)$
   (d) $A(-6, 6)$; $B(-2, 2)$

10. If points $A(-1, 6)$ and $B(2, 3)$ undergo the translation $(x + 2, y - 5)$, how can you describe quadrilateral $ABB'A'$?

11. If a triangle undergoes a dilation of 2, what is the ratio of the area of the image to the area of the original triangle?

7

More Coordinate Geometry

In many ways, this chapter is a continuation of chapters 5 and 6. If anything in this chapter is unfamiliar to you, it may have been explained more completely in one of those earlier chapters. There are also some references to basic geometry, which is discussed in chapters 8–10. Be sure to look there as well if a geometric term eludes you.

Remember how you were graphing lines just by plugging values of x into an equation and figuring out the corresponding y-coordinates? Well, now it's time to get a little more sophisticated. There is a much faster way to graph a line, by simply analyzing its equation.

SLOPE

Most linear equations are given in **slope-intercept form**, which is denoted like this:

$$y = mx + b$$

The m in this equation represents the line's **slope**, which indicates how steep the line is. Take any two points (x_1, y_1) and (x_2, y_2) on a line. The steepness of the line between those two points is measured by how high up the line goes in relation to how far to the right it goes. More familiarly:

$$\text{slope} = \frac{\text{rise}}{\text{run}}$$

The "rise" is the difference between the y-coordinates, which you can calculate by subtracting one from the other. The "run" is determined the same way—by subtracting one x-coordinate from the other. This leads you to the **slope formula**: $m = \dfrac{y_2 - y_1}{x_2 - x_1}$

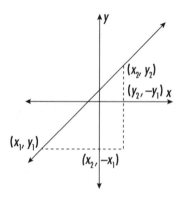

Remember it this way: The *rise* is the *y*'s.

EXAMPLE 1

Find the slope of the line determined by $M(-4, -1)$ and $N(3, 6)$.

SOLUTION

Plug the coordinates into the formula. Let $(x_1, y_1) = (-4, -1)$ and $(x_2, y_2) = (3, 6)$:

$$m = \frac{6-(-1)}{3-(-4)} = \frac{7}{7} = 1$$

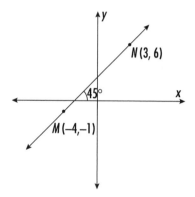

Note: It doesn't matter which points you designate to be (x_1, y_1) and (x_2, y_2), as long as you're consistent. You get the same value if you switch the order of the points:

$$m = \frac{-1-6}{-4-3} = \frac{-7}{-7} = 1$$

As you can see, a line with a slope of 1 makes a 45° angle with the x-axis. With this knowledge, you can determine a lot about a line just by looking at it.

A line that goes up and to the right has a **positive** slope; if the line goes down and to the right, the slope is **negative**.

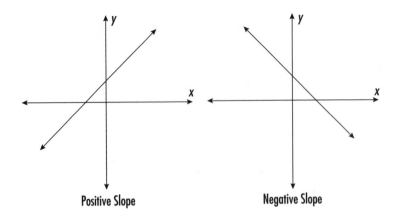

Positive Slope   Negative Slope

HORIZONTAL AND VERTICAL LINES

If a line is **horizontal**, it doesn't rise at all. Therefore, its slope equals zero.

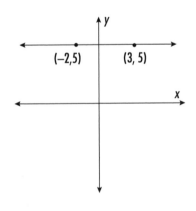

$$m = \frac{5-5}{3-(-2)} = \frac{0}{5} = 0$$

The equation for a horizontal line is $y = b$, in which b is a constant.

A **vertical** line has an undefined slope, because there's no change in the x-coordinates:

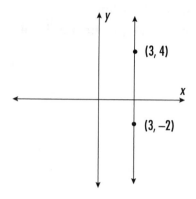

$$m = \frac{4-(-2)}{3-3} = \frac{6}{0} = \infty$$

The equation for a vertical line is $x = a$, in which a is a constant. You can sum up this information with this chart:

If the Line...	Angle Formed with x-axis	Slope
has negative slope	greater than 45° equal to 45° less than 45	$m < -1$ $m = -1$ $-1 < m < 0$
is horizontal	—	$m = 0$
has a positive slope	less than 45° equal to 45° greater than 45°	$0 < m < 1$ $m = 1$ $m > 1$
is vertical	—	$m = \infty$

FINDING THE EQUATION OF A LINE

In the linear equation $y = mx + b$, the b represents the **y-intercept**, or the point at which the line intersects the y-axis. There are two ways to determine the equation of a line:

1. When you know the slope and a point on the line.

EXAMPLE 2

Find the equation of the line that has a slope of 2 and passes through the point $(-4, -5)$.

SOLUTION

There are two methods for doing this. The first involves the slope-intercept formula:

$$y = mx + b$$

You know the slope already ($m = 2$), so substitute that in the equation:

$$y = 2x + b$$

Now substitute the coordinates $(-4, -5)$ into the equation and solve for b:

$$-5 = 2(-4) + b$$
$$-5 = -8 + b$$
$$3 = b$$

The equation is $y = 2x + 3$. From this formula, you can discern that (a) the slope of the line is 2 and (b) the y-intercept of the line is $(0, 3)$:

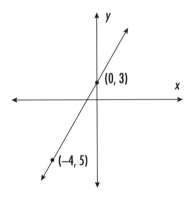

The other method involves the **point-slope** formula, in which m is the slope and (x_1, y_1) is the point you know:

$$y - y_1 = m(x - x_1)$$

Substitute the values you know and simplify:

$$y - (-5) = 2[x - (-4)]$$
$$y + 5 = 2x + 8$$
$$y = 2x + 3$$

2. When you know two points.

EXAMPLE 3
Find the equation of the line containing the points (–4, 1) and (2, 4).

SOLUTION
Find the slope of the line using the slope formula:

$$m = \frac{y_2 - y_1}{x_2 - x_1}$$
$$= \frac{4 - 1}{2 - (-4)} = \frac{3}{6} = \frac{1}{2}$$

Now you can repeat the work in Example 2, and you have two points to choose from.

$y = \dfrac{1}{2}x + b$ $\qquad$ $y = \dfrac{1}{2}x + b$

$4 = \dfrac{1}{2}(2) + b$ $\qquad\quad OR \qquad$ $1 = \dfrac{1}{2}(-4) + b$

$4 = 1 + b$ $\qquad\qquad\qquad\qquad$ $1 = -2 + b$

$3 = b$ $\qquad\qquad\qquad\qquad\quad$ $3 = b$

No matter which point you choose, the equation is $y = \dfrac{1}{2}x + 3$.

PARALLEL AND PERPENDICULAR LINES
Any two parallel lines in the coordinate plane have the same slope.

EXAMPLE 4
Find the equation of a line that is parallel to $y = 4x - 1$ and goes through the point (–2, 0).

SOLUTION

The slope of the line $y = 4x - 1$ is 4, so the slope of the line in question is also 4. Now you can repeat the steps you've seen before:

$$y = 4x + b$$
$$0 = 4(-2) + b$$
$$0 = -8 + b$$
$$8 = b$$

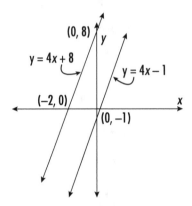

The equation of the new line is $y = 4x + 8$.

The slopes of two perpendicular lines are negative reciprocals; their product is –1.

For example, the negative reciprocal of 5 is $-\frac{1}{5}$, and the negative reciprocal of $\frac{4}{7}$ is $-\frac{7}{4}$.

EXAMPLE 5

Find the equation of a line that is perpendicular to $y = -\frac{2}{3}x + 1$ and goes through the point (4, –1).

SOLUTION

The slope of the line $y = -\frac{2}{3}x + 1$ is $-\frac{2}{3}$, so the slope of any line

perpendicular to that line is $\frac{3}{2}$. You know the rest:

$$y = \frac{3}{2}x + b$$
$$-1 = \frac{3}{2}(4) + b$$
$$-1 = 6 + b$$
$$-7 = b$$

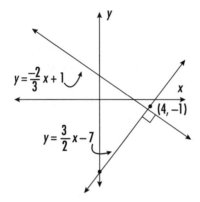

The equation is $y = \frac{3}{2}x - 7$.

EXERCISES, SET 7A

Here are some sample problems pertaining to slopes and equations of lines. The answers are in chapter 16.

1. Identify whether the slope of each of the following lines is positive, negative, 0, or undefined.

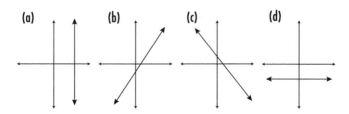

(a)　(b)　(c)　(d)

2. **(a)** Which of the following lines has a slope greater than one? **(b)** Which one has a slope between 0 and –1?

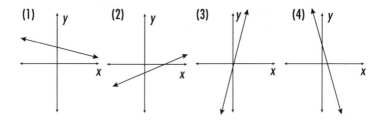

(1)　(2)　(3)　(4)

3. Find the equation of the line with the given slope that passes through the given point.
   (a) $m = -2$; $(0, 3)$
   (b) $m = 3$; $(-1, 4)$
   (c) $m = \dfrac{1}{2}$; $(-4, 7)$
   (d) $m = 0.4$; $(5, 1)$
   (e) $m = -\dfrac{2}{3}$; $(-1, -4)$
   (f) $m = p$; $(0, q)$

4. Find the equation of the line determined by each of the following pairs of points.

(a) (3, 4) and (0, 1)

(b) (−2, 5) and (−4, 1)

(c) (−3, 0) and (3, −4)

(d) (6, −3) and (6, 5)

(e) $\left(\dfrac{1}{2}, 3\right)$ and $\left(3, \dfrac{7}{2}\right)$

(f) (−4, 2) and (8, 2)

5. Which of the following lines is parallel to the line $y = \dfrac{3}{2}x + 3$?

(1) $y = \dfrac{2}{3}x + 3$

(2) $3y = -2x + 5$

(3) $2y = 3x - 2$

(4) $y = -\dfrac{3}{2}x + 1$

6. Which of the following lines is perpendicular to the line $y = \dfrac{3}{2}x + 3$?

(1) $y = \dfrac{2}{3}x + 3$

(2) $3y = -2x + 5$

(3) $2y = 3x - 2$

(4) $y = -\dfrac{3}{2}x + 1$

7. Find the equation of each of the following lines.
   (a) The line parallel to $y = 4x - 1$ and passing through (1, 7).

   (b) The line parallel to $y = \dfrac{5}{4}x + 3$ and passing through (–8, –3).

   (c) The line perpendicular to $y = -2x + 4$ and passing through (3, 1).

   (d) The line perpendicular to $y = \dfrac{1}{7}x - \dfrac{2}{7}$ and passing through (2, –10).

DISTANCE

Now it's time to turn your attention from lines to line segments.

The **Pythagorean Theorem**, which we'll discuss more in chapter 9, says that the sum of the squares of the two legs of a right triangle equals the hypotenuse squared. You've probably seen it written like this (in which a and b are the legs and c is the hypotenuse):

$$a^2 + b^2 = c^2$$

Well, you can look at any line segment on the coordinate plane as the hypotenuse of a right triangle:

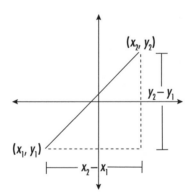

Let the distance between the two points equal d. The length of the horizontal leg is equal to the difference between the x-coordinates $(x_2 - x_1)$, and the length of the vertical leg is equal to the difference between the y-coordinates $(y_2 - y_1)$. Using these terms, you can substitute into the Pythagorean Theorem to find the **distance formula**.

> The formula for the distance between two points (x_1, y_1) and (x_2, y_2) is: $d = \sqrt{(x_2 - x_1)^2 + (y_2 - y_1)^2}$

EXAMPLE 6
On the coordinate plane, find the distance between points (3, –5) and (–6, 1).

SOLUTION
Plug the coordinates into the distance formula (again, the order doesn't matter as long as you're consistent):

$$d = \sqrt{(-6-3)^2 + [(1-(-5)]^2}$$
$$= \sqrt{(-9)^2 + 6^2}$$
$$= \sqrt{81 + 36}$$
$$= \sqrt{117}$$
$$= 3\sqrt{13}$$

MIDPOINT
As you learned from chapter 6, the formula for the **midpoint** of a line segment is: $(\bar{x}, \bar{y}) = \left(\dfrac{x_1 + x_2}{2}, \dfrac{y_1 + y_2}{2} \right)$.

The formula is based on the common-sense principle that the coordinates of a midpoint are the average values of the x- and y-coordinates. There are two types of problems in which this formula is used.

EXAMPLE 7
Find the midpoint of the segment between $P(5, -3)$ and $Q(-1, 3)$.

SOLUTION:
It couldn't be more basic. Just plug 'em in:

$$(\bar{x}, \bar{y}) = \left(\frac{5 + (-1)}{2}, \frac{-3 + 3}{2} \right)$$
$$= \left(\frac{4}{2}, \frac{0}{2} \right)$$
$$= (2, 0)$$

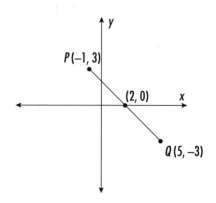

EXAMPLE 8

If the midpoint of a segment is (–2, 3) and one of the endpoints of that segment is (–4, –3), find the coordinates of the other endpoint.

SOLUTION

Use the midpoint formula to solve for each coordinate one at a time.

Let $(\bar{x}, \bar{y}) = (-2, 3)$, $(x_1, y_1) = (-4, -3)$ and $(x_2, y_2) = (x, y)$:

$$\bar{x} = \frac{x_1 + x_2}{2} \qquad\qquad y = \frac{y_1 + y_2}{2}$$
$$-2 = \frac{-4 + x}{2} \qquad\qquad 3 = \frac{-3 + y}{2}$$
$$-4 = -4 + x \qquad\qquad 6 = -3 + y$$
$$0 = x \qquad\qquad 9 = y$$

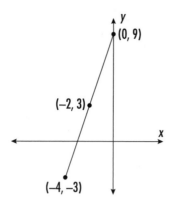

The coordinates of the other endpoint are **(0, 9)**.

AREAS

Here's a preliminary look at three important area formulas (you'll work more with them in chapters 9 and 10):

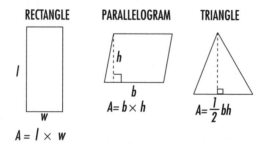

Finding areas using coordinate geometry is easy if you remember these formulas. There's usually no length to calculate; just count the units.

EXAMPLE 9

Given the vertices $M(2, 2)$, $U(7, 2)$, and $D(4, 6)$, find the area of $\triangle MUD$.

SOLUTION

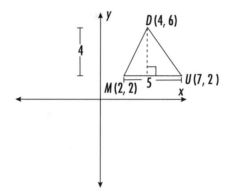

The base of the triangle is 5 units long, and the height is 4 units.

Plug those values into the area for a triangle: $A = \frac{1}{2}(5)(4) = 10$

The area of $\triangle MUD$ is **10** square units.

Area problems aren't always quite so easy, though. If there are no dimensions that are parallel with either axis, it's best to work indirectly.

EXAMPLE 10

Given the vertices $S(-4, -1)$, $P(3, -3)$, $U(5, 0)$, and $D(-1, 5)$, find the area of quadrilateral $SPUD$.

SOLUTION

Graph all four vertices, then circumscribe a rectangle on the coordinate plane like this:

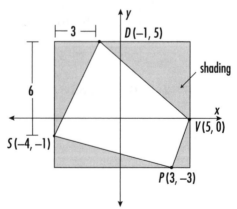

You can now find the area of the quadrilateral by subtracting the collective area of the four shaded triangles from the big rectangle. The area of the big rectangle is 9 × 8, or 72 square units. Now, calculate the area of the three outer triangles, using the formula $A = \frac{1}{2}bh$:

Triangle 1: $A = \frac{1}{2}(6)(3) = 9$

Triangle 2: $A = \frac{1}{2}(6)(5) = 15$

Triangle 3: $A = \frac{1}{2}(3)(2) = 3$

Triangle 4: $A = \frac{1}{2}(7)(2) = 7$

Total area of three triangles: 9 +15 + 3 + 7 = 34.

Subtract 34 from the rectangle's area (72), and you're left with **38** square units.

CIRCLES

Here's another enticing little nugget of information that will get you ready for the next chapter on Euclidean geometry. It's the **equation of a circle**. As you'll read in chapter 13, a circle is the locus of points that are a certain distance from a point. That distance is the **radius** of the circle.

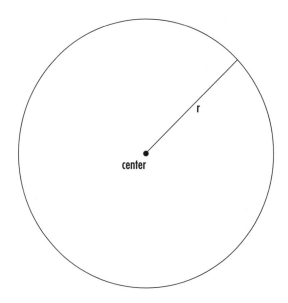

center

In the formula below, the radius is denoted as r, and the co-ordinates of the center of the circle are (h, k):

$$(x-h)^2 + (y-k)^2 = r^2$$

EXAMPLE 11

Find the equation of a circle that has a radius of 4 and is centered at the point $(-3, 1)$.

SOLUTION

Just plug in the numbers.

$$(x-h)^2 + (y-k)^2 = r^2$$
$$[x-(-3)]^2 + (y-1)^2 = 4^2$$
$$(x+3)^2 + (y-1)^2 = 16$$

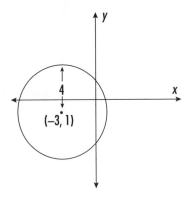

EXAMPLE 12

If the endpoints of the diameter of a circle are $(-1, 1)$ and $(7, 3)$, what are the coordinates of the center of that circle?

SOLUTION

As you'll see in the next chapter, the diameter of a circle runs through the center of that circle. Therefore, the center of the circle is the midpoint of the diameter. Plug the points into the midpoint formula and solve:

$$\left(\overline{x},\overline{y}\right)=\left(\frac{x_1+x_2}{2},\frac{y_1+y_2}{2}\right)$$

$$=\left(\frac{-1+7}{2},\frac{1+3}{2}\right)$$

$$=\left(\frac{6}{2},\frac{4}{2}\right)$$

$$=(3,2)$$

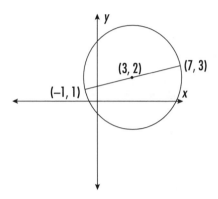

EXERCISES, SET 7B

These problems feature distance, midpoint, areas, and circles. Have a ball. The answers are in chapter 16.

1. Find the distance between the following pairs of points.
   (a) (6, –4) and (2, –7)
   (b) (–2, –3) and (–2, 4)
   (c) (–8, 3) and (4, –2)
   (d) (0, 8) and (2, 0)
   (e) (2, –9) and (5, –9)
   (f) (–4, 1) and (2, 2)
   (g) (–3, –1) and (1, 3)
   (h) (6, 6) and (–3, –9)

2. Find the midpoint of the segment between each of the following pairs of points.
   (a) (5, 3) and (5, 9)
   (b) (0, 8) and (−10, 0)
   (c) (2, 7) and (6, −3)
   (d) (−5, −1) and (−9, 10)
   (e) (−3, −8) and (16, 5)
   (f) (0.7a, 1.2b) and (1.3a, 4.8b)
   (g) (a, b) and (c, d)

3. Find the equation of the circle with the given center and radius.
   (a) (3, 2); $r = 4$
   (b) (−2, −6); $r = \sqrt{5}$
   (c) (5, −2); $r = 3.5$
   (d) $\left(\dfrac{1}{2}, -\dfrac{4}{3}\right)$; $r = \dfrac{2}{9}$
   (e) (♣, ♦); $r = $ ♥

4. Graph the following circles.
   (a) $x^2 + y^2 = 25$
   (b) $(x - 2)^2 + (y - 1)^2 = 9$
   (c) $\left(x - \dfrac{1}{2}\right)^2 + \left(y + \dfrac{7}{2}\right)^2 = \dfrac{25}{4}$
   (d) $(2 - x)^2 + (4 + y)^2 = 36$
   (e) $x^2 + 4x + 4 + y^2 - 6y + 9 = 16$
   (f) $x^2 + 10x + y^2 - 2y = -10$

5. (a) Graph the circles $(x + 2)^2 + (y - 3)^2 = 25$ and $(x - 6)^2 + (y + 3)^2 = 25$.
   (b) Where do they intersect?

6. Find the area of each polygon.
   (a) $A(-3, -2)$; $B(5, -2)$; and $C(1, 4)$
   (b) $A(-4, -4)$; $B(5, 0)$; and $C(-2, 6)$
   (c) $A(-3, -1)$; $B(6, -1)$; $C(6, 5)$; and $D(-3, 5)$
   (d) $A(-3, 2)$; $B(4, 2)$; $C(7, 8)$; and $D(0, 8)$
   (e) $A(-10, -1)$; $B(-2, -1)$; $C(0, 7)$; and $D(-5, 7)$
   (f) $A(-11, 5)$; $B(-6, -5)$; $C(5, 3)$; and $D(-2, 6)$

7. (a) Find the equation of the locus of points equidistant from $D(-2, -5)$ and $F(6, 11)$. (b) Graph it.

PROOFS USING COORDINATES

To get you geared up for the next three chapters (which are all about geometric proofs), this last section of the chapter deals with proofs using the techniques to prove that polygons have certain properties by analyzing their coordinates. That's why many textbooks refer to these as **analytic proofs** or **coordinate proofs**.

This portion also incorporates the properties of certain polygons that are discussed in chapters 9 (triangles) and 10 (quadrilaterals). If you can memorize those characteristics (some of which you're about to see) and understand the distance, slope, and midpoint formulas, you'll be great at these proofs.

You'll use the **distance formula** to prove that segments are the same length, including:

- sides of an isosceles or equilateral triangle
- opposite sides of a parallelogram or rectangle
- diagonals of a rectangle

EXAMPLE 13

Given points $F(-1, -1)$, $G(6, 0)$, and $H(2, 3)$, prove that $\triangle FGH$ is an isosceles triangle.

SOLUTION

An isosceles triangle has two equal sides. Therefore, use the distance formula to find the length of each side:

$$FG = \sqrt{[(6-(-1)]^2 + [0-(-1)]^2} \qquad GH = \sqrt{(2-6)^2 + (3-0)^2}$$
$$= \sqrt{7^2 + 1^2} \qquad\qquad = \sqrt{(-4)^2 + 3^2}$$
$$= \sqrt{49+1} \qquad\qquad = \sqrt{16+9}$$
$$= \sqrt{50} \qquad\qquad = \sqrt{25}$$
$$= 5\sqrt{2} \qquad\qquad = 5$$

So far, there's nothing helpful.

$$FH = \sqrt{[2-(-1)]^2 + [3-(-1)]^2}$$
$$= \sqrt{3^2 + 4^2}$$
$$= \sqrt{9+16}$$
$$= \sqrt{25}$$
$$= 5$$

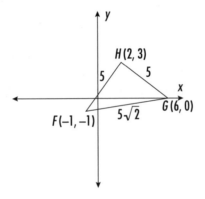

That's got it. Since $\overline{GH}$ and $\overline{FH}$ have the same length, $\triangle FGH$ is isosceles.

The **slope formula** is used chiefly to prove that two lines are parallel (i.e., opposite sides of a parallelogram, rectangle, or trapezoid) or perpendicular (for right angles in a right triangle, rectangle, or square).

EXAMPLE 14

Prove that the triangle in Example 13 is a right triangle.

SOLUTION

Find the slope of all three sides of the triangle using the slope formula:

$$m = \frac{y_2 - y_1}{x_2 - x_1}$$

Slope of $\overline{FG}$:   Slope of $\overline{GH}$:   Slope of $\overline{FH}$:

$$m = \frac{0 - (-1)}{6 - (-1)}$$ $$m = \frac{3 - 0}{2 - 6}$$ $$m = \frac{3 - (-1)}{2 - (-1)}$$

$$= \frac{1}{7}$$ $$= -\frac{3}{4}$$ $$= \frac{4}{3}$$

Since the slopes of $\overline{GH}$ and $\overline{FH}$ are negative reciprocals $\left(-\frac{3}{4} \times \frac{4}{3}\right) = -1$, the two sides are perpendicular. Therefore, $\angle FHG$ is a right angle and $\triangle FGH$ is a right triangle.

The **midpoint formula** is called for usually when you have to prove that a segment (i.e., the side or a diagonal of a polygon) is bisected, or to prove that a segment is the median of a triangle. You can also use it in the situation below.

EXAMPLE 15

Given the triangle in Example 13, prove that the segment determined by the midpoints of $\overline{FH}$ and $\overline{GH}$ is parallel to $\overline{FG}$.

SOLUTION

As you'll see in chapter 9, the segment determined by the midpoints of two sides of a triangle is parallel to the third side. Now's your chance to prove it. First, use the midpoint formula to find the midpoints of $\overline{FH}$ and $\overline{GH}$ and label those points X and Y:

$$(\bar{x}, \bar{y}) = \left(\frac{x_1 + x_2}{2}, \frac{y_1 + y_2}{2}\right)$$

Midpoint of $\overline{FH}$:	Midpoint of $\overline{GH}$:

$$\left(\bar{x},\bar{y}\right)=\left(\frac{-1+2}{2},\frac{-1+3}{2}\right) \qquad \left(\bar{x},\bar{y}\right)=\left(\frac{6+2}{2},\frac{0+3}{2}\right)$$

$$=\left(\frac{1}{2},\frac{2}{2}\right) \qquad\qquad\qquad =\left(\frac{8}{2},\frac{3}{2}\right)$$

$$=\left(\frac{1}{2},1\right) \qquad\qquad\qquad =\left(4,\frac{3}{2}\right)$$

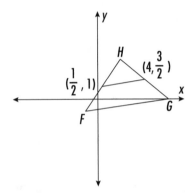

You have the coordinates, and you already know that the slope of $\overline{FG}$ is $\frac{1}{7}$ (from Example 2). Find the slope of $\overline{XY}$ using the slope formula (and don't be afraid of complex fractions):

$$m=\frac{y_2-y_1}{x_2-x_1}$$

Slope of $\overline{XY}$:

$$m=\frac{\dfrac{3}{2}-1}{4-\dfrac{1}{2}}=\frac{\dfrac{1}{2}}{\dfrac{7}{2}}$$

$$=\frac{1}{2}\times\frac{2}{7}$$

$$=\frac{1}{7}$$

Line segments $\overline{FG}$ and $\overline{XY}$ have the same slope, so they're parallel.

PROVING THAT SOMETHING *ISN'T* TRUE

Proving that something is false is sometimes just as useful as declaring something to be true. The process is the same, only you prove that something is not possible.

EXAMPLE 16

Given the points $C(-3, -3)$, $R(5, 1)$, $U(2, 5)$, and $D(-2, 3)$, prove that quadrilateral $CRUD$ is not a parallelogram.

SOLUTION

From the diagram below, you can tell that the quadrilateral is not a parallelogram. (If it looks like a parallelogram, you may have drawn it wrong.)

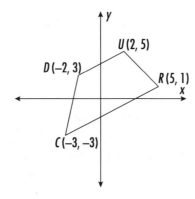

As with most of these analytic proofs, there is more than one way to solve this problem.

Method One: Prove that opposite sides of the parallelogram aren't congruent using the distance formula. Pick sides $\overline{CR}$ and $\overline{DU}$:

$$CR = \sqrt{(x_2 - x_1)^2 + (y_2 - y_1)^2} \qquad DU = \sqrt{(x_2 - x_1)^2 + (y_2 - y_1)^2}$$

$$\quad = \sqrt{[5-(-3)]^2 + [1-(-3)]^2} \qquad \quad = \sqrt{[2-(-2)]^2 + (5-3)^2}$$

$$\quad = \sqrt{8^2 + 4^2} \qquad\qquad\qquad\quad = \sqrt{4^2 + 2^2}$$

$$\quad = \sqrt{64 + 16} \qquad\qquad\qquad\quad = \sqrt{16 + 4}$$

$$\quad = \sqrt{80} = 4\sqrt{5} \qquad\qquad\qquad = \sqrt{20} = 2\sqrt{5}$$

The two sides have different lengths. Since opposite sides of a parallelogram are congruent, $CRUD$ is not a parallelogram.

<u>Method Two</u>: Prove that opposite sides of the quadrilateral aren't parallel using the slope formula: $m = \dfrac{y_2 - y_1}{x_2 - x_1}$

Slope of $\overline{CR}$:

$$m = \frac{1-(-3)}{5-(-3)}$$
$$= \frac{4}{8} = \frac{1}{2}$$

Slope of $\overline{RU}$:

$$m = \frac{1-5}{5-2}$$
$$= -\frac{4}{3}$$

Slope of $\overline{DU}$:

$$m = \frac{5-3}{2-(-2)}$$
$$= \frac{2}{4} = \frac{1}{2}$$

Slope of $\overline{CD}$:

$$m = \frac{3-(-3)}{-2-(-3)}$$
$$= \frac{6}{1} = 6$$

The slopes of opposite sides $\overline{CR}$ and $\overline{DU}$ are the same, so those two sides are parallel. However, opposite sides $\overline{RU}$ and $\overline{CD}$ have different slopes, so they are not parallel. Therefore, $CRUD$ is not a parallelogram. (In fact, it's a trapezoid.)

WHEN THERE ARE NO NUMBERS

Sometimes, a coordinate proof doesn't refer to an actual polygon. You might have to prove that a polygon has a certain property by using variables instead of numbers.

EXAMPLE 17

Using analytic geometry, prove that the diagonals of a rectangle are congruent.

SOLUTION

Now you don't have any numbers to work with. You have to set up a rectangle and assign coordinate values that are variables:

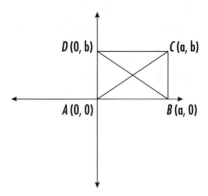

Rectangle $ABCD$ has coordinates $A(0, 0)$, $B(a, 0)$, $C(a, b)$, and $D(0, b)$. To prove that the diagonals have the same length, use the distance formula: $d = \sqrt{(x_2 - x_1)^2 + (y_2 - y_1)^2}$

Use it just as you normally would—just use the letters instead of the numbers:

$$AC = \sqrt{(a-0)^2 + (b-0)^2}$$
$$= \sqrt{a^2 + b^2}$$

$$BD = \sqrt{(0-a)^2 + (b-1)^2}$$
$$= \sqrt{(-a)^2 + b^2}$$
$$= \sqrt{a^2 + b^2}$$

No matter what the values of a and b are, the diagonals have the same length, $\sqrt{a^2 + b^2}$.

EXERCISES, SET 7C

Prove (or disprove) the following. The answers are in chapter 16.

1. Given vertices $M(7, -1)$, $O(1, -1)$, and $P(-3, 5)$, prove that MOP is an isosceles triangle.

2. Prove that MOP is *not* equilateral.

3. Given vertices $L(-6, 0)$, $I(2, -4)$, $M(7, 1)$, and $P(-1, 5)$, prove that $LIMP$ is a parallelogram.

4. Prove that $LIMP$ is *not* a rectangle.

5. Given vertices $P(-6, 1)$, $I(3, -2)$, and $G(-4, 7)$, prove that PIG is a right triangle.

6. Given vertices $D(-2, 2)$, $U(3, 0)$, $M(1, 5)$, and $P(-4, 7)$, prove that $DUMP$ is a rhombus.

7. Prove that $DUMP$ is *not* a square.

   For the following, there are no numbers to work with.

8. Prove that the diagonals of a square bisect each other.

9. Prove that a rectangle is a parallelogram with at least one right angle.

10. Prove that the diagonals of a rhombus are perpendicular.

8

Geometric Concepts

This is the first of four chapters devoted to the subject that, for many students, can be a real struggle: geometric proofs. This chapter is an introduction to several basic geometric concepts, many of which you learned in Course I.

Pay close attention to the material in this chapter, as well as the theorems, postulates, and definitions in chapters 9 and 10. There are a bunch of mini-proofs scattered throughout the unit, but the big-time stuff happens in chapter 11.

You've seen the basic structure of a two-column proof: statements on the left, and the corresponding reason that backs up that statement on the right. There are plenty of examples all over the place.

THE BASICS

Euclidean geometry is named after the Greek mathematician Euclid. Euclidean geometry incorporates three building blocks:

> A **point** indicates a position in space, but has no dimensions.

You may recognize the concept of points from the last chapter on coordinate geometry.

> A **line** is a series of points that extends infinitely in two opposite directions. Two points determine a line.

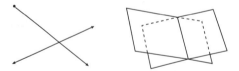

If two or more points are in the same line, they're **collinear** (as in co-**line**-ar). The two main subsets of a line are **rays**, which start at one point and extend infinitely in one direction, and **line segments**, which have a specific length.

A **plane** is a flat surface that extends forever in all directions. Three points determine a plane.

If three or more points are in the same plane, they're **coplanar** (as in co-**plane**-ar). (**Note:** That's why the best-made stools have only three legs; a three-legged stool will never wobble.)

Two lines intersect in a point, and two planes intersect in a line.

Planes contain **angles**, which are formed by two rays with a common starting point (or **vertex**), and **polygons**, or shapes. (You'll see more of these in chapters 9 and 10.) You won't encounter any three-dimensional geometry until Course III.

EQUALITY AND CONGRUENCY

The goal of many proofs is to prove that two things are **congruent** (the same size and shape). Congruency is denoted by the symbol "≅". If two line segments have equal length, for example, then they are congruent.

There are three basic properties of equality and congruency that you should know. Students sometimes remember them as the "*RST*" properties:

Property	Rule	Example
Reflexive	Anything is equal (or congruent) to itself.	$\angle A \cong \angle A$.
Symmetric	You can always switch the order of the elements on either side of the "=" or "≅" sign.	If $\angle A \cong \angle B$, then $\angle B \cong \angle A$.
Transitive	Two things that are equal (or congruent) to a separate third thing are equal (or congruent to each other).	If $\angle A \cong \angle B$ and $\angle B \cong \angle C$, then $\angle A \cong \angle C$.

Your textbook might also include a theorem that states: "Congruence in segments and angles is reflexive, symmetric, and transitive."

In addition to those three (the *R* and *T* show up a lot in proofs), you should know these:

Addition Property of Equality: If $a = b$ and $c = d$, then $a + b = c + d$.

Subtraction Property of Equality: If $a = b$ and $c = d$, then $a - b = c - d$.

Multiplication Property of Equality: If k is a constant and $a = b$, then $ka = kb$.

The bottom line of these three properties is that you can do whatever you want to both sides of an equals sign.

> **Substitution Property:** If two quantities are equal, then one may be substituted for the other in any expression at any time.

Don't confuse the Substitution Property with the Transitive Property. As you'll see in the many proofs you do, the two properties are related, but they're not the same. You'll usually get penalized if you use the wrong one.

Substitution Property:	**Transitive Property:**
If $a + b = c$ and $b = d$, then $a + d = c$.	If $a = b$ and $b = c$, then $a = c$.

LINES AND SEGMENTS

Here are the highlights of the theorems involving linear sets of points.

> **Segment Addition Postulate:** If a point B is between points A and C, then A, B, and C are collinear, and $AB + BC = AC$.

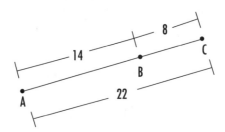

Basically, this means that if two segments are collinear, you can add their lengths. You're about to get your first example of a proof. (Take a moment to compose yourself.)

EXAMPLE 1

Given: $BU = RP$ Prove: $BR = UP$

SOLUTION

This is about as basic as it gets.

SOLUTION

This is about as basic as it gets.

Statements	Reasons
1. $BU = RP$	1. Given
2. $UR = UR$	2. Reflexive Property of Equality
3. $BU + UR = UR + RP$	3. Addition Property of Equality
4. $BR = UP$	4. Segment Addition Postulate

As you learned in chapter 7, the **midpoint** of a line segment is the one point that is equidistant from the endpoints of that segment. Each line segment has exactly one midpoint.

> The midpoint M of a line segment $\overline{AB}$ divides the segment into segments $\overline{AM}$ and $\overline{MB}$ such that:
>
> $$\overline{AM} \cong \overline{MB}$$
>
> $$AM = MB = \frac{1}{2}(AB)$$
>
> A———————M———————B

Any line or part of a line that passes through the midpoint of a line segment is the **segment bisector**.

EXAMPLE 2

If Y is the midpoint of $\overline{XZ}$, $XY = 5x - 8$, and $YZ = 3x + 2$, what is the value of x?

SOLUTION

Since Y is the midpoint, XY and YZ are equal:

```
        5x+8          3x+2
   ┌──────────┬──────────┐
   X          Y          Z
```

Therefore, you can set the two lengths equal to each other and solve:

$$5x - 8 = 3x + 2$$
$$2x = 10$$
$$x = 5$$

PARALLELS AND PERPENDICULARS

You also saw parallel and perpendicular lines in chapter 7. They look like this:

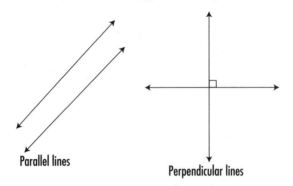

Parallel lines

Perpendicular lines

> Two distinct lines are **parallel** if and only if they lie in the same plane and do not intersect. **Perpendicular** lines intersect at a 90° angle.

If you have a line *l* and a point *P* that is not on that line, there is exactly one line parallel to *l* and one line perpendicular to *l* that go through point *P*.

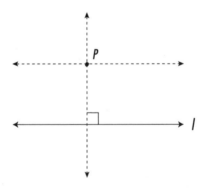

ANGLES

When two lines intersect, an angle is formed. Many of the theorems you're about to see might seem like common sense as well—that's because they are. Memorize them anyway, because you have to refer to them officially when you write proofs.

Any two lines that intersect form two pairs of **vertical angles,** and vertical angles are congruent.

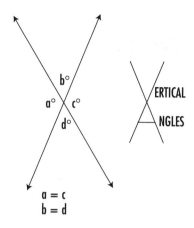

a = c
b = d

EXAMPLE 3

In the diagram below, what is the value of d?

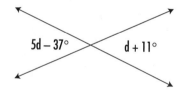

SOLUTION

The two angles in question are vertical angles, so you can set them equal to each other:

$$5d - 37 = d + 11$$
$$4d = 48$$
$$d = \mathbf{12}$$

You can add measures of adjacent angles just as well as you can add segment lengths.

Angle Addition Postulate: If a ray BD lies within the interior of $\angle ABC$, then m$\angle ABD$ + m$\angle DBC$ = m$\angle ABC$.

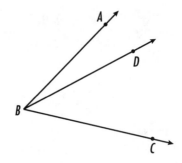

An **angle bisector** is a ray that divides an angle into two smaller congruent angles.

EXAMPLE 5

If $\overline{MN}$ is the angle bisector of $\angle LNP$, what is the value of b?

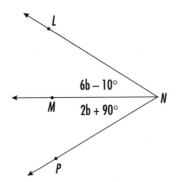

SOLUTION

Since $\overline{MN}$ is the angle bisector, then $\angle LNM$ and $\angle MNP$ have equal measure. Set the measures of the two angles equal to each other.

$$6b - 10 = 2b + 90$$
$$4b = 100$$
$$b = \mathbf{25}$$

You should also be familiar with the basics of angle measure. There are 180° in a line (which is also referred to as a straight angle), and two perpendicular lines form four right angles, each of which measures 90°.

An angle that measures 90° is a **right angle**, which is usually denoted with a little box at the vertex, like this:

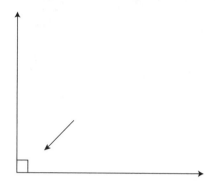

All right angles are congruent.

EXAMPLE 5

In the diagram below, what is the value of *d*?

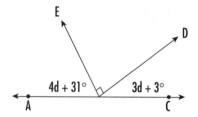

SOLUTION

Since $\overline{AC}$ is a line, the sum of all three angles is 180. The middle angle is a right angle, which measures 90. Therefore, you can set up the following equation:

$$(4d + 31) + 90 + (3d + 3) = 180$$
$$7d + 124 = 180$$
$$7d = 56$$
$$d = 8$$

As we discussed in chapter 4, you should always double-check your answers whenever you have to do algebra:

$$4(8) + 31 = 63$$
$$3(8) + 3 = 27$$

Since $63 + 27 = 90$, you might recognize that the sum of the measures of $\angle ABE$ and $\angle DBC$ in Example 4 is 90°. That means that the angles are complementary.

If the sum of the measures of two angles is 90°, then the angles are **complementary**. If the measure of an angle is x, then its complement can be represented as **90 – x.**

If the sum of the measures of two angles is 180°, then the angles are **supplementary**. If the measure of an angle is x, then its supplement can be represented as **180 – x.**

Note: Many students confuse these two terms. Think of it this way: "If you got a *90* on an exam, your parents would *compliment* you." (Sure, it's stupid. But it'll help you remember.)

If two angles are congruent and supplementary, then they are right angles.

Algebra problems involving complements and supplements are common in Course II. Remember to use the algebraic terms in the definitions above.

EXAMPLE 6
If the supplement of an angle is equal to four times its complement, what is the measure of the angle?

SOLUTION
You'll have to use your ability to construct algebraic equations on this one. Let the measure of the angle equal x:

supplement	equals	four times	complement
$180 - x$	$=$	$4 \times$	$(90 - x)$

$$180 - x = 4(90 - x)$$
$$180 - x = 360 - 4x$$
$$-180 = -3x$$
$$60 = x$$

Check your work: The complement of 60 is 30, and the supplement of 60 is 120. Since 120 equals 4 × 30, you know you're right.

EXAMPLE 7

If two supplementary angles are in a ratio of 5 : 7, what is the measure of the larger angle?

SOLUTION

Let the measures of the angles equal $5x$ and $7x$, respectively. Then add them up and solve for x:

$$5x + 7x = 180$$
$$12x = 180$$
$$x = \mathbf{15}$$

You aren't finished yet. Since the larger angle is represented as $7x$, the measure of the larger angle is 7×15, or **105°**.

EXERCISES, SET 8A

Now try these. The answers are in chapter 16.

1. If $m + n = 15$ and $p = m$, which of the following is true based on the Substitution Property?
   (1) $m + p = 150$
   (2) $m + n + p = 15 + p$
   (3) $p + n = 15$
   (4) $p + 15 = m + 15$

2. If M is the midpoint of GH, $GH = 3x - 1$, and $GM = x + 2$, find the value of x.

3. Find the value of g in each of the following.

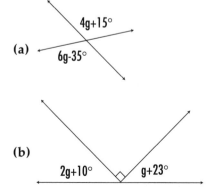

(a) 4g+15° 6g-35°

(b) 2g+10° g+23°

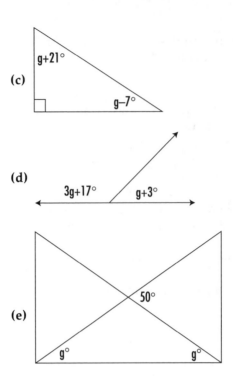

(c) $g+21°$ $g-7°$

(d) $3g+17°$ $g+3°$

(e) $50°$ $g°$ $g°$

4. A line and a plane could intersect in
   (1) a point
   (2) a line
   (3) the empty set
   (4) all of the above

5. If two angles are supplementary, find the measure of the acute angle if the ratio of the two measures is
   (a) 1:2
   (b) 1:3
   (c) 1:4
   (d) 1:5
   (e) 2:7
   (f) 3:7
   (g) 4:11
   (h) 5:13

6. If $\overline{US}$ bisects $\angle FUD$ and m$\angle FUS = 2x - 15$, find x if m$\angle FUD =$
   (a) 62
   (b) 50
   (c) 106
   (d) 142
   (e) m

7. (a) When the measure of an angle is subtracted from the measure of its supplement, the result is 100. Which of the following represents the equation for this statement?
   (1) $(180 - x) - x = 100$
   (2) $x - (180 - x) = 100$
   (3) $x + 100 = 180 - (x + 100)$
   (4) $x + (180 - x) = 100$

   (b) What is the measure of the acute angle?

8. If the supplement and complement of an angle are in each of the following ratios, find the measure of the angle.
   (a) 3:1
   (b) 4:1
   (c) 5:1
   (d) 5:2
   (e) 8:3

ANGLES AND PROOFS

The backbone of many geometric proofs is finding that two angles are congruent to each other. There are many theorems that you can use to prove that two angles are equal in measure.

Let's look back at parallel lines again. No doubt, you've seen a diagram like this, in which two parallel lines are cut by a third line, called a **transversal**:

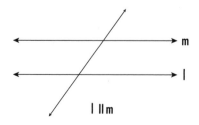

If two parallel lines are cut by a transversal, then:

Corresponding angles are congruent:

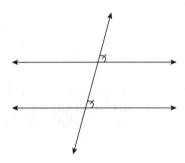

Alternate interior angles are congruent:

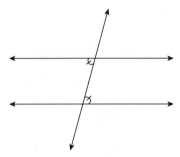

Interior angles on the same side of the transversal are supplementary:

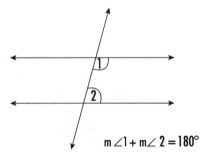

$$m\angle 1 + m\angle 2 = 180°$$

EXAMPLE 7

In the diagram below, if lines l and m are parallel, what is the value of p?

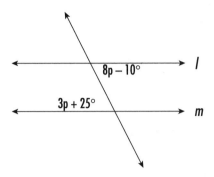

SOLUTION

The two angles in question are alternate interior angles, so they're congruent to each other:

$$8p - 10 = 3p + 25$$
$$5p = 35$$
$$p = 7$$

The converse of each of these theorems is also true:

> If two lines are cut by a transversal and:
>
> - corresponding angles are congruent;
> - alternate interior angles are congruent; or
> - interior angles on the same side of the transversal are supplementary, then the lines are parallel.

You can use these theorems to prove that two lines are parallel.

EXAMPLE

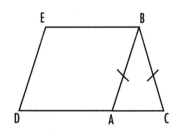

Given: $\overline{AB} \cong \overline{BC}$ Prove: $\overline{AB}$ is parallel to $\overline{DE}$
$\angle BCA \cong \angle EDA$

SOLUTION
The proof looks like this:

Statements	Reasons
1. $\overline{AB} \cong \overline{BC}$	1. Given
2. $\angle BAC \cong \angle BCA$	2. If two sides of a triangle are congruent, then the angles opposite them are congruent.*
3. $\angle BCA \cong \angle EDA$	3. Given
4. $\angle BAC \cong \angle EDA$	4. Transitive Property (2, 3)
5. $\overline{AB}$ is parallel to $\overline{DE}$	5. If corresponding angles are congruent, then the lines are parallel.

* **Note:** This theorem isn't discussed until the next chapter on triangles, but we included it here to help the proof along.

Another way to prove that two lines are parallel is to show that each line is perpendicular to a third line.

If two lines are perpendicular to the same line, then they are parallel. If a line is perpendicular to one of two parallel lines, then it is perpendicular to the other line.

There are two more theorems left in this chapter that relate angles to each other, and they involve complementary and supplementary angles.

If two angles are complementary to congruent angles, then the two angles are congruent.
If two angles are supplementary to congruent angles, then the two angles are congruent.

EXAMPLE 9

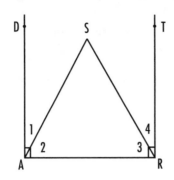

Given: $\overline{DA} \perp \overline{AR};\ \overline{AR} \perp \overline{RT}$

Prove: $\triangle ASR$ is isosceles.
$\angle 1 \cong \angle 4$

SOLUTION

Statements	Reasons
1. $\overline{DA} \perp \overline{AR}$	1. Given
2. $m \angle DAR = 90$	2. Definition of perpendicular lines
3. $\angle 1$ and $\angle 2$ are complementary	3. Definition of complementary
4. $\overline{AR} \perp \overline{RT}$	4. Given
5. $m \angle ART = 90$	5. Definition of perpendicular lines
6. $\angle 3$ and $\angle 4$ are complementary	6. Definition of complementary
7. $\angle 1 \cong \angle 4$	7. Given
8. $\angle 2 \cong \angle 3$	8. If two angles are complementary to congruent angles, then the two angles are congruent
9. $\triangle ASR$ is isosceles	9. Definition of isosceles triangle*

*Yeah, we know. We haven't talked about isosceles triangles yet. We will, though, in chapter 9, which is all about triangles.

EXERCISES, SET 8B

In the meantime, try these exercises and a few preliminary proofs. The answers are in chapter 16.

1. If lines *l* and *m* are parallel in each of the following diagrams, solve for *p*.

(a)

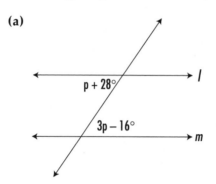

(b)

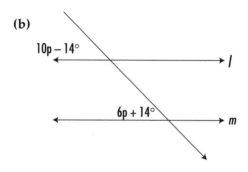

(c)

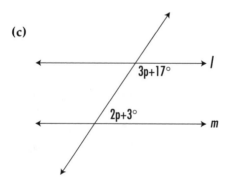

(d)

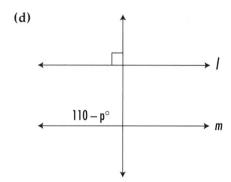

$110 - p°$

2. Write a proof that illustrates that when two parallel lines are cut by a transversal, alternate interior angles are congruent.

3. Lines 1, 2, 3, and 4 are all in the same plane. If line 1 is perpendicular to line 2, line 2 is perpendicular to line 3, and line 4 is parallel to line 3, what is the relationship between line 1 and line 4?

4. If $\angle A$ is congruent to $\angle B$ and the measure of an angle supplemental to $\angle A$ is 140, solve for q if the measure of an angle supplemental to $\angle B = 6q + 14$.

5. If $\angle A$ and $\angle B$ are complementary, and $\angle B$ and $\angle C$ are supplementary, what do you know about the measure of $\angle C$?
   (1) m$\angle C < 90$
   (2) m$\angle C = 90$
   (3) m$\angle C > 90$
   (4) Nothing

6.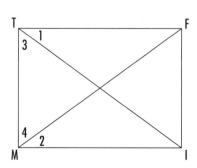

Given: rectangle *MIFT*   Prove: ∠3 ≅ ∠4
          ∠1 ≅ ∠2

Exercises 7 and 8 pertain to the diagram below.

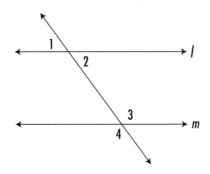

7. Given: lines *l* and *m*;   1 and ∠4 are supplementary

    Prove: *l* is parallel to *m*

8. Given: *l* is parallel to *m*

    Prove: ∠1 and ∠3 are supplementary

9

Triangles

Triangles figure very prominently in both algebraic exercises and geometric proofs, as you'll see when you realize how huge this chapter is.

PARTS OF A TRIANGLE

Your standard triangle has three sides and three angles. (Okay. You knew that.) The **altitude** of a triangle is a line segment drawn from one vertex perpendicular to the opposite side, and the **median** is a line segment drawn from one vertex to the midpoint of the opposite side.

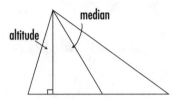

Note: An altitude can lie outside the triangle if the triangle is obtuse.

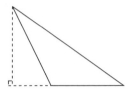

THE RULE OF 180

One of the first rules you learn about triangles is that the sum of the measures of its three angles is 180°.

EXAMPLE 1

In the triangle, what is the value of *m*?

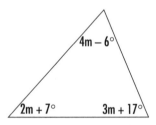

SOLUTION

Add the three angles and set the sum equal to 180:

$$(2m + 7) + (3m + 17) + (4m - 6) = 180$$
$$9m + 18 = 180$$
$$9m = 162$$
$$m = 18$$

To check your work, plug 18 in for *m* in each of the three angles, and make sure their sum is 180:

$$2(18) + 7 = 43$$
$$3(18) + 17 = 71 \qquad 43 + 71 + 66 = 180$$
$$4(18) - 6 = 66$$

EXTERIOR ANGLES

An exterior angle is formed when you extend one of the sides of the triangle past a vertex, like this:

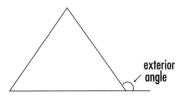

exterior angle

Exterior Angle Theorem: The measure of an exterior angle equals the sum of the two non-adjacent (or remote) interior angles.

EXAMPLE 2

The measures of two angles in a triangle are $7x$ and $2x + 20$. If the measure of an exterior angle drawn from the third vertex is $12x - 7$, what is the value of x?

SOLUTION

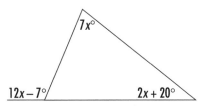

The measure of an exterior angle equals the sum of the measures of the two non-adjacent interior angles:

$$12x - 7 = 7x + (2x + 20)$$
$$12x - 7 = 9x + 20$$
$$3x = 27$$
$$x = 9$$

HOW BIG CAN A SIDE BE?

Your textbook might say something like this:

"The length of any side of a triangle must be less than the sum of the lengths of the other two sides and greater than the absolute value of their difference.

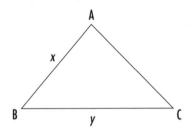

If $AB = x$ and $BC = y$, then $|x-y| < AC < x + y$."

Huh?

Do it like this: If you're given the lengths of two sides of a triangle, subtract the two numbers, then add them. The length of the third side has to be somewhere between those two numbers.

EXAMPLE 3

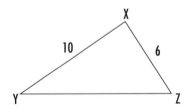

Which of the following is not a possible length of side $\overline{YZ}$?

(1) 4

(2) 8.5

(3) 12

(4) 15.5

SOLUTION

The range of possible values is $|10-6| < YZ < 10 + 6$. That means that YZ is between 4 and 16. Since YZ is *greater* than 4, it can't *equal* 4. Therefore, the answer is **(1)**.

Note: In questions like these, when the answer choices are listed in order from greatest to least or least to greatest, the answer has to be on one end or the other.

There is a standard relationship between the sides and angles of a triangle that makes common sense:

> The bigger the side, the bigger the angle opposite that side, and vice versa.

EXAMPLE 4

In $\triangle FBI$, $m\angle F = 55$ and $m\angle I = 64$. Which side of $\triangle FBI$ is the longest?

SOLUTION

There's no diagram to accompany this problem, and you really don't need one. You know the size of two of the angles, so find the third using the Rule of 180:

$$m\angle F + m\angle B + m\angle I = 180$$
$$55 + m\angle B + 64 = 180$$
$$m\angle B = 61$$

Now that you know the measures of all three angles, it's clear that $\angle I$ is the largest angle. That means that the side opposite $\angle I$, or $\overline{FB}$, is the largest side.

HOW MANY CONGRUENT SIDES?

There are three specific types of triangles that appear throughout Course II: **isosceles**, **equilateral**, and **right**. If a triangle has three sides of unequal length, it's **scalene**.

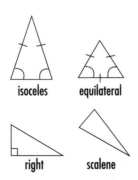

isoceles   equilateral

right   scalene

An **isosceles triangle** has two congruent sides and two congruent angles. As the following two theorems indicate, these characteristics are related:

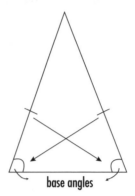

base angles

> If two sides of a triangle are congruent, then the angles opposite those two sides are congruent. (Other textbooks might phrase it like this: Base angles of an isosceles triangle are congruent.) If two angles of a triangle are congruent, then the sides opposite those two sides are congruent.

EXAMPLE 5
If $\angle A \cong \angle B$, what is the value of x?

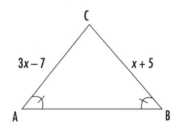

SOLUTION

Since the two base angles are congruent, the two sides, $\overline{BC}$ and $\overline{AC}$, are also congruent (equal in length):

$$3x - 7 = x + 5$$
$$2x = 12$$
$$x = 6$$

These two theorems can be a great help in proofs, as you're about to see.

If all three sides of a triangle are the same length (as are all three angles), that triangle is **equilateral** (which comes from "equi-," meaning "equal," and "lateral," which means "side.")

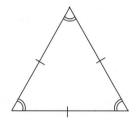

The measure of each of the three angles in an equilateral triangle is 60°.

EXERCISES, SET 9A

Here's your first taste of the triumph and tribulation of triangles. The answers are in chapter 16.

1. In each of the following triangles, solve for x.

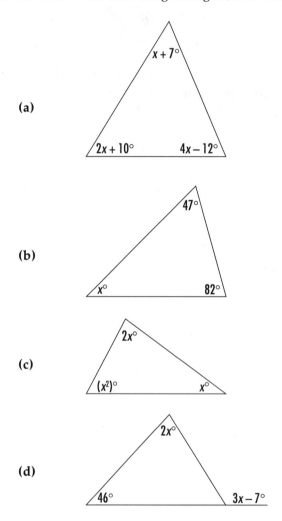

(a)

(b)

(c)

(d)

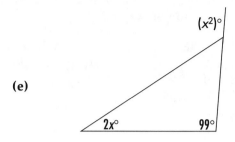

(e)

2. In $\triangle ABC$, the measure of an exterior angle drawn at C is four times the measure of $\angle B$. If $m\angle A = 132$, what is the measure of B?

3. In the two diagrams below, $\overline{RU}$ and $\overline{TU}$ are angle bisectors. Find the value of x.

(a)

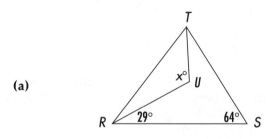

(b)

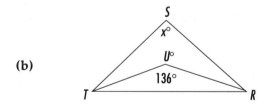

4. If $BC = BD$, what is the measure of $\angle DBC$?

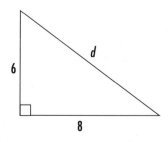

5. In $\triangle FGH$, m $\angle F = 55$ and m $\angle G = 62$. What is the largest side of $\triangle FGH$?

6. In $\triangle BED$, $BE = 10$ and $ED = 18$. Which of the following represents the range of possible lengths of BD?
   (1) $-8 < BD < 28$
   (2) $-8 < BD < 8$
   (3) $8 < BD < 28$
   (4) $28 < BD < 180$

7. What is the range of values of the perimeter of $\triangle BED$?

8. Which of the following sets CANNOT represent the lengths of the sides of a triangle?
   (1) $\{3, 4, 5\}$
   (2) $\{3, 4, 6\}$
   (3) $\{3, 4, 7\}$
   (4) $\{4, 4, 7\}$

9. Determine whether any of the following sets of numbers can represent the lengths of the sides of a triangle.
   (a) $\{15, 9, 12\}$
   (b) $\{2, 5, 2\}$
   (c) $\{0.5, 0.7, 1.2\}$
   (d) $\left\{\dfrac{1}{3}, \dfrac{2}{5}, \dfrac{3}{7}\right\}$
   (e) $\{x, x, x\}$
   (f) $\{x, x, x + 1\}$

10. Two sides of isosceles triangle DEF measure 6 and 13, respectively. (a) What is the set of possible lengths of the third side? (b) What is the perimeter of $\triangle DEF$?

11. In $\triangle JKL$, $\angle J$ is obtuse. Which side is the longest?

12. In isosceles triangle *DOG*, *DG* = *OG* and point *H* lies between *D* and *O*. Which of the following must be true?

(1) m∠*DHG* = 90

(2) *GH* > *GO*

(3) *DO* = *DG*

(4) m∠*GDO* < m∠*GHO*

RIGHT TRIANGLES

Behold the mystical right triangle!

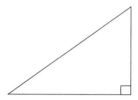

The properties of the right triangle (so named because of the right angle it contains) are numerous. The most famous theorem about right triangles was put forth by the Greek mathematician Pythagoras (whether he was buddies with Euclid is unknown):

> **The Pythagorean Theorem:** In a right triangle, the square of the length of the hypotenuse is equal to the sum of the squares of the two legs.

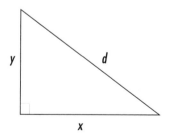

As you learned in chapter 7, the Pythagorean Theorem is the basis of the distance formula.

EXAMPLE 6

What is the length of $\overline{MN}$?

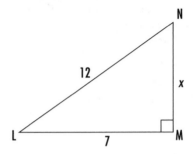

SOLUTION

Plug the lengths into the formula and solve:

$$(LM)^2 + (MN)^2 = (LN)^2$$
$$7^2 + x^2 = 12^2$$
$$49 + x^2 = 144$$
$$x^2 = 95$$
$$x = \sqrt{95}.$$

Usually, at least one of the measurements is irrational. There are several circumstances, though, when all three measurements are integers. These are called Pythagorean triplets, and the most common of these are the **3:4:5** triangle and the **5:12:13** triangle:

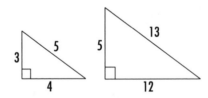

The two other sets of Pythagorean triplets that you'll probably see are **8:15:17** and **7:24:25**. Multiples of each of these triplets also work.

EXAMPLE 7

What is the length of $\overline{ST}$?

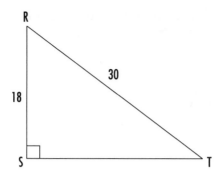

SOLUTION

The hypotenuse of $\triangle RST$ is 30, or 5 × 6. One leg is 18, or 3 × 6. The other leg must therefore be 4 × 6, or **24**.

Note: If you don't recognize that $\triangle RST$ is a 3:4:5 triangle, you can always use the Pythagorean Theorem and your calculator.

There are two specific right triangles that have an even more specific relationship between the sides. Your textbook might refer to them as **special right triangles**:

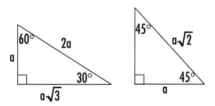

These relationships are good for finding the areas of various polygons.

EXAMPLE 8

What is the area of $\triangle PQR$?

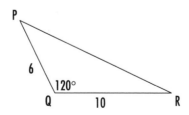

SOLUTION

You already know that the base of the triangle is 10. You have to determine the height, which also happens to be the long leg of a 30:60:90 triangle:

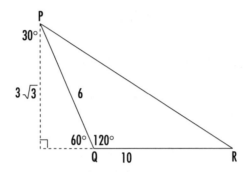

Plug the values for the base (10) and the height ($3\sqrt{3}$) into the formula for the area of a triangle:

$$A = \frac{1}{2}(10)(3\sqrt{3})$$
$$= 15\sqrt{3}$$

EXERCISES, SET 9B

The problems hereunder involve the right triangle in all its majesty. The answers are in chapter 16.

1. Which of the following is not a set of Pythagorean triplets?
(1) {3, 4, 5}
(2) {7, 24, 25}
(3) {8, 15, 17}
(4) {9, 12, 16}

2. Solve for d in each of the following right triangles.

(a)

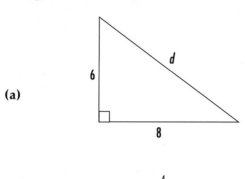

(b)

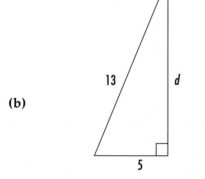

(c)

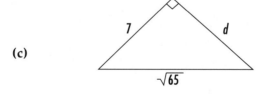

(d)

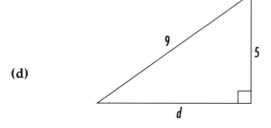

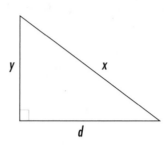

(e)

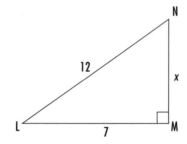

(f)

3. The diagonal of a square has a length of 14. In radical form, what is the length of each side of the square?

4. If the area of a square is 45, what is the length of its diagonal?

5.

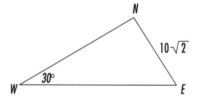

If $NE = 10\sqrt{2}$,

(a) what is the value of WN?

(b) what is the length WE?

(c) what is the area of $\triangle WEN$?

(**Hint**: Drop a perpendicular from point N.)

6. If the length of a side of an isosceles right triangle is x,
   (a) what is the perimeter of the triangle?
   (b) what is the area of the triangle?

7. If the hypotenuse of a 30:60:90 triangle has a length of 24, what is the combined length of the legs?

8. Find the area of an equilateral triangle with a perimeter of
   (a) 12
   (b) 20
   (c) $3s$

9. If the base angles of an isosceles trapezoid measure 60° and the two bases have lengths of 12 and 22, respectively,
   (a) what is the perimeter of the trapezoid?
   (b) what is the area of the trapezoid? (**Note**: For information about the trapezoid, consult chapter 10.)

10. Triangle STU has the vertices $S(2, -3)$, $T(7, -3)$, and $U(2, 7)$. Without using the distance formula, find the length of $\overline{TU}$.

SIMILAR TRIANGLES
From the world of right triangles, we move to this:

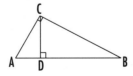

When you draw the altitude of a right triangle from the vertex of the right angle to its hypotenuse, as in the diagram above, you create two more triangles. Now there are three: the smallest one, $\triangle ADC$; the medium-sized one, $\triangle CDB$; and the original, $\triangle ABC$:

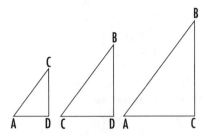

All three are the same shape, but they're not the same size.

> If two polygons are the same shape but not the same size, then they're **similar polygons**. The symbol for similarity is "~". Corresponding angles of similar polygons are congruent.

Most of the work with similar polygons involves triangles. If two triangles are similar, then the ratio between corresponding sides is consistent. (That is, the sides are proportional.) The proportion works for all linear measurements, including altitudes, medians, and perimeters.

EXAMPLE 9

In the diagram below, $\triangle RED$ is similar to $\triangle SOX$. If the sides of $\triangle RED$ are 3, 5, and 6, respectively, and the largest side of $\triangle SOX$ is 18, how long is the smallest side of $\triangle SOX$?

SOLUTION

The two triangles look like this:

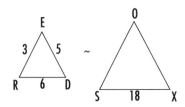

Once you're sure which sides are proportional to each other, it's only a matter of a little algebra. Set up the proportion and cross-multiply, like this:

$$\frac{3}{x} = \frac{6}{18}$$

$$6x = 54$$

$$x = 9$$

The smallest side of △ SOX is **9** units long.

Note: A shrewd math person (like yourself) might notice the consistent relationship without having to do any algebra. The largest side of △ SOX (18) is three times the size of the largest side of △ RED (6). Therefore, the smallest side of △ SOX is three times the size of the smallest side of △ RED: 3 × 3 = 9.

Another common diagram involving similar triangles looks like this, in which the triangles share a vertex angle and the bases are parallel:

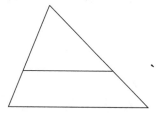

As before, each corresponding side is proportional.

EXAMPLE 10

Given the similar triangles BAT and MAN in the following diagram, compute the following:

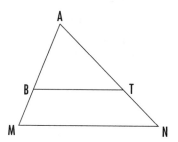

(a) If AB = 6, BT = 7, and MN = 14, find AM.

(b) If AM is 3 more than AB, AT = 14, and TN = 6, find AB.

(c) If BT is 7 more than BM, AB = 6, and MN = 12, find BM.

SOLUTION

As you'll see, these will get progressively harder.

(a) The proportion for this problem is as basic as it gets:

$$\frac{AB}{BT} = \frac{AM}{MN}$$

$$\frac{6}{7} = \frac{x}{14}$$

$$7x = 84$$

$$x = 12$$

(b) This ratio compares the pairs of sides that share point

$$A: \frac{AB}{AM} = \frac{AT}{AN}$$

As a good rule of thumb, set the length you're looking for (in this case, AB) equal to x. That means $AM = x + 3$. Further, $AN = AT + TN$, or 20:

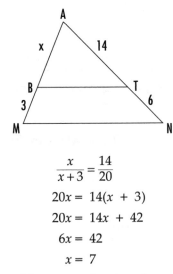

$$\frac{x}{x+3} = \frac{14}{20}$$

$$20x = 14(x + 3)$$

$$20x = 14x + 42$$

$$6x = 42$$

$$x = 7$$

(c) This sort of problem can also involve a quadratic, in which there are two possible answers—one negative, and one positive. Since you're looking for a distance, throw out the negative value.

$$\frac{AB}{BT} = \frac{AM}{MN}$$

Let $BM = x$ and $BT = x + 7$. Also, remember that $AM = AB + BM$, or $x + 6$:

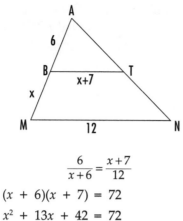

$$\frac{6}{x+6} = \frac{x+7}{12}$$

$$(x + 6)(x + 7) = 72$$

$$x^2 + 13x + 42 = 72$$

$$x^2 + 13x - 30 = 0$$

$$(x - 2)(x + 15) = 0$$

$$x = \{2, -15\}$$

Get rid of the negative, because there's no such thing as a negative distance. Therefore, $BM = \mathbf{2}$.

The diagram of triangles BAT and MAN in the example above helps explain the next theorem, concerning the midpoints of two sides of a triangle. Suppose that AB was exactly half of AM and AT was exactly half of AN:

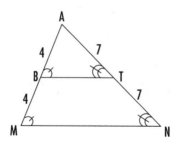

Since $\triangle BAT$ and $\triangle MAN$ are similar, the proportion must remain consistent; BT must be exactly half of MN. Also, all corresponding angles are congruent ($\angle ABT \cong \angle AMN$, for example). Therefore, $\overline{BT}$ and $\overline{MN}$ are parallel.

The segment formed by the midpoints of two sides of a triangle is (a) parallel to the third side and (b) half the length of the third side.

EXAMPLE 11

Triangle FGH has vertices $F(3, 1)$, $G(7, 7)$, and $H(-1, 5)$. If the midpoints of $\overline{FG}$ and $\overline{GH}$ are connected to form segment $\overline{XY}$, (a) compare the lengths of $\overline{FH}$ and $\overline{XY}$, and (b) prove that $\overline{FH}$ is parallel to $\overline{XY}$.

SOLUTION

This problem is a nice review of the coordinate geometry work you did in chapter 7. You'll use all three big theorems: midpoint, distance, and slope. First, find the midpoint of each side using the midpoint formula:

$$(\bar{x}, \bar{y}) = \left(\frac{x_1 + x_2}{2}, \frac{y_1 + y_2}{2} \right)$$

Midpoint of $\overline{FG}$ Midpoint of $\overline{GH}$

$$(\bar{x}, \bar{y}) = \left(\frac{3+7}{2}, \frac{1+7}{2} \right)$$
$$= \left(\frac{10}{2}, \frac{8}{2} \right)$$
$$= (5, 4)$$

$$(\bar{x}, \bar{y}) = \left(\frac{7+(-1)}{2}, \frac{7+5}{2} \right)$$
$$= \left(\frac{6}{2}, \frac{12}{2} \right)$$
$$= (3, 6)$$

Now plot all the points, including $X(5, 4)$ and $Y(3, 6)$:

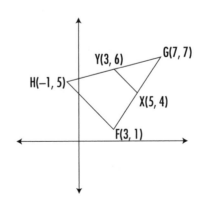

(a)   Find the length of the two segments using the distance formula: $d = \sqrt{(x_2 - x_1)^2 + (y_2 - y_1)^2}$

$$FH = \sqrt{(-1-3)^2 + (1-5)^2}$$
$$= \sqrt{(-4)^2 + (-4)^2}$$
$$= \sqrt{16+16}$$
$$= \sqrt{32} = 4\sqrt{2}$$

$$XY = \sqrt{(3-5)^2 + (6-4)^2}$$
$$= \sqrt{(-2)^2 + 2^2}$$
$$= \sqrt{4+4}$$
$$= \sqrt{8} = 2\sqrt{2}$$

$\overline{FH}$ is twice as long as $\overline{XY}$.

(b)   To prove that the two segments are parallel, use the slope
formula: $m = \dfrac{y_2 - y_1}{x_2 - x_1}$.

Slope of $\overline{FH}$:

$$m = \frac{5-1}{-1-3}$$
$$= \frac{4}{-4}$$
$$= -1$$

Slope of $\overline{XY}$:

$$m = \frac{6-4}{3-5}$$
$$= \frac{2}{-2}$$
$$= -1$$

The slopes are the same, so the two line segments are parallel.

Sometimes, you might have to prove that two triangles are similar before you set up the proportions. In that case, you can use the
AA Theorem:

Angle-Angle (AA) Theorem of Similarity: If two angles of a
triangle are congruent to their corresponding angles of another
triangle, then the triangles are similar.

CONGRUENCY THEOREMS

When two triangles are the same shape *and* the same size, they're
congruent. What you're about to read about plays a huge part in
geometric proofs. There are five major theorems you'll use to prove
that two triangles are congruent.

Before we get into those theorems, though, it's important to recognize **corresponding parts** of a triangle:

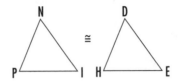

If $\triangle PIN \cong \triangle HED$, then:

Corresponding angles	Corresponding sides
$\angle P \cong \angle H$	$\overline{PI} \cong \overline{HE}$
$\angle I \cong \angle E$	$\overline{IN} \cong \overline{ED}$
$\angle N \cong \angle D$	$\overline{PN} \cong \overline{HD}$

Generally, the vertices of congruent triangles are written in the same order.

Here are the first four of the Big Five theorems that you'll use to prove two triangles congruent.

Side-Side-Side (SSS) Theorem: If all three sides of a triangle are congruent to their corresponding sides of another triangle, then the triangles are congruent.

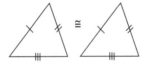

Side-Angle-Side (SAS) Theorem: If two sides and the angle between them are congruent to their corresponding parts of another triangle, then the triangles are congruent.

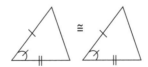

> **Angle-Side-Angle (ASA) Theorem:** If two angles and an included side of a triangle are congruent to their corresponding parts of another triangle, then the triangles are congruent.

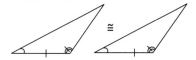

> **Angle-Angle-Side (AAS) Theorem:** If two angles and a side opposite one of them are congruent to their corresponding parts of another triangle, then the triangles are congruent.

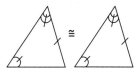

As we'll explore in chapter 11, it's always good to have a plan before you start a geometric proof. Which one of these three would you use to prove the following?

EXAMPLE 12

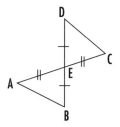

Given: Segments $\overline{AC}$ and $\overline{BD}$ intersect each other at point E and also bisect each other.

Prove: $\triangle ABE \cong \triangle CDE$.

SOLUTION

Since the two segments bisect each other, it must be true that $\overline{AE} \cong \overline{EC}$ and $\overline{BE} \cong \overline{ED}$. You have two sides so far. Further, $\angle AEB$ and $\angle DEC$ are vertical angles, so they're congruent as well. These angles are *between* the two sets of congruent sides, so you should use Side-Angle-Side.

The proof looks like this:

Statements	Reasons
1. $\overline{AC}$ and $\overline{BD}$ bisect each other.	1. Given
2. $\overline{AE} \cong \overline{EC}$; $\overline{BE} \cong \overline{ED}$	2. Definition of bisector
3. $\angle AEB \cong \angle DEC$	3. Vertical angles are congruent
4. $\triangle ABE \cong \triangle CDE$	4. SAS $\cong$ SAS

Which theorem would you use in this next example?

EXAMPLE 13

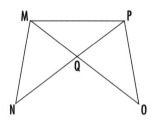

Given: $\angle N \cong \angle O$; $\angle NMQ \cong \angle OPQ$; $\overline{MQ} \cong \overline{PQ}$

Prove: $\triangle MNP \cong \triangle POM$

SOLUTION

You might recognize that the best theorem to use is Angle-Angle-Side, because the given information includes two angles and a side. The problem many students have on problems like these is that the two triangles that you're trying to prove congruent overlap each other. The key is separating the triangles out in your mind. Or, you can draw them out on scratch paper if it helps:

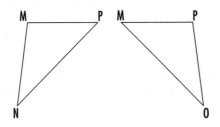

Here's the proof:

Statements	Reasons
1. $\angle N \cong \angle O$	1. Given
2. $\overline{MQ} \cong \overline{PQ}$	2. Given
3. $\angle PMQ \cong \angle MPQ$	3. If two sides of a triangle are congruent, then the angles opposite them are congruent.
4. $\angle NMQ \cong \angle OPQ$	4. Given
5. m $\angle PMQ$ + m $\angle NMQ$ = m $\angle MPQ$ + m $\angle OPQ$	5. Addition Property of Equality
6. $\angle NMP \cong \angle QPM$	6. Substitution Property
7. $\overline{MP} \cong \overline{MP}$	7. Reflexive Property of Equality
8. $\triangle MNP \cong \triangle POM$	8. AAS $\cong$ AAS

Note: Your teacher might suggest that you add a few steps. For example, you might have to add that m $\angle NMP$ = m $\angle NMQ$ + m $\angle PMQ$ by reason of the Angle Addition Postulate. Be sure that the proofs you write conform to your teacher's instructions.

There will be many other chances to work with these theorems in the exercises that appear at the end of this chapter, as well as in chapter 11.

Guess what: There is no ASS theorem. (Imagine the fun we'd all have if there were.) Here's why:

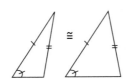

The corresponding angles are congruent, and there are also two congruent sides. Therefore, the only way you can use two sides and an angle to prove congruency is if the angle is between the sides.

Hypotenuse-Leg (HL or Hy-Leg) Theorem: If the hypotenuse and a leg of one right angle are congruent to their corresponding parts of another triangle, then the triangles are congruent.

Note: This theorem works *only* for right triangles, which makes sense because the only triangle that has a hypotenuse is a right triangle.

EXAMPLE 14

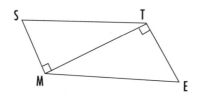

Given: Parallelogram $METS$; $\overline{SM}\perp\overline{MT}$; $\overline{MT}\perp\overline{TE}$.
Prove: $\triangle SMT \cong \triangle ETM$

SOLUTION

Since the two sets of segments are perpendicular, $\triangle SMT$ and $\triangle ETM$ are right triangles. Therefore, you can use Hy-Leg.

Statements	Reasons
1. $METS$ is a parallelogram	1. Given
2. $\overline{ST} \cong \overline{ME}$ (hypotenuse)	2. Opposite sides of a parallelogram are congruent.
3. $\overline{MT} \cong \overline{MT}$ (leg)	3. Reflexive Property of Equality
4. $\triangle SMT \cong \triangle ETM$	4. HL $\cong$ HL

So far, we've used corresponding parts of triangles to prove that they're congruent. As you might imagine, you can also work in reverse.

CPCTC

Once you've proven that two triangles are congruent, you can prove that any two corresponding parts (angles or sides) are also congruent.

> Corresponding parts of congruent triangles are congruent (CPCTC).

If a proof asks you prove that two segments are congruent, for example, you can look and see if the segments are corresponding parts of two congruent triangles. Then you can prove that the triangles are congruent and use CPCTC.

EXAMPLE 15

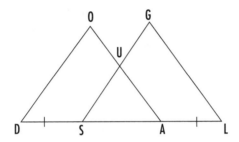

Given: $\overline{DO}$ is parallel to $\overline{SG}$

$\overline{OA}$ is parallel to $\overline{GL}$

$DS = AL$

Prove: $\overline{SG} \cong \overline{OA}$

SOLUTION

The two segments, $\overline{SG}$ and $\overline{OA}$, are corresponding sides of $\triangle SGL$ and $\triangle DOA$. Therefore, you can prove that the triangles are congruent; CPCTC will follow.

Statements	Reasons
1. $\overline{DO}$ is parallel to $\overline{SG}$	1. Given
2. $\angle D \cong \angle GSL$	2. Corresponding angles are congruent.
3. $DS = AL$	3. Given
4. $SA = SA$	4. Reflexive Property of Equality
5. $DS + SA = SA + AL$	5. Addition Property of Equality

6. $\overline{DA} \cong \overline{SL}$	6. Substitution Principle
7. $\overline{OA}$ is parallel to $\overline{GL}$	7. Given
8. $\angle DAO \cong \angle SLG$	8. Corresponding angles are congruent.
9. $\triangle DOA \cong \triangle SGL$	9. ASA $\cong$ ASA
10. $\overline{SG} \cong \overline{OA}$	10. CPCTC

EXERCISES, SET 9C

We bet you can guess where the answers to these questions are, you brilliant so-and-so.

1. The smaller of two similar triangles has a perimeter of 25, and the larger has a perimeter of 100. If the largest side of the smaller triangle is 11 units long, how long is the largest side of the larger triangle?

2. In the diagram, the altitude $\overline{FO}$ of right triangle GLF is drawn.

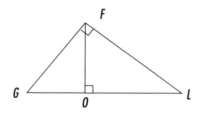

   (a) If $GO = 2$ and $FO = 4$, find OL, GF, and FL.
   (b) If $FO = 9$ and FL is three times as long as GF, find GF, GO, FL, and OL.
   (c) If $FO = 12$ and OL is 7 more than GO, find GO, OL, GF, and FL.

3. In similar triangles *ABC* and *XYZ*, *AB* is three times as long as its counterpart, *XY*. If m∠C = 96, what is the measure of ∠Z?

4.

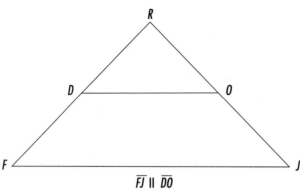

$$\overline{FJ} \parallel \overline{DO}$$

(a) If *DR* = 5, *DO* = 9, and *FJ* = 18, find *FR*.
(b) If *OR* = 4 *DO* = 10, and *FJ* = 15, find *OJ*.
(c) If *DR* = 6, *FD* = 9, and *OJ* = *RO* + 2, find *RO*.
(d) If *FD* = 4, *RO* = *DR* + 4, and *OJ* = *DR* − 2, find *DR*.

5. Which congruency theorem would you use to prove the triangles congruent?
   (a)

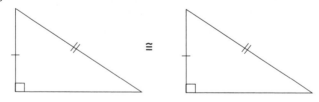

   (b)

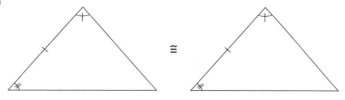

(c)

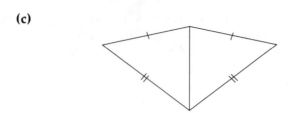

(d)

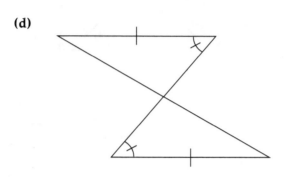

(e)

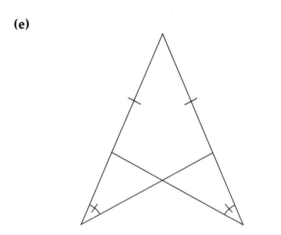

6. The area of a triangle is 15. If the altitude of a similar triangle is three times the length of the altitude of the first triangle, what is the area of the second triangle?

Try these proofs. If you get stuck, there's more information about writing proofs (as well as more proofs to try) in chapter 11.

7.

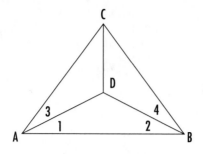

(a) Given: $\angle 1 \cong \angle 2$

$\angle ADC \cong \angle BDC$

Prove: $\overline{AC} \cong \overline{BC}$

(b) Given: $\overline{AC} \cong \overline{BC}$

$\angle 3 \cong \angle 4$

Prove: $\angle 1 \cong \angle 2$

8.

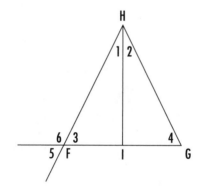

(a) Given: $\overline{HI}$ bisects $\angle FHG$

$\overline{HI} \perp \overline{FG}$

Prove: $\angle 4 \cong \angle 5$

(b) Given: $\overline{FH} \cong \overline{GH}$

Prove: $m\angle 6 = m\angle 1 + m\angle 2 + m\angle 3$

9.

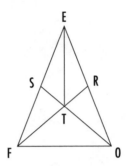

Given: $\overline{ST} \cong \overline{TR}$
             $\angle STE \cong \angle RTE$
             $\angle 1 \cong \angle 2$
Prove: **(a)** $\triangle EFO$ is isosceles
            (b) $\triangle TFO$ is isosceles

CHAPTER 10

Quadrilaterals and Other Polygons

This chapter contains a lot of information about the properties of various four-sided figures, or **quadrilaterals**.

As you try to memorize all the theorems and properties of quadrilaterals (as well as those of triangles in chapter 9), remember this: If it looks like it's true, it probably is.

For example, say you're not sure if the diagonals of a rhombus are perpendicular. (A rhombus, as you'll read later, is a quadrilateral with four congruent sides.) Draw a few of them:

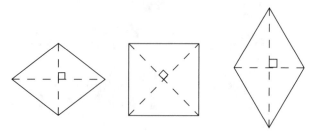

In each of these diagrams, the diagonals are perpendicular to each other. If you're ever hung up on a problem, it often pays to jump-start your brain by drawing a picture.

THE FOUR-SIDED FAMILY

You may have seen this quadrilateral chart in your textbook:

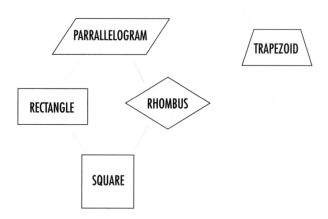

The chart indicates how the quadrilaterals that appear in Course II are related. The farther down the chart you go, the more specialized the quadrilateral is. At the top is the standard quadrilateral ("quad-" means "four," and "lateral" means "side"), which has only one standard property:

The sum of the measures of the four angles in a quadrilateral is 360°.

EXAMPLE 1

In quadrilateral *CLAM*, $\angle C$ is twice as big as $\angle L$, $\angle A$ is 70° larger than $\angle L$, and $\angle M$ is 22° smaller than $\angle C$. What is the measure of $\angle L$?

SOLUTION

Let m $\angle L = x$. Since $\angle C$ is twice as big as $\angle L$, m $\angle C = 2x$. To finish out the algebra, m $\angle A = x + 70$, and m $\angle M = 2x - 22$. The rest is easy:

$$m\angle C + m\angle L + m\angle A + m\angle M = 360$$
$$2x + x + (x + 70) + (2x - 22) = 360$$
$$6x + 48 = 360$$
$$6x = 312$$
$$x = 52$$

Double-check your work by finding the measure of the other angles:

$$m\angle C = 2 \times 52 = 104$$
$$m\angle L = 52$$
$$m\angle A = 52 + 70 = 122$$
$$m\angle M = 2(52) - 22 = 82$$
$$104 + 52 + 122 + 82 = 360$$

PARALLELOGRAMS

Most of the quadrilaterals in this chapter are some form of **parallelogram**, which is a quadrilateral with two pairs of parallel sides.

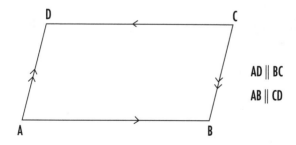

AD ∥ BC

AB ∥ CD

The angles of a parallelogram have the following properties:
- opposite angles are congruent
- consecutive angles are supplementary (the sum of any two angles in a row is 180)

EXAMPLE 2

In parallelogram *FORK*, m $\angle R = 3x + 5$ and m $\angle K = 5x + 23$. What is the measure of each angle?

SOLUTION

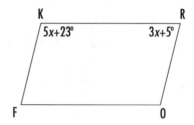

In *FORK*, $\angle R$ and $\angle K$ are consecutive angles. Therefore, the sum of their measures is 180°.

$$(3x + 5) + (5x + 23) = 180$$
$$8x + 28 = 180$$
$$8x = 152$$
$$x = 19$$
$$m\angle R = 3(19) + 5, \text{ or } \mathbf{62}$$
$$m\angle K = 5(19) + 23, \text{ or } \mathbf{118}$$

Check: 62 + 118 = 180. Bingo.

Note: Be sure to read each problem carefully before you enter your answer. Many students solve for *x* and think they're finished. In this problem, *x* = 19 is only a partial answer.

There is much more to know about the sides and diagonals of a parallelogram:

- opposite sides are parallel

- opposite sides are congruent

- diagonals bisect each other

EXAMPLE 3

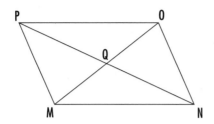

Given: Parallelogram *MNOP*; diagonals $\overline{MO}$ and $\overline{NP}$ intersect at point *Q*.

Prove: △MNQ ≅ △OPQ.

SOLUTION
If you choose to use Side-Side-Side, the proof looks like this:

Statements	Reasons
1. *MNOP* is a parallelogram	1. Given
2. $\overline{MN} \cong \overline{OP}$	2. Opposite sides of a parallelogram are congruent
3. Diagonals $\overline{MO}$ and $\overline{NP}$ intersect at *Q*	3. Given
4. $\overline{MQ} \cong \overline{QO}$; $\overline{PQ} \cong \overline{QN}$	4. Diagonals of a parallelogram bisect each other
5. △*MNQ* ≅ △*OPQ*	5. SSS ≅ SSS

Note: Since ∠*OPQ* ≅ ∠*QNM* and ∠*POQ* ≅ ∠*QMN* (alternate interior angles), and ∠*PQO* ≅ ∠*MQN* (vertical angles), you can use SAS, ASA, or AAS to write this proof.

If you can prove that a quadrilateral has any of the properties listed above, you can prove that the quadrilateral is a parallelogram. There's also one other theorem you can use:

> If a quadrilateral has two sides that are both parallel and congruent, then the quadrilateral is a parallelogram.

EXAMPLE 4

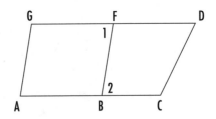

Given: $\overline{ABC}$, $\overline{GFD}$
$\angle 1 \cong \angle 2$
F is the midpoint of $\overline{GD}$
$\overline{AB} \cong \overline{FD}$

Prove: Quadrilateral ABFG is a parallelogram.

SOLUTION

The key is to prove that sides $\overline{GF}$ and $\overline{AB}$ are both parallel and congruent (see steps 2 and 7):

Statements	Reasons
1. $\angle 1 \cong \angle 2$	1. Given
2. $\overline{GF}$ is parallel to $\overline{AB}$	2. If alternate interior angles are congruent, then lines are parallel.
3. F is the midpoint of $\overline{GD}$	3. Given
4. GF = FD	4. Definition of midpoint
5. AB = FD	5. Given
6. GF = AB	6. Substitution Property of Equality
7. $\overline{GF} \cong \overline{AB}$	7. Definition of congruence
8. ABFG is a parallelogram	8. If two sides of a quadrilateral are both parallel and congruent, then the quadrilateral is a parallelogram.

The formula for the area of a parallelogram derives from the area of a triangle. Each diagonal divides a parallelogram into two congruent triangles:

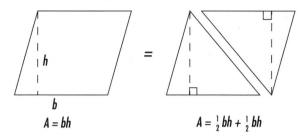

$$A = bh \qquad A = \tfrac{1}{2}bh + \tfrac{1}{2}bh$$

Make sure that your height measurement is perpendicular to the base.

A **rectangle** is a special parallelogram. It has every property of a parallelogram, as well as these extras:

- all four angles are congruent (they're right angles)
- diagonals are congruent

EXAMPLE 5

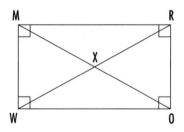

Given: Rectangle $WORM$, diagonals $\overline{WR}$ and
$\overline{OM}$ intersect at point X.

Prove: $\overline{WR} \cong \overline{OM}$

SOLUTION

Since $\overline{WR} \cong \overline{OM}$ and $\overline{WR} \cong \overline{OM}$ are corresponding parts of $\triangle WRM$ and $\triangle ORM$, prove that the triangles are congruent using Side-Angle-Side, then use CPCTC.

Statements	Reasons
1. *WORM* is a rectangle	1. Given
2. $\overline{MR} \cong \overline{MR}$	2. Reflexive Property of Equality
3. $\angle WMR$ and $\angle ORM$ are right angles	3. Definition of a rectangle
4. $\angle WMR \cong \angle ORM$	4. All right angles are congruent.
5. $\overline{WM} \cong \overline{OR}$	5. Opposite sides of a rectangle are congruent.
6. $\triangle WRM \cong \triangle ORM$	6. SAS $\cong$ SAS
7. $\overline{WR} \cong \overline{OM}$	7. Corresponding parts of congruent triangles are congruent.

The most common way to prove that a quadrilateral is a rectangle is to show that it's a parallelogram with a right angle.

You first saw the formula for the **area of a rectangle** in chapter 3 (remember all that FOIL stuff?). It's probably the most basic area formula there is: length (l) × width (w).

EXAMPLE 6
The vertices of rectangle *TUNA* are $T(1, -1)$, $U(4, 0)$, $N(2, 6)$, and $A(-1, 5)$. What is the area of the rectangle?

SOLUTION

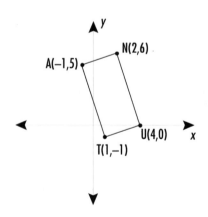

They told you it's a rectangle, so all you have to do is to find the length of two consecutive sides of the rectangle using the distance formula.

$$TU = \sqrt{(4-1)^2 + [0-(-1)]^2}$$
$$= \sqrt{3^2 + 1^2}$$
$$= \sqrt{9+1}$$
$$= \sqrt{10}$$

$$UN = \sqrt{(2-4)^2 + (6-0)^2}$$
$$= \sqrt{(-2)^2 + 6^2}$$
$$= \sqrt{4+36}$$
$$= \sqrt{40} = 2\sqrt{10}$$

To find the area, multiply the length times the width.

$$\sqrt{10} \times 2\sqrt{10} = 2\sqrt{100} = \mathbf{20}$$

RHOMBUSES

A **rhombus** is also a special parallelogram that has every property of a parallelogram. Extra properties of rhombuses (or rhombi, depending on the textbook) include:

- all four sides are congruent
- diagonals are perpendicular
- diagonals bisect the opposite angles

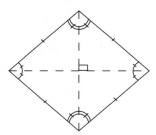

Because the diagonals of a rhombus are perpendicular, you can think of a rhombus as a collection of four congruent right triangles.

EXAMPLE 7

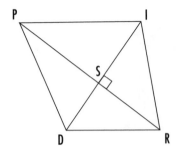

Given: Rhombus *DRIP*; diagonal $\overline{DI}$ and $\overline{RP}$
intersect at point *S*.

Prove: $\triangle DSP \cong \triangle ISP$

SOLUTION
Given the many properties of a rhombus, you can use almost any
triangle congruence theorem. Let's use Hypotenuse-Leg:

Statements	Reasons
1. *DRIP* is a rhombus	1. Given
2. $\overline{DI} \perp \overline{RP}$	2. Diagonals of a rhombus are perpendicular.
3. $\angle DSP$ and $\angle ISP$ are right angles	3. Definition of perpendicular lines
4. $\triangle DSP$ and $\triangle ISP$ are right triangles	4. Definition of right triangles
5. $\overline{DP} \cong \overline{IP}$	5. All sides of a rhombus are congruent.
6. $\overline{PS} \cong \overline{PS}$	6. Reflexive Property of Equality
7. $\triangle DSP \cong \triangle ISP$	7. HL $\cong$ HL

The formula for the **area of a rhombus** is $\frac{1}{2}(d_1 \times d_2)$, in which d_1 and d_2 are the lengths of the two diagonals. If you circumscribe a rectangle (WXYZ) on a rhombus (ABCD), you can see that the area of the rectangle is $(d_1 \times d_2)$:

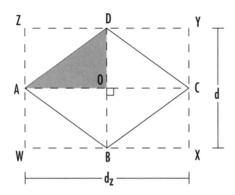

The diagonals of the rhombus meet at point O. Right triangle AOD has exactly half the area of rectangle $AODZ$, and the same is true for the other three right triangles in the rhombus. Therefore, the area of the rhombus is half the area of the rectangle.

SQUARES

If a rectangle and a rhombus loved each other very, very much and got married, their children would be squares. Since every square is both a rectangle and a rhombus, it has all the properties of both quadrilaterals.

A square is:

- a rectangle with four equal sides and
- a rhombus with four equal angles

You can also find the area of a square using the formula for the area of a rhombus or that of a rectangle:

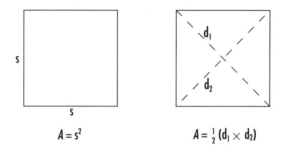

$A = s^2$

$A = \frac{1}{2}(d_1 \times d_2)$

A square can be divided into two 45:45:90 triangles; this might help you remember the relationship between the sides of the triangle (also known as an isosceles right triangle).

EXAMPLE 8

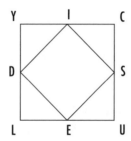

In the diagram above, square *LUCY* is circumscribed on square *DESI*. If the area of *DESI* is 16, what is the area of *LUCY*?

SOLUTION

The key thing to note here is that the length of diagonal $\overline{DS}$ is the same as the length of side $\overline{LY}$ of *LUCY*. If the area of *DESI* is 16, then each side of the square has a length of 4. Look at $\triangle DES$; it's a 45:45:90 triangle with a side of length 4. If you remember that the ratio of the sides of a 45:45:90 triangle is $1:1:\sqrt{2}$, you can work out that $DS = 4\sqrt{2}$. (Otherwise, you can use the Pythagorean Theorem.)

The area of *LUCY* is therefore $4\sqrt{2} \times 4\sqrt{2}$, or **32** square units.

Note: Can you see that since square *DESI* is also a rhombus, it makes sense that its area is half the area of *LUCY*?

TRAPEZOIDS

A **trapezoid** is a quadrilateral with *exactly one* pair of parallel sides. The parallel sides are the **bases**, and the sides of a trapezoid that are not parallel are called the **legs**. A segment connecting the midpoints of the legs is called the **median**, and it is parallel to either base.

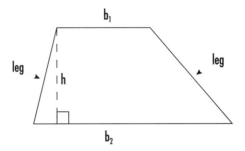

EXAMPLE 9

A quadrilateral has the vertices $B(-4, -6)$, $U(6, -1)$, $R(3, 8)$, and $P(-3, 5)$. Determine whether $BURP$ is a trapezoid.

SOLUTION

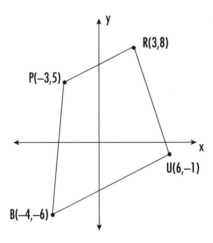

Find the slope of each of the sides of $BURP$ using the slope formula:

$$m = \frac{y_2 - y_1}{x_2 - x_1}$$

Slope of $\overline{BU}$:
$$m = \frac{-1-(-6)}{6-(-4)}$$
$$= \frac{5}{10}$$
$$= \frac{1}{2}$$

Slope of $\overline{UR}$:
$$m = \frac{8-(-1)}{3-6}$$
$$= \frac{9}{-3}$$
$$= -3$$

Slope of $\overline{RP}$:
$$m = \frac{5-8}{-3-3}$$
$$= \frac{-3}{-6}$$
$$= \frac{1}{2}$$

Slope of $\overline{PB}$:
$$m = \frac{-6-5}{-4-(-3)}$$
$$= \frac{-11}{-1}$$
$$= 11$$

Since $\overline{BU}$ and $\overline{RP}$ have the same slope, those two sides are parallel. The other two have different slopes, so they are *not* parallel. Thus, quadrilateral $BURP$ is a trapezoid.

The formula for the area of a trapezoid is somewhat related to that of the triangle:

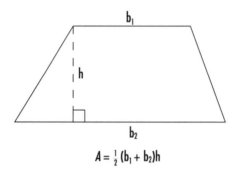

$$A = \tfrac{1}{2}(b_1 + b_2)h$$

The idea is to take the average length of the bases and multiply that by the height. When you look at it that way, it's the same as the area of a rectangle:

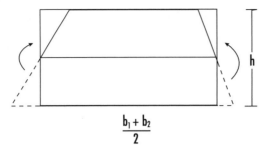

$$\frac{b_1 + b_2}{2}$$

An **isosceles trapezoid** is a trapezoid with congruent legs. The base angles and the diagonals of an isosceles trapezoid are congruent.

EXAMPLE 10
Determine whether the trapezoid in Example 9 is isosceles.

SOLUTION
In an isosceles trapezoid, the two non-parallel sides have the same length. You can find the length of each non-parallel side using the distance formula:

$$d = \sqrt{(x_2 - x_1)^2 + (y_2 - y_1)^2}$$

From Example 9, you know that the non-parallel sides are $\overline{UR}$ and $\overline{PB}$:

Length of $\overline{UR}$:

$$d = \sqrt{(3-6)^2 + [8-(-1)]^2}$$
$$= \sqrt{(-3)^2 + 9^2}$$
$$= \sqrt{9+81}$$
$$= \sqrt{90} = 3\sqrt{10}$$

Length of $\overline{PB}$:

$$d = \sqrt{[-4-(-3)]^2 + (-6-5)^2}$$
$$= \sqrt{(-1)^2 + (-11)^2}$$
$$= \sqrt{1+121}$$
$$= \sqrt{122}$$

Since the two non-parallel sides are not equal in length, *ABCD* is *not* an isosceles trapezoid.

Finding the area and perimeter of an isosceles trapezoid can be a sneaky proposition, because the information you get might not seem to be enough (even though it is).

EXAMPLE 11

Find the (a) perimeter and (b) area of isosceles trapezoid *DINK*.

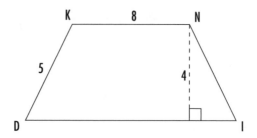

SOLUTION

At first glance, you might think that they forgot something. With a little figuring, though, you can get this in no time. Since the legs of an isosceles trapezoid are equal in length, you know that *DK* = *IN* = 5. One perpendicular from point *N* to the base $\overline{DI}$ is indicated. Drop another one from point *K*, and label the points *A* and *B*.

Isosceles trapezoids can be broken up into a rectangle and two congruent right triangles. Look at $\triangle DAK$. Since the length of its hypotenuse is 5 and one leg is 4 units long, you might be able to recognize $\triangle DAK$ as a 3:4:5 right triangle (if not, you can find *DA* using the Pythagorean Theorem). Thus, *DA* = 3. Since $\triangle DAK \cong \triangle BIN$, *BI* also equals 3.

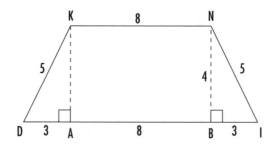

Since *ABNK* is a rectangle, *AB* = *KN* = 8. That means that *DI* = 3 + 8 + 3, or 14. Add up the sides and you have the perimeter: 5 + 14 + 5 + 8 = **32**.

The area is a snap, because you already know all the dimensions you need:

$$A = \frac{1}{2}(b_1 + b_2)h$$
$$= \frac{1}{2}(8+14)(4)$$

$$= 44 \text{ square units}$$

REGULAR POLYGONS

The sides of a **regular polygon** are congruent to each other, and so are the angles. The examples of regular polygons you've seen so far are equilateral triangles and squares. There are two rules to know concerning these regular polygons

The **sum of the measures** of the interior angles of a regular polygon with n sides is:

$$180(n - 2)$$

You can derive the second rule from the first one:

The **measure of each interior angle** in a regular polygon with n sides is:

$$\frac{180(n-2)}{n}$$

EXAMPLE 12

What is the measure of each interior angle of a regular octagon?

SOLUTION

An octagon has eight sides ("octo-" means "eight," as in "octopus"), and a regular octagon looks like a stop sign:

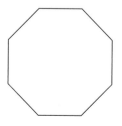

Use the formula. There are eight sides, so $n = 8$:

$$x = \frac{180(8-2)}{8}$$
$$= \frac{180(6)}{8}$$
$$= \frac{1080}{8}$$
$$= 135$$

Each angle measures **135°**.

EXAMPLE 13

If the measure of an interior angle of a regular polygon is 150°, how many sides does the polygon have?

SOLUTION

You'll use the same formula, but there's a little algebra involved this time:

$$150 = \frac{180(n-2)}{n}$$
$$150n = 180(n-2)$$
$$150n = 180n - 360$$
$$-30n = -360$$
$$n = 12$$

The polygon has **12** sides.

EXERCISES, SET 10A

The answers to these problems are in chapter 16.

1. (a) In quadrilateral *MILK*, if $\angle M$ is twice as big as $\angle I$, $\angle I$ is 42° larger than $\angle L$, and $\angle K$ is 2° larger than $\angle I$, what is the measure of all four angles? (b) In parallelogram *DRUM*, m $\angle D = 4x - 13$ and m $\angle R = 2x + 31$; what is the measure of all four angles?

2. Solve for q in each of the following parallelograms.

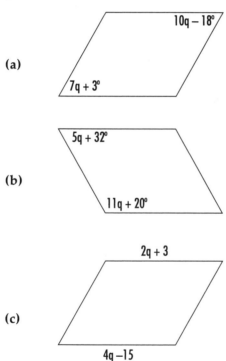

(a)

$10q - 18°$

$7q + 3°$

(b)

$5q + 32°$

$11q + 20°$

(c)

$2q + 3$

$4q - 15$

3. If the diagonals of a quadrilateral are congruent but not perpendicular, the quadrilateral could be each of the following EXCEPT
   (1) a rectangle
   (2) a rhombus
   (3) a parallelogram
   (4) an isosceles trapezoid

4. Find the area of each of the following.

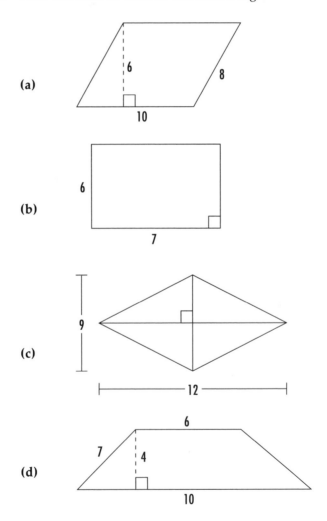

(a)

(b)

(c)

(d)

5. In parallelogram *BACH*, if *BA* = *AC* and *BC* = *AH*, then the quadrilateral is
   (1) a rectangle
   (2) a square
   (3) a rhombus
   (4) all of the above

6. A quadrilateral has vertices (–6, 2), (–2, –4), (3, 1), and (–3, 5). What type of quadrilateral is it?

7. What is the sum of the measures of the angles in **(a)** a regular hexagon? **(b)** a regular octagon? **(c)** a regular 35-sided figure?

8. Find the number of sides a regular polygon has if each angle within it measures:
   (a) 156° **(b)** 162° **(c)** 150° **(d)** 168° **(e)** 174°

9.

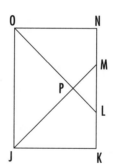

Given: Rectangle *JKNO*
$\overline{JM} \cong \overline{OL}$

Prove: **(a)** △ *PML* isisosceles
(b) △ *JPO* is isosceles

10.

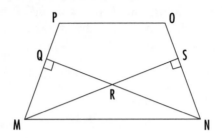

Given: Isosceles trapezoid *MNOP*

$\overline{QN} \perp \overline{MP}$; $\overline{MS} \perp \overline{ON}$

Q is the midpoint of $\overline{PM}$

S is the midpoint of $\overline{ON}$

Prove: $\overline{MR} \cong \overline{RN}$

11.

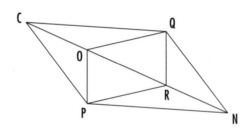

Given: Parallelogram *PNQC*
Parallelogram *PRQO*
$\overline{CR} \cong \overline{ON}$

Prove: $\angle COP \cong \angle QRN$

Geometric Proofs

The last three chapters have been a review of the geometric theorems, postulates, definitions, and characteristics that you have to know in order to compose geometric proofs. Here's where you put them all together and construct a two-column proof.

For many students, geometric proofs are the toughest aspect of the Sequential II course. That's because much of the stuff you have to prove can seem so maddeningly obvious. You have to fight the urge to say, "Of course these line segments are congruent! Just look at them!"

As always, the process gets a lot easier if you practice. (The logic proofs we discussed in chapter 1 are related.) When you write a proof, make sure that:

- each statement progresses logically to the next one
- each reason relates to its statement properly
- each reason is logistically valid
- each reason is stated correctly, as your teacher has directed

As you work in this chapter, feel free to look back at chapters 8, 9, and 10 to refresh your memory.

MAKING A PLAN

One of the biggest mistakes you can make when you write a proof is to start writing without knowing what you're doing. If you don't have a clear objective, you'll end up wandering around just stating stuff that you know is true. Then you'll wonder why your proof has 23 statements.

Before you put pencil to paper, take a long look at the diagram and think to yourself, "How can I do this?" Get an idea of the last theorem or two you'll use. That way, you'll have a definite target to aim for.

WORKING BACKWARDS

As you conceive your plan, you'll start with your last line, then write the line that leads to your last line, then the line before that, and so forth. In fact, one of the best ways to write a proof is to work backwards and write your statements in reverse order. Let's start with a relatively easy example of the process.

EXAMPLE 1

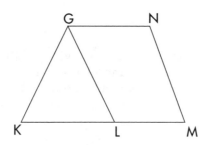

Given: Trapezoid *KMNG*   Prove: $\overline{GL}$ bisects $\angle KGN$

$\overline{KG} \cong \overline{KL}$

SOLUTION

An angle bisector is defined as a line that cuts an angle into two congruent angles. Therefore, your last line will be this:

Statement	Reason
$\overline{GL}$ bisects $\angle KGN$	Definition of angle bisector

In order for $\overline{GL}$ to be the angle bisector, the angles on either side of $\overline{GL}$ must be congruent:

Statement	Reason
$\angle KGL \cong \angle NGL$	?????

Now you have to wrack your brain and search for a way to prove that those two angles are congruent. Look at what you're given: $KMNG$ is a trapezoid. That means that the bases ($\overline{GN}$ and $\overline{KM}$) are parallel. If you look at $\overline{GL}$ as a transversal, you know that $\angle NGL$ and $\angle KLG$ are congruent because they're alternate interior angles. You've made some progress.

Now look at the only other bit of information you were given: $\overline{KG} \cong \overline{KL}$. This means that $\triangle KGL$ is isosceles, and $\angle KGL \cong \angle KLG$. Now you're getting somewhere! If both $\angle NGL$ and $\angle KGL$ are congruent to $\angle KLG$, then they must be congruent to each other.

Your proof should look like this:

Statements	Reasons
1. $KMNG$ is a trapezoid	1. Given
2. $\overline{GN}$ is parallel to $\overline{KM}$	2. Definition of a trapezoid
3. $\angle NGL \cong \angle KLG$	3. Alternate interior angles are congruent.
4. $\overline{KG} \cong \overline{KL}$	4. Given
5. $\angle KGL \cong \angle KLG$	5. If two sides of a triangle are congruent, the angles opposite those sides are congruent.
6. $\angle KGL \cong \angle NGL$	6. Transitive Property (3, 5)
7. $\overline{GL}$ bisects $\angle KGN$	7. Definition of angle bisector

Notice how the statements you wrote first appear last in the proof? That's an example of how working backwards can be beneficial. Once you plot your strategy and analyze the information you're given, the proof falls into place.

Here's another drawn-out look at the proof-writing technique of working backwards. This one's a bit more complicated.

EXAMPLE 2

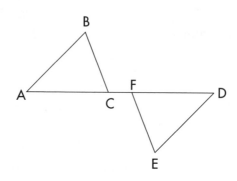

Given: $\overline{AB} \cong \overline{DE}$; $\overline{AB}$ is parallel to $\overline{DE}$; $\overline{AF} \cong \overline{CD}$

Prove: $\angle BCF \cong \angle CFE$

SOLUTION

Note that the two angles that you have to prove are congruent; $\angle BCF$ is supplemental to $\angle BCA$, and $\angle CFE$ is supplemental to $\angle EFD$. It's also true that $\angle BCA$ and $\angle EFD$ are corresponding parts of $\triangle ABC$ and $\triangle DEF$. If you can prove that the two triangles are congruent, you're home free.

Based on what you've decided so far, work on scratch paper in reverse order. Each successive statement supports the one before it. In this proof, your last line will read:

Statement	Reason
$\angle BCF \cong \angle CFE$	Supplements of congruent angles are congruent.

What's the line right before it going to be? It has to involve supplementary angles:

Statement	Reason
$\angle BCF$ is supplementary to $\angle BCA$; $\angle CFE$ is supplementary $\angle EFD$	Definition of supplementary angles

You still need to add one more piece of information to support your last line. Since supplements of congruent angles are congruent, you have to show which are the congruent angles:

Statement	Reason
$\angle BCA \cong \angle EFD$	CPCTC

Since you used CPCTC, you have to specify which triangles are congruent; $\angle BCA$ and $\angle EFD$ are corresponding parts of triangles $\triangle ABC$ and $\triangle EFD$:

Statement	Reason
$\triangle ABC \cong \triangle DEF$	?????

You've got some important preliminary stuff out of the way, and your proof is taking shape. Don't bother numbering any statements yet, because you don't know how many statements you'll need. So far, your proof looks like this:

Statements	Reasons
$\triangle ABC \cong \triangle DEF$	?????
$\angle BCA \cong \angle EFD$	CPCTC
$\angle BCF$ is supplementary to $\angle BCA$; $\angle CFE$ is supplementary to $\angle EFD$	Definition of supplementary angles
$\angle BCF \cong \angle CFE$	Supplements of congruent angles are congruent.

Now, you have to figure out how to prove that $\triangle ABC$ and $\triangle DEF$ are congruent. With the various triangle congruence theorems in mind, look at the given information:

- $\overline{AB} \cong \overline{DE}$: These are corresponding **sides**. This clue is a gift. (Many clues are like this; they just state information you need, and you don't have to figure anything out.)

- $\overline{AB}$ is parallel to $\overline{DE}$: This means that $\overline{AD}$ is a transversal, so $\angle BAC$ and $\angle FDE$ are alternate interior angles (which are congruent). You have an **angle**.

- $\overline{AF} \cong \overline{CD}$: Using the subtraction property of equality, you can subtract CF from AF and CD and prove that $AC = FD$. There's another **side**.

You can use Side-Angle-Side!

Now you have to piece together the proof, working one step at a time. You know exactly where you're headed, so you shouldn't have to wander around aimlessly.

Here's the proof:

Statements	Reasons
1. $\overline{AB} \cong \overline{DE}$	1. Given
2. $\overline{AB}$ is parallel to $\overline{DE}$	2. Given
3. $\angle BAC \cong \angle FDE$	3. Alternate interior angles are congruent.
4. $AF = CD$	4. Given
5. $CF = CF$	5. Reflexive Property of Equality
6. $AF - CF = CD - CF$	6. Subtraction Property of Equality
7. $AC = FD$	7. Substitution Principle
8. D$ABC \cong$ DDEF	8. SAS $\cong$ SAS
9. $\angle BCA \cong \angle EFD$	9. CPCTC
10. $\angle BCF$ is supplementary to $\angle BCA$; $\angle CFE$ is supplementary to $\angle EFD$	10. Definition of supplementary
11. $\angle BCF \cong \angle CFE$	11. Supplements of congruent angles are congruent

Here's one more. Then you're on your own. (Be warned; it's a toughie.)

EXAMPLE 3

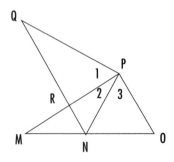

Given: $\overline{QRN}$, $\overline{MRP}$ Prove: $\overline{QP} \cong \overline{MP}$

$\angle PNO \cong \angle PON$

$\overline{MP} \perp \overline{PO}$

$m \angle 1 = m \angle 3$

$\overline{QN} \cong \overline{MO}$

SOLUTION

The process is the same, despite the complicated nature of the proof.

$\overline{QP}$ and $\overline{MP}$ are corresponding parts of $\triangle QPN$ and $\triangle MPO$. If you can prove that the two triangles are congruent, you can use CPCTC on the last step and be home free. Therefore, your last line will be:

Statement	Reason
$\overline{QP} \cong \overline{MP}$	CPCTC

The next to last line will involve the two congruent triangles.

Statement	Reason
$\triangle QPN \cong \triangle MPO$	?????

You've gotten off to a good start, but now is the moment of truth. How can you prove that these triangles are congruent?

The perpendicular lines are the key. Since $\overline{MP} \perp \overline{PO}$, $\triangle MPO$ is a right triangle. That means that $\triangle QPO$ is also probably a right angle. (Angles 1, 2, and 3 should suggest to you that the angles are related somehow.) When you see right triangles, your first instinct should be Hy-Leg.

The hypotenuses are easy; they told you that $\overline{QN} \cong \overline{MO}$. The legs will take a little more work. Look at $\triangle PON$. Since $\angle PNO \cong \angle PON$, $\triangle PON$ is an isosceles triangle. As you know from chapter 9, if two angles of a triangle are congruent, then the sides opposite them are also congruent. Thus, $\overline{PN} \cong \overline{PO}$; you've got your legs.

You have your plan of attack. The challenge is to make sure the proof fulfills the four qualifications listed at the beginning of the chapter.

Your final result should look like this:

Statements	Reasons
1. $m \angle 1 = m \angle 3$	1. Given
2. $m \angle 2 \cong m \angle 2$	2. Reflexive Property of Equality
3. $m \angle 1 + m \angle 2 = m \angle 2$ $+ m \angle 3$	3. Additive Property of Equality
4. $m \angle QPN = m \angle MPO$	4. Substitution Principle
5. $\overline{MP} \perp \overline{PO}$	5. Given
6. $\angle MPO$ is a right angle	6. Definition of a right angle
7. $m \angle QPN = m \angle MPO = 90$	7. Substitution Principle
8. $\triangle QPN$ and $\triangle MPO$ are right triangles	8. Definition of a right triangle
9. $\overline{QN} \cong \overline{MO}$	9. Given
10. $\angle PNO \cong \angle PON$	10. Given
11. $\overline{PN} \cong \overline{PO}$	11. If two angles in a triangle are congruent, then the sides opposite them are congruent.
12. $\triangle QPN \cong \triangle MPO$	12. HL $\cong$ HL
13. $\overline{QP} \cong \overline{MP}$	13. CPCTC

EXERCISES, SET 11A

The following proofs will incorporate theorems and definitions from chapters 8 through 10. Prove each of the following, and remember to sketch out a plan of attack before you start.

1.

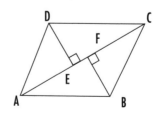

Given: Parallelogram *ABCD*
$\overline{DE} \perp \overline{AC}$; $\overline{FB} \perp \overline{AC}$
Prove: $\overline{AE} \cong \overline{FC}$

2.

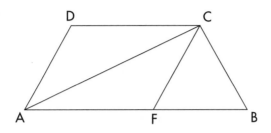

Given: Isosceles trapezoid *ABCD*
m∠*CFB* = m∠*CBF*
m∠*DAC* = m∠*ACF*
Prove: *AFCD* is a parallelogram.

3.

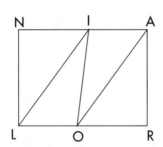

Given: Rectangle *LRAN*
$\overline{NI} \cong \overline{OR}$
Prove: △*LOI* ≅ △*AIO*

4.

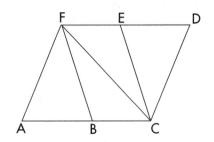

Given: Parallelogram *BCEF*

   E is the midpoint of $\overline{DF}$

   B is the midpoint of $\overline{AC}$

Prove: $\overline{AF} \cong \overline{CD}$

5.

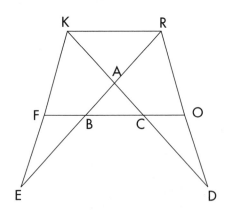

Given: Isosceles trapezoid *FORK*

   EF = OD

Prove: $\triangle ARK$ is isosceles

6.

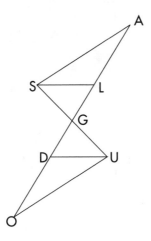

(a) Given: $\overline{ODGLA}$; $\overline{OA}$ and $\overline{US}$ bisect
each other

$\overline{AL} \cong \overline{OD}$

Prove: $\overline{SL} \cong \overline{DU}$

(b) Given: $\overline{ODGLA}$; $\overline{US}$ bisects $\overline{OA}$

D is the midpoint of $\overline{OG}$

L is the midpoint of $\overline{GA}$

Prove: $\overline{SL} \cong \overline{DU}$

7.

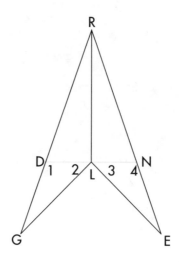

(a) Given: $\angle G \cong \angle E$; $\overline{RL} \perp \overline{DN}$
   $\overline{RL}$ bisects $\angle DRN$
   Prove: $\angle 2 \cong \angle 3$

(b) Given: $\overline{DL} \cong \overline{LN}$; $\overline{RL} \perp \overline{DN}$
   $\angle 2 \cong \angle 3$
   Prove: $\overline{LG} \cong \overline{EL}$

(c) Given: $\overline{RL} \perp \overline{DN}$; $\angle RDL \cong \angle RNL$
   Prove: $\angle 1 \cong \angle 4$

INDIRECT PROOFS (PROVING THAT SOMETHING *ISN'T* TRUE, PART DEUX)

Remember the unit in chapter 7 about proving through coordinate geometry that something is *not* true? This portion of the chapter is a lot like that. In indirect proofs, you show that something is false by proving that it can't be true.

EXAMPLE 4

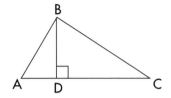

Given: $\overline{DB}$ is an altitude of $\triangle ABC$
$DC > DA$

Prove: $\overline{DB}$ *does not* bisect $\angle ABC$

SOLUTION

The first statement of an indirect proof is the opposite of what you're trying to prove:

Statement	Reason
$\overline{DB}$ bisects $\angle ABC$	Definition of angle bisector

Your goal is to keep working logically until one of your statements contradicts the given information. Follow along with the following indirect proof:

Statements	Reasons
1. $\overline{DB}$ **bisects** $\angle ABC$	1. Assumed
2. $\angle ABD \cong \angle DBC$	2. Definition of angle bisector
3. $\overline{DB} \cong \overline{DB}$	3. Reflexive Property of Equality
4. $\overline{DB}$ is an altitude of $\triangle ABC$	4. Given
5. $\overline{DB} \perp \overline{AC}$	5. Definition of altitude
6. $\angle ADB$ and $\angle CDB$ are right angles	6. Definition of perpendicular lines
7. $\angle ADB \cong \angle CDB$	7. All right angles are congruent.
8. $\triangle ADB \cong \triangle CDB$	8. ASA $\cong$ ASA
9. $\overline{AD} \cong \overline{DC}$	9. CPCTC

Aha! One of the given statements says that $AD > DC$. Statement 10 in the proof states that $\overline{AD}$ and $\overline{DC}$ are congruent, which contradicts that given statement. Since it is impossible for $\overline{DB}$ to bisect $\angle ABC$, you have proven (indirectly) that $\overline{DB}$ does *not* bisect $\angle ABC$.

EXERCISES, SET 11B

Prove each of the following indirectly. The answers are in chapter 16.

1.

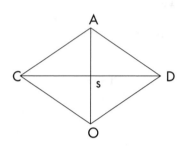

Given: Quadrilateral $CODA$

diagonals $\overline{CD}$ and $\overline{AO}$ intersect at point S

m $\angle SCO = 45$

Prove: Quadrilateral $CODA$ is not a square.

2.

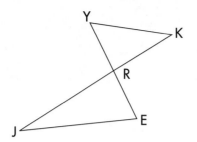

Given: $\overline{JK}$ bisects $\overline{YE}$ at R
$\quad\quad\quad JR > RK$
Prove: $\overline{YK}$ is not parallel to $\overline{JE}$

3. Prove indirectly that if a segment drawn from a vertex of an equilateral triangle to the opposite side of that triangle is not an altitude, then it is also not a median.

CHAPTER 12

Introduction to Trigonometry

As far as trigonometry is concerned, you'll only scratch the surface during Sequential II. The trig you'll need to know is restricted to right triangles only.

As you learned from our discussion of triangles in chapter 9, each right angle has two **legs**, a and b, and a **hypotenuse**, c.

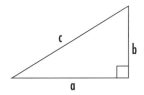

TRIGONOMETRIC RATIOS

The Pythagorean Theorem, however, only relates the sides to each other; the lengths of the sides of a triangle and the measures of its angles are related through **trigonometric ratios**. Look at these three similar right triangles:

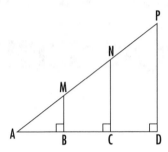

The angle A in the lower left-hand corner, has the same measure in all three triangles. Because they're all similar triangles, you know this: $\dfrac{BM}{AM} = \dfrac{CN}{AN} = \dfrac{DP}{AP}$

In other words, the ratio of the length of the side opposite $\angle A$ to the length of the hypotenuse of the triangle is consistent. This ratio is known as the **sine** ratio (which is commonly abbreviated as "sin"):

$$\sin \angle A = \frac{opposite}{hypotenuse}$$

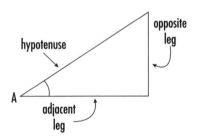

If your textbook doesn't use our alphabet to refer to angles, it might use Greek letters θ (referred to as "theta") and ϕ ("phi") instead.

There are two other ratios you'll have to know that pertain to the right triangle: the **cosine** (indicated by "cos") and **tangent** (or "tan"). Each involves two of the three sides (the side **opposite** the angle, the side **adjacent** to the angle, and the **hypotenuse**.)

$$\cos \angle A = \frac{adjacent}{hypotenuse} \qquad\qquad \tan \angle A = \frac{opposite}{adjacent}$$

It is from these three ratios that the term **SOHCAHTOA** was born: **S**ine equals **O**pposite over **H**ypotenuse, **C**osine equals **A**djacent over **H**ypotenuse, and **T**angent equals **O**pposite over **A**djacent. This is the easiest and most common method of remembering which trig ratio is which.

Whatever you do, memorize these ratios.

EXAMPLE 1
Find the sine, cosine, and tangent of $\angle A$ and $\angle B$.

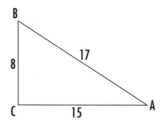

SOLUTION
The key is differentiating the opposite side from the adjacent side in each case.

$$\sin \angle A = \frac{opposite}{hypotenuse} = \frac{8}{17} = 0.4706 \qquad \sin \angle B = \frac{opposite}{hypotenuse} = \frac{15}{17} = 0.8824$$

$$\cos \angle A = \frac{adjacent}{hypotenuse} = \frac{15}{17} = 0.8824 \qquad \cos \angle B = \frac{adjacent}{hypotenuse} = \frac{8}{17} = 0.4706$$

$$\tan \angle A = \frac{opposite}{adjacent} = \frac{8}{15} = 0.5333 \qquad \tan \angle B = \frac{opposite}{adjacent} = \frac{15}{8} = 1.8750$$

Look at the similarity between $\sin \angle A$ and $\cos \angle B$. They're the same, because the side *opposite* $\angle A$ is the side *adjacent* to $\angle B$. Furthermore, $\angle C$ is a right angle, which means that $m \angle A + m \angle B = 90$. Therefore, $m \angle A = 90 - m \angle B$.

The sine of any angle is equal to the cosine of that angle's complement:

$$\sin \theta = \cos (90 - \theta)$$

SPECIAL TRIANGLES

Remember the 30:60:90 and 45:45:90 triangles we talked about in chapter 9? Those are useful here to help you remember the trig ratios that come up a lot.

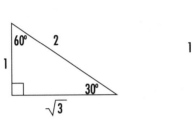

$$\sin 30° = \frac{1}{2} \qquad \sin 60° = \frac{\sqrt{3}}{2} \qquad \sin 45° = \frac{1}{\sqrt{2}} \text{ or } \frac{\sqrt{2}}{2}$$

$$\cos 30° = \frac{\sqrt{3}}{2} \qquad \cos 60° = \frac{1}{2} \qquad \cos 45° = \frac{1}{\sqrt{2}} \text{ or } \frac{\sqrt{2}}{2}$$

$$\tan 30° = \frac{1}{\sqrt{3}} \text{ or } \frac{\sqrt{3}}{3} \qquad \tan 60° = \sqrt{3} \qquad \tan 45° = 1$$

If you use your calculator a lot, you should be able to recognize these ratios in decimal form. For example, if you're doing a trig problem and you get an answer 0.8666, you should recognize that as the decimal version of $\frac{\sqrt{3}}{2}$.

USING YOUR CALCULATOR

Any calculator you use in Sequential II should be equipped with trig buttons, because the problems you're about to learn can involve any angle between 0° and 90°. Since you can't always construct a triangle to determine a trig ratio, you can use your calculator. (Consider yourself lucky; a few years ago, most teachers made you look up trig ratios on a huge, clumsy chart.)

Note: Before you do any trig work on your calculator, make sure it is in **degree mode**. You can tell if the "DEG" appears somewhere in the rectangular display. If it doesn't, hit the "DRG" button (which differentiates **D**egrees, **R**adians, and **G**radients) until the "DEG" comes up.

EXAMPLE 2

Find the value of cos 26°.

SOLUTION

It couldn't be simpler. Enter "26" into your calculator and press "cos". You should get 0.898794. Normally, most trig ratios are rounded off to four decimal points. Your final answer is **0.8988**.

INVERSE TRIGONOMETRY

Naturally, if you can use your calculator to find the sine of an angle, you can also work in reverse using **inverse trigonometry**. On your calculator, inverse trig usually appears as a second function command right above the trig buttons. The inverse sine, for example, looks like this: $\sin^{-1}$.

EXAMPLE 3

If tan q = 1.1504, find the value of θ to the nearest degree.

SOLUTION

Enter 1.1504 into your calculator. Then hit the second function button (which is probably labeled "2ND" or "INV"), then the tangent button. If your calculator is in degree mode, you should get 49.000779. When you round off to the nearest degree, as instructed, you get **49°**.

EXERCISES, SET 12A

Here are some brush-up exercises about the use of trigonometry in a right triangle. The answers are in chapter 16.

1. Use your calculator to find the following.
   (a) $\sin 21°$
   (b) $\cos 15°$
   (c) $\tan 73°$
   (d) $\sin^{-1}\left(\dfrac{\sqrt{5}}{4}\right)$
   (e) $\cos^{-1}\left(\dfrac{2}{\sqrt{7}}\right)$
   (f) $\tan^{-1}\left(\dfrac{5}{3}\right)$

2. Set up the trigonometric equation that is relevant to each diagram.
   (a)

   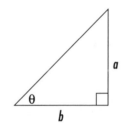

   (b)

   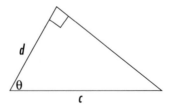

   (c)

   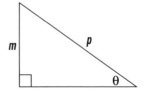

3. Which of the following is equal to sin *x*?
   (1) cos *x*
   (2) cos (90 – *x*)
   (3) sin (90 – *x*)
   (4) tan *x*

4. Find the value of *x* in each of the following to the nearest tenth.
   (a)

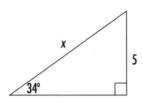

   (b)

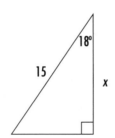

   (c)

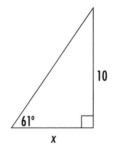

   (d)

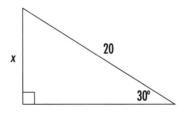

5. Find the value of θ in each of the following to the nearest tenth.

(a)

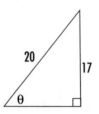

(b)

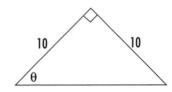

(c)

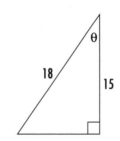

(d)

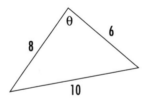

(e)

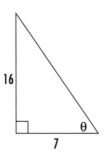

6. Solve for x.

   (a) $\sin x = \cos 41°$

   (b) $\sin x = \cos x$

   (c) $\sin x = \cos\left(\dfrac{x}{2}\right)$

   (d) $\sin 2x = \cos 3x$

   (e) $\sin x^2 = \cos x$

7. Fill in this chart.

	0°	30°	45°	60°	90°
sin					
cos					
tan					

8. Write this same chart out 27,000 times (or until you memorize it).

GEOMETRY

In Sequential II, you'll often use trig to determine the length of a side or the measure of an angle. From there, the problem could expand into areas and perimeters.

EXAMPLE 4

Find the value of x to the nearest tenth.

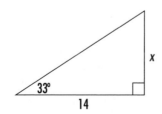

33°

14

x

SOLUTION

You'll use SOHCAHTOA to solve problems like this every time; the key is determining which parts of the right triangle are involved. You know that the angle measures 33°. The leg adjacent to the angle has a length of 14, and the length you're looking for is x, the opposite leg. Therefore, use tangent (the TOA):

$$\tan q = \frac{opposite}{adjacent}$$

$$\tan 33° = \frac{x}{14}$$

Find the value of tan 33° to four decimal places, cross-multiply, and solve:

$$0.6494 = \frac{x}{14}$$

$$14(0.6494) = x$$

$$9.0916 = x$$

When you round off to the nearest tenth, your answer becomes **9.1**.

Of course, these can get pretty complex.

EXAMPLE 5

If m $\angle EAB$ = 24 and BD = 14, find (a) the perimeter and (b) the area of rhombus $ABCD$ to the nearest tenth.

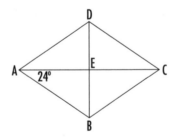

SOLUTION

Before you get started, it's important to remember that the diagonals of a rhombus bisect each other and are perpendicular. Therefore, $\triangle EAB$ is a right triangle, and EB equals half the length of diagonal $\overline{BD}$, or 7.

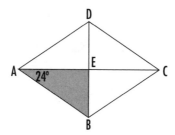

To find the perimeter of the rhombus, you can find the length of one side ($\overline{AB}$) and multiply it by 4 (because a rhombus has four equal sides). You know the length of the leg opposite $\angle EAB$, and you want to find the length of the hypotenuse $\overline{AB}$. Therefore, use sine (the SOH in SOHCAHTOA):

$$\sin \angle EAB = \frac{EB}{AB}$$

$$\sin 24° = \frac{7}{AB}.$$

Since $\sin 24° = 0.4067$, enter that into the equation and cross-multiply:

$$0.4067 = \frac{7}{AB}$$
$$AB(0.4067) = 7$$
$$AB = \frac{7}{0.4067}$$
$$AB = 17.212$$

Multiply this value by 4 and you get 68.848, which becomes **68.8** when you round it off to the nearest tenth.

To find the area of the rhombus, you can find the area of one of the right triangles and multiply by 4. The only measurement that's missing is AE, which is the length of the leg adjacent to $\angle EAB$. The opposite leg is still 7, so use the tangent (the TOA):

$$\tan \angle EAB = \frac{EB}{AE}$$

$$\tan 24° = \frac{7}{AE}$$

$$0.4452 = \frac{7}{AE}$$

$$0.4452(AE) = 7$$

$$AE = \frac{7}{0.4452}$$

$$AE = 15.7$$

Now use the formula for the area of $\triangle EAB$ (since it's a right triangle, AE is the base and EB is the height):

$$A = \frac{1}{2}bh$$
$$= \frac{1}{2}(15.7)(7)$$
$$= 54.95.$$

The area of the rhombus is 54.95×4, or **219.8** square units.

OTHER APPLICATIONS

Many textbooks include trig problems that apply to more tangible, real-life situations. The problems still involve right triangles, and the process is pretty much the same deal.

EXAMPLE 6

A woman is treading water in New York Harbor near the Statue of Liberty, which has an observation deck that is 165 feet above sea level. If she notices (somehow) that the angle of elevation from her head to the observation deck is 38°, how far is she from the base of the statue (to the nearest foot)?

SOLUTION

This problem is a simple trig exercise dressed up as a Coast Guard rescue mission. The key term is **angle of elevation**, which tells you that the woman's line of sight makes a 38° with the level of the water:

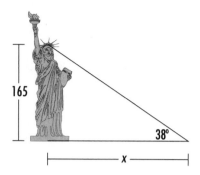

The height of the statue represents the opposite leg, and you want to find the length of the adjacent leg. Use tangent (TOA):

$$\tan 38° = \frac{165}{x}$$

$$0.7813 = \frac{165}{x}$$

$$0.7813x = 165$$

$$x = \frac{165}{0.7813}$$

$$x = 211.19$$

When you round it off to the nearest foot, your answer becomes **211** feet.

Here's one more example that's a little more complicated and involves the **angle of depression**.

EXAMPLE 7

Max and Mandy are riding on a horizontal ski lift, heading toward a support pole that is 45 feet tall. At a certain point, Max notices (somehow) that the angle of depression to the base of the support pole is 36°. Three minutes later, Mandy recognizes that the angle of depression is 51°. To the nearest *tenth* of a foot, how far along did they travel during that three-minute interval?

SOLUTION

Draw the diagram first.

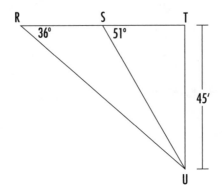

You have two triangles to work with: $\triangle RTU$ and $\triangle STU$. First, find RT using the tangent:

$$\tan 36° = \frac{TU}{RT}$$

$$0.7265 = \frac{45}{RT}$$

$$RT = \frac{45}{0.7265}$$

$$= 61.94 \text{ feet}$$

Now, find ST in the same manner:

$$\tan 51° = \frac{TU}{ST}$$

$$1.2349 = \frac{45}{ST}$$

$$ST = \frac{45}{1.2349}$$

$$= 36.44 \text{ feet}$$

Now that you have both distances, you can subtract to find RS:

$$RT - ST = RS$$
$$61.94 - 36.44 = RS$$
$$25.50 = RS.$$

Max and Mandy traveled a total of **25.5** feet.

DISCUSSION QUESTION

Why would anyone ever be on a *horizontal* ski lift? Wouldn't that defeat the purpose? Explain.

EXERCISES, SET 12B

What follow are some more practice questions that show you how the wonders of basic trigonometry affect our everyday lives. Find all measurements to the nearest *tenth*. The answers are in chapter 16.

1. If *KR* = 20, find the perimeter and area of rectangle *DREK*.

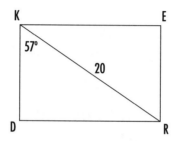

2. Find the perimeter and area of isosceles trapezoid *ABCD*. (Hint: Drop a perpendicular from *D* to $\overline{AB}$ and label it $\overline{DH}$.)

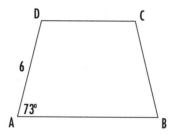

3. **(a)** If the area of $\triangle ABC$ is 20, find the measures of $\angle A$ and $\angle B$.

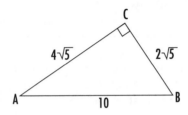

(b) Find the measure of $\angle EAB$.

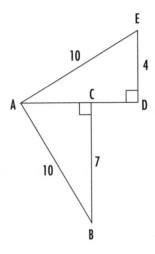

(c) Find the measure of $\angle QPO$.

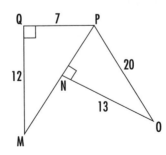

4. Find the perimeter and area of isosceles trapezoid COMB.

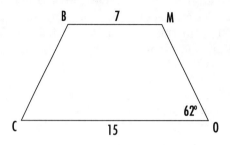

5.

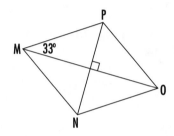

If PN = 30, find the following:
(a) MO
(b) MP
(c) the perimeter of MNOP

6.

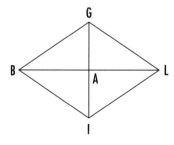

If BL = 30 and GI = 14, find the measure of ∠GLA and the perimeter of rhombus BILG.

7. A pirate seeking buried treasure is walking along with his treasure map when he reaches the edge of a cliff. He looks down into the depths and sees a big "X" on the ground, 70 feet from the base of the cliff. If the angle of depression from the pirate to the X is 53°, how tall is the cliff?

8. Milton is making an enormous flag for the kingdom of Aucampia. The flag is shaped like a right triangle, and the angle facing the short leg of the triangle must measure 36°. **(a)** If the long leg of the flag is 18 feet long, how long is the short leg? **(b)** How much material does Milton need?

9. Milton sits looking at the 55-foot flagpole with the Aucampian flag atop it. If the angle of elevation from Milton's shoes to the top of the flagpole is 37°, how far is he from the base of the flagpole?

10. A rescue plane maintaining a constant altitude of 2,000 feet sees a man in a rowboat in the water below. The angle of depression from the plane to the man is 28°. After a few moments, the angle of depression has increased to 44°. How far has the plane traveled during that time?

13

Locus and Constructions

You'll be happy to know that this chapter contains no theorems or formulas to memorize, no complicated algebra, and no mind-bending logic. In this chapter, we'll discuss what a locus is and how it pertains to constructions using a compass.

Most **loci** (the plural of locus) involve bisectors and points that are a consistent distance from other points and lines. That's why you use a compass for all your constructions; the compass is designed to maintain a certain distance between the pointy end and the pencil. (If it doesn't, it's a piece of crap—get a new one.)

WHAT'S A LOCUS?

A **simple locus** is just a series of points that satisfy certain specifications. There are several simple loci with which you should be familiar.

Locus	What it looks like
All points that are a specific distance d from a certain point form a **circle** with radius d centered at that point.	
All points that are a specific distance d from a certain line form **two parallel lines**, each d units from the given line.	

EXAMPLE 1

Define the locus of points that are 5 cm from a certain point D.

SOLUTION

The locus of points is a circle with a radius of 5 centered at point D.

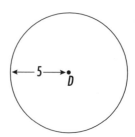

Most simple loci are sets of points that are **equidistant** from two things. These are the ones that figure prominently in constructions.

Locus	What It Looks Like
All points equidistant from two points A and B form the perpendicular bisector of line segment .	
All points equidistant from two parallel lines form a third line parallel to the other two and midway between them.	
All points equidistant from two intersecting lines form two perpendicular lines, each of which bisects a pair of vertical angles.	
All points equidistant from the sides of a given angle form the angle bisector of that angle.	

COMPOUND LOCI

Questions concerning loci can get more complicated when more than one is involved. You may have to discern how many points of intersection there are between two separate loci.

EXAMPLE 2

How many points of intersection are there between the locus of points 4 feet from a certain line and the locus of points 6 feet from a point on that line?

SOLUTION

Problems like this one require a lot of visualization. Look at the line first. The set of points 4 feet from that line is two parallel lines.

Now look at the second locus; it's a circle with a radius of 6 feet:

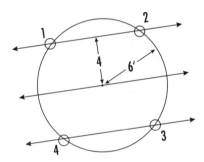

There are **four** points of intersection.

WHAT'S A CONSTRUCTION?

You can use a compass to construct loci involving equidistant points. When the arcs drawn from two certain points intersect, for example, you know that the point of intersection is equidistant from both points.

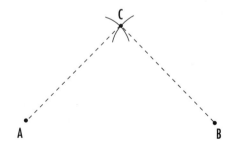

$\overline{AC}$ and $\overline{BC}$ both represent radii of circles drawn from points A and B, so C is equidistant from both A and B.

BISECTING STUFF

As we've noted, the **perpendicular bisector of a line segment** is the locus of points that are equidistant from the segment's endpoints.

STEP 1

Open your compass until it's over half as long as $\overline{AB}$. Then place the pointy end of your compass on A and make two arcs like so:

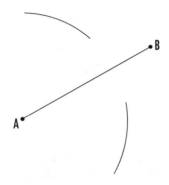

STEP 2
Without changing the width of your compass, put the pointy end on B and find where the two arcs intersect. Label these two points C and D.

STEP 3
Connect C and D with your straightedge.

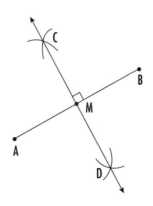

Note: This technique should also be used to construct the **midpoint of a line segment**. The midpoint, point M in the diagram above, is the point at which a segment intersects its perpendicular bisector.

An **angle bisector** is the locus of points that are equidistant from both sides of the angle.

Step 1
Put the metal point of the compass on point B and create an arc that intersects both $\overline{BA}$ and $\overline{BC}$. Label those points of intersection D and F:

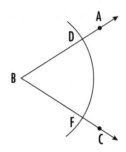

Step 2
Without changing the width of your compass, put the pointy end on point D and make an arc inside the angle. Then put the pointy end on point F and find the point inside the angle where the two arcs intersect. Label this point E.

Step 3
Draw ray BE. This is the angle bisector.

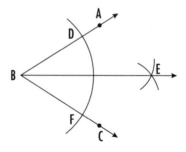

PERPENDICULAR LINES

The instructions for constructing perpendicular lines are very similar to those for constructing a perpendicular bisector. To construct a **perpendicular line through a point on the line**, there's only one added step.

Step 1

Put the pointy end of your compass on point C and make an arc that intersects line AB in two places, J and K, like so:

Step 2

Construct the perpendicular bisector of $\overline{JK}$.

Constructing a **perpendicular line through a point not on the line** is a comparable exercise.

Step 1

With the point of your compass on P, draw an arc (#1) that intersects $\overline{AB}$ in two places:

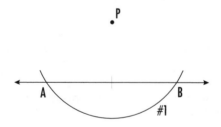

Step 2

Rather than repeat the perpendicular bisector drill, you only need to find one more point. Without altering the width of your compass, place its point on A and draw an arc (#2) on the side opposite P.

Step 3

Put the pointy end on B and find where the two arcs intersect below the line.

Step 4:
Draw the line defined by P and Q:

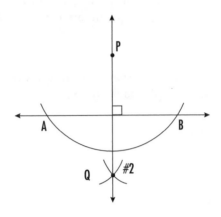

COPYING STUFF

The other half of the construction world involves reconstructing, or copying, various shapes.

Copying a **line segment** is probably the most basic of all constructions. Follow this two-step process.

Step 1

Make the compass exactly as wide as segment $\overline{AB}$.

Step 2

Choose a point E on line $\overline{CD}$, place the pointy end on that point, and make an arc that intersects with the line at F.

Segment $\overline{EF}$ is a copy of segment $\overline{AB}$.

Copying an **angle** is a bit more time consuming:

Step 1
With the pointy end of the compass on point A, make an arc that intersects both rays of angle A. Label these points M and N.

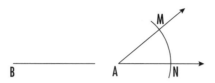

Step 2
From point B on a separate line, without changing the width of your compass, draw the same arc. Label the point of intersection point P.

Step 3
Make your compass as wide as segment $\overline{MN}$. Without changing that setting, place the pointy end on point P and make an arc that intersects the first arc at point Q.

Step 4
Connect points B and Q.

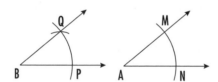

PARALLEL LINES
Constructing a parallel line requires the same work you do to copy an angle and relies on the principle that if corresponding angles are congruent, the lines are parallel (see chapter 8 for more details).

Step 1
Draw a transversal from point P that intersects with the line. Label the point of intersection Q:

Step 2

With the pointy end of the compass on Q, draw an arc (#1) that intersects both the line and the transversal. Label these points of intersection A and B.

Step 3

Without changing the width of your compass, draw the same arc (#2) with the pointy end on P. The arc intersects the transversal at point C:

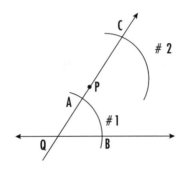

Step 4

Make your compass as wide as segment $\overline{AB}$. Without changing that width, place the pointy end on point C and make an arc that intersects with arc #2. Label this point of intersection D.

Step 5

Connect points P and D with your straightedge.

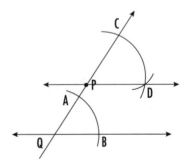

COORDINATE GEOMETRY

Sometimes, you have to determine the graphic equation of a locus of points. Equations for lines come up a lot.

EXAMPLE 3

What is the equation of the locus of points that are equidistant from points $A(1, 3)$ and $B(7, 3)$?

SOLUTION

To get a grip on the situation, it helps to draw a diagram:

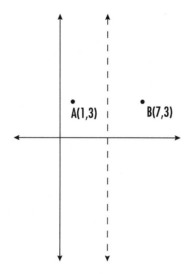

The locus of points is going to be the perpendicular bisector of segment $\overline{AB}$. Since the two points form a horizontal line, the locus will be a vertical line. The equation of any vertical line is $x = a$, in which a is a constant.

The line will go through the midpoint of the segment, which is halfway between 1 and 7. Take the average of these two points:

$$\frac{1+7}{2} = \frac{8}{2} = 4$$

The equation of the locus is $x = \mathbf{4}$.

Of course, these can get much harder if the line in question isn't horizontal or vertical. If you have any trouble with this answer, refer back to the section about perpendicular lines in chapter 8.

EXAMPLE 4

What is the equation of the locus of points that are equidistant from points $M(-6, 5)$ and $N(2, 1)$?

SOLUTION

As you can see, the line in question is not parallel to either axis:

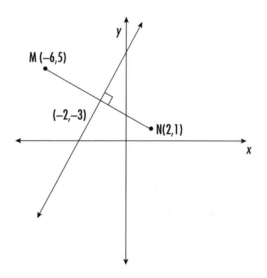

You'll need to find the slope of $\overline{MN}$:

$$m = \frac{y_2 - y_1}{x_2 - x_1}$$

$$= \frac{1 - 5}{2 - (-6)}$$

$$= \frac{-4}{8} = -\frac{1}{2}$$

Slopes of perpendicular lines are negative reciprocals, so the slope of the line in question is 2. You can plug this into the slope-intercept formula:

$$y = 2x + b$$

Now you have to find a point on the line. The only point that you know is on the perpendicular bisector is the midpoint of $\overline{MN}$:

$$(\bar{x}, \bar{y}) = \left(\frac{x_1 + x_2}{2}, \frac{y_1 + y_2}{2} \right)$$

$$= \left(\frac{-6+2}{2}, \frac{5+1}{2} \right)$$

$$= \left(\frac{-4}{2}, \frac{6}{2} \right)$$

$$= (-2, 3)$$

Plug the information you know into the slope-intercept formula, and simplify:

$$y = 2x + b$$
$$3 = 2(-2) + b$$
$$3 = -4 + b$$
$$7 = b$$

The equation of the line is $y = 2x + 7$. Note that the line intersects the y-axis at (0, 7).

You also might have to use the formula for the equation of a circle.

EXAMPLE 5

What is the equation of the locus of points that are 3 units from the point (–5, 4)?

SOLUTION

Once you recognize this locus as a circle (a locus of points equidistant from a certain point), the rest is easy. Use the formula for a circle, and remember that (h, k) is the center and r is the radius:

$$(x - h)^2 + (y - k)^2 = r^2$$
$$[x - (-5)]^2 + (y - 4)^2 = 3^2$$
$$(x + 5)^2 + (y - 4)^2 = 9$$

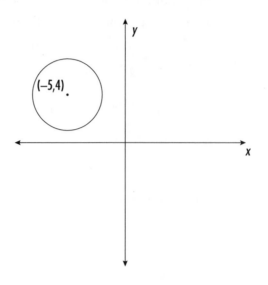

EXERCISES, SET 13A

Try these locus problems. The answers are in chapter 16.

    1. Draw and describe the locus of points that are:
        (a) 5 cm from a certain point P.
        (b) 2 cm from a certain line m.
        (c) equidistant from two perpendicular lines.
        (d) equidistant from the centers of two tangent, congruent circles A and B.

    2. Write the equation of the locus of points that are:
        (a) equidistant from $A(-2, 3)$ and $B(4, 3)$.
        (b) equidistant from $A(1, 4)$ and $B(1, -6)$.
        (c) equidistant from $A(-4, 3)$ and $B(2, 5)$.
        (d) four units from the point $(2, -5)$.

3. Write an equation for the locus of coordinate points in which:
   (a) the ordinates are twice the abscissas.
   (b) each ordinate equals three more than half of each abscissa.
   (c) the abscissa equals one.
   (d) all points are 4 units from the line $x = 3$.
   (e) the abscissa equals the ordinate.
   (f) the sum of the squares of the abscissa and the ordinate is 16.

4. Identify the number of points of intersection between the following compound loci:
   (a) all points 4 cm from a line and 5 cm from a point on that line.
   (b) all points equidistant from two intersection lines and 3 cm from the point of intersection.
   (c) all points 2 units from the point $(-1, 3)$ and all points 3 units from the point $(5, 5)$.
   (d) all points 3 units from the point $(2, -3)$ and all points 4 units from the origin.
   (e) all points 5 units from the point $(4, 7)$ and all points 6 units from the point $(3, 7)$.
   (f) all points two units from the x-axis and three units from the y-axis.
   (g) all points equidistant from the origin and $(0, 6)$, and all points that satisfy the equation $(x - 2)^2 + (y - 1)^2 = 25$.

5. How many points of intersection are there between the locus of points 3 cm from M and the locus of points equidistant from M and P if (a) $MP = 4$? (b) $MP = 6$? (c) $MP = 8$?

6. How many points are equidistant from points X and Y and also 5 cm from line XY?

7. How many points are equidistant from the four vertices of a rectangle?

8. Find the point(s) at which the locus of points equidistant from (−3, 3) and (−7, 3) intersects with the locus of points equidistant from points (4, 2) and (4, −8).

9. If $\triangle DEF$ is equilateral, how many points of intersection are there between the locus of points that are equidistant from rays $\overline{DE}$ and $\overline{DF}$, and the locus of points equidistant from points E and F?

10. Lines l and m are eight units apart. At how many points does the locus of points 6 units from a point on line m intersect with the locus of points 5 units from line l and the locus of points 4 units from line m?

Note: When you practice constructions on your own, make sure you have good equipment—a reliable compass and a straightedge. You should basically know if you get a question right by looking at the finished product. For example, if your perpendicular bisector makes a 30° angle with the original line, something's probably wrong.

14

Permutations and Combinations

This chapter concerns the number of ways you can arrange or choose objects!

FACTORIAL!

You're going see a lot of exclamation points in the work you review here! If you see the term *n*!, it's not a direction to scream "N" at the top of your lungs! You pronounce it "*n* **factorial**!" So there!

The term *n*! stands for the product of all integers between 1 and *n*, inclusive. For example, $5! = 5 \times 4 \times 3 \times 2 \times 1$.

PERMUTATIONS

Each possible arrangement of a set of items is called a **permutation**. Permutations are different from combinations, which you'll read about later, because the order in which things appear matters.

Let's say, for example, that you have portraits of each of the four Beatles, and you want to hang them in a row over your bed.

There are *four* possibilities for the first position; you can put John, Paul, George, or Ringo there. Once you've chosen the first portrait, though, you have to decide which one to put in the second spot. You've already chosen one, so three are remaining; there are *three* possibilities.

The same logic holds true for the final two spots. There are *two* Beatles left for position No. 3, and when it's time to hang the last picture, there's only *one* left.

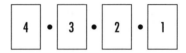

This is where the factorial stuff comes from. It's a lot easier to recognize that you can arrange four items 4! ways than it is to list all the possibilities manually:

JPGR	PJGR	GJPR	RJPG		
JPRG	PJRG	GJRP	RJGP		
JGPR	PGJR	GPJR	RPJG	**or**	4! = 24
JGRP	PGRJ	GPRJ	RPGJ		
JRPG	PRJP	GRJP	RGJP		
JRGP	PRPJ	GRPJ	RGPJ		

A set of *n* items can be arranged in a total of *n*! ways if you use each item *only once*.

RESTRICTIONS

What if Ringo is your favorite and you want him to be on the far left? How many possible permutations are there now? As you might imagine, there are fewer than 24.

There is only one possibility for the first portrait. Each of the other three could be in the next slot, followed by two, then one.

The number of permutations is 1 × 3 × 2 × 1, or 6. (Incidentally, you could have just looked at the list of 24 permutations above to get the answer; there are six possible arrangements in the Ringo column on the far right.)

The best way to answer questions with restrictions is to figure out how many possibilities there are for each position in the array.

EXAMPLE 1

In how many ways can the digits 2, 3, 5, and 7 be arranged to form a number that is less than 4,000? How many of those four-digit numbers are even?

SOLUTION

There are four places in the number, and one place is restricted. Deal with it first, then fill in the unrestricted places.

The number must be less than 4,000, so the first digit has only two possibilities: 2 or 3. The rest of the places don't have restrictions:

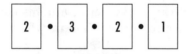

You can form **12** four-digit numbers that are less than 4,000.

Now, work on the second part. If the four-digit number is even, then the last digit must be 2. There's only *one* possibility for the ones digit. Further, if the 2 is in the ones place, then the only digit that can be in the thousands place is the 3 (otherwise, the number would be greater than 4,000). Thus, there's only one possibility for the first digit. Fill in the rest normally—there are *two* numbers left for the hundreds place, and *one* left for the tens place.

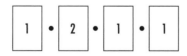

There are **2** even numbers less than 4,000. (Those numbers are 3,752 and 3,572.)

REPETITION

Each of these exercises so far has assumed that you can't repeat a digit in the arrangement. If repetition is possible, however, there's a simple formula to follow.

A set of n items can be arranged in a total of n^n ways if you use each item *more than once*.

EXAMPLE 2

How many three-digit numbers can be formed from the set of digits {2, 3, 4} if repetition is allowed?

SOLUTION

There are 3 items in the set, so you can form 3^3, or **27** different three-digit numbers. Here they are:

222	223	224	332	334	442	443	234	324
333	232	242	323	343	424	434	243	423
444	322	422	233	433	244	344	342	432

Another potential hitch involves arranging sets of items in which some items are duplicated. If a set of n items contains an item that appears p times, the number of ways in which those items can be arranged is: $\dfrac{n!}{p!}$

This formula expands to accommodate the number of repeated items. To find the number of possible arrangements of n letters, in which one letter appears p times and another letter appears q times (remember that p and q are greater than 1), the formula looks like this: $\dfrac{n!}{p!q!}$

And so on. The most common examples involve arranging letters in a word.

EXAMPLE 3

How many possible arrangements are there of the letters in the word "BOOKKEEPER"?

SOLUTION

There are 10 letters in "BOOKKEEPER," and there's a lot of repetition: three E's, two O's, and two K's. Therefore, you can express the number of arrangements like this:

$$\frac{10!}{3!\,2!\,2!}$$

Some teachers let you leave it like this, especially since the number is so huge. It's easy enough to figure out, though, if you have to:

$$\frac{10!}{3!\,2!\,2!} = \frac{10\times9\times8\times7\times6\times5\times4\times3\times2\times1}{(3\times2\times1)\times(2\times1)\times(2\times1)} = 172{,}800$$

In the problems so far, every element has been involved in the arrangements. That's not always the case.

LIFE WITH LEFTOVERS: $_nP_r$

There are many instances when some items are selected and others are left out. When this occurs, there are two formulas you need to memorize. The first involves permutations:

> If you choose r items from a group of n items, the number of ways you can arrange those items is denoted as $_nP_r$:
>
> $$_nP_r = \frac{n!}{(n-r)!}$$

Use this formula when the order in which you choose the items matters.

EXAMPLE 4

Seven runners are competing in the 100-yard dash in the Olympics. How many different lineups of medal winners can there be?

SOLUTION

As in most races, the order in which the racers finish matters. Therefore, use the permutations rule. There are 7 runners, but only 3 get medals

$$\begin{aligned}
_7P_3 &= \frac{7!}{(7-3)!} \\
&= \frac{7!}{4!} \\
&= \frac{7\times6\times5\times4\times3\times2\times1}{4\times3\times2\times1} \\
&= 7\times6\times5 \\
&= 210
\end{aligned}$$

The race could end in **210** different ways that involve the top three finishers.

Note: As you might have seen from this example, there's another way to look at the $_nP_r$ formula.

> The term $_nP_r$ represents the product of the r highest factors of n!

In the example above, $_7P_3$ equals the product of the first 3 factors of 7!, or $7 \times 6 \times 5$. The total is 210.

EXERCISES, SET 14A

Here are some drills to try before you go further. The answers are in chapter 16.

1. Calculate the following:
   (a) 4!
   (b) 6!
   (c) $_8P_3$
   (d) $_{10}P_4$
   (e) $_{10}P_6$
   (f) $_5P_5$
   (g) $_5P_0$

2. Determine the number of ways that the letters in the following words can be arranged.
   (a) ZERO
   (b) SCORN
   (c) DINGBAT
   (d) CHEETOS
   (e) RIBOFLAVIN
   (f) BIKINI
   (g) BARFBAG
   (h) AARDVARK
   (i) MARMALARD
   (j) MISSISSIPPI

3. Find the number of permutations of the word HOTSPUR under each of the following situations:

   (a) There are no restrictions.
   (b) The first letter has to be R.
   (c) The fourth letter must be R.
   (d) The first two letters have to be vowels.
   (e) The last three letters must be consonants.
   (f) There must be consonants in every odd-numbered space.
   (g) The first two letters must be SH.
   (h) The word SPOT must appear within the word.

4. Find the number of four-digit numbers that can be formed from the set {3, 4, 5, 6, 7} under each of the following situations:

   (a) Any number can be used at any time.
   (b) You can use each number exactly once.
   (c) The number must be odd.
   (d) The number is less than 4,000.
   (e) The number is greater than 5,000.

5. In each case, solve for x.

   (e) $_xP_5 = 1$
   (f) $_6P_x = 120$
   (g) $_7P_x = 840$
   (h) $_xP_{(x-2)} = 60$

6. At a wedding, a bride is posing for a picture with her maid of honor and four bridesmaids. In how many ways can they be arranged if the bride and the maid of honor have to be in the middle?

7. The United Nations celebrates a certain international holiday by displaying four Belgian flags, two Argentinean flags, and three South Korean flags. (a) In how many ways can they be arranged? (b) If the Argentinean flags must be on either end, how many possible arrangements are there?

8. Both the Jackson and Osmond families have five members. If the two families are to march single file in the Thanksgiving Day parade, in how many ways can they be arranged such that no Osmond is next to a Jackson?

9. Six boys and five girls are in line for Rolling Stones tickets. How many arrangements of the children are possible if **(a)** the boys and girls alternate? **(b)** three girls are first in line? **(c)** the five boys are all next to each other?

10. When you divide $n!$ by $(n - 2)!$, what do you get?

ORDER DOESN'T MATTER: $_nC_r$

The other half of this chapter involves selecting a group of items from a larger set when you don't care which order they appear in.

Look back at Example 4 above. Let's say the three medal winners are Bannister, Fosbury, and Owens. These three can finish in six possible ways:

Gold	Silver	Bronze	
B	*F*	*O*	
B	*O*	*F*	
F	*B*	*O*	{*B, F, O*}
F	*O*	*B*	
O	*B*	*F*	
O	*F*	*B*	

These are the six permutations of *B*, *F*, and *O*. But the group {*B, F, O*} is only one **combination** of athletes that could end up on the medal platform. In most situations, therefore, there are much fewer combinations than permutations.

> From a group of n items, the number of subsets you can choose containing r items is denoted as $_nC_r$:
>
> $$_nC_r = \frac{n!}{r!(n-r)!}$$

Let's alter Example 4 slightly.

EXAMPLE 5

Seven runners are competing in a qualifying heat for the 100-yard dash in the Olympics. If the top three finishers move on to the next round, how many different groups can move on to become finalists?

SOLUTION

This example is different from Example 4 because the order doesn't matter—the winners all move on to the next round regardless of how they finish, as long as they're among the top three. Because of this, use the combinations formula:

$$_7C_3 = \frac{7!}{3!(7-3)!}$$
$$= \frac{7!}{3!\,4!} = \frac{7\times6\times5\times4\times3\times2\times1}{(3\times2\times1)\times(4\times3\times2\times1)}$$
$$= 35$$

There are **35** possible combinations.

Note: There's an easier way to find $_nC_r$ as long as you remember that $_nP_r = \frac{n!}{(n-r)!}$:

$$_nC_r = \frac{n!}{r!(n-r)!}$$
$$= \frac{n!}{(n-r)!} \times \frac{1}{r!}$$
$$= {_nP_r} \times \frac{1}{r!}$$
$$= \frac{_nP_r}{r!}$$

Now you can calculate $_7C_3$ like this:

$$_7C_3 = \frac{_7P_3}{3!} = \frac{7\times6\times5}{6} = 35$$

OTHER FACTS ABOUT COMBINATIONS

Here's something you may have noticed from the combinations formula. Let's look at a combinations problem in which you have to choose from the group {A, B, C, D, E}. The table on the left lists the three-letter combinations, and the table on the right lists the two-letter combinations:

In	Out
ABC	DE
ABD	CE
ABE	CD
ACD	BE
ACE	BD
ADE	BC
BCD	AE
BCE	AD
BDE	AC
CDE	AB

In	Out
AB	CDE
AC	BDE
AD	BCE
AE	BCD
BC	ADE
BD	ACE
BE	ACD
CD	ABE
CE	ABD
DE	ABC

Look closely at the two tables—they contain the same combinations, but in a different order. That leads you to this point: When you select three items out of five, you're *leaving out the other two.* Given that, it must be true that $_5C_3 = {}_5C_2.$

In any combinations problem, $_nC_r = {}_nC_{n-r}.$

EXAMPLE 6

The term $_8C_5$ is equal to which of the following?

(1) $_8P_5$ (2) $\dfrac{8!}{5!}$ (3) $_8C_3$ (4) $\dfrac{8!}{3!}$

SOLUTION

If you know the formula, you can avoid all the calculations and pick **(3)**, which is the right answer.

Here are some other bits of important info:

- $_nC_n = 1$ There's only one way to select all the members of a set.

- $_nC_0 = 1$ There's only one way to select none of the members of a set.

- $_nC_1 = n$ There are n ways to select any one of n items.

USING YOUR CALCULATOR

Of course, a lot of this calculation is unnecessary if your calculator has $_nP_r$ and $_nC_r$ buttons and your teacher lets you use it. Your calculator may be different, but most of them follow this procedure:

To calculate $_6P_2$, for example:

- enter 6 into the calculator
- press "$_nP_r$"
- enter 2.
- press "=".

Your answer should be 30.

If your teacher doesn't let you use a calculator on an exam, it isn't too hard to memorize the formulas. Just keep practicing. Here's one more example (the calculations are omitted):

EXAMPLE 7

The U.S. Amateur Association must choose four cities to host the quarterfinals of the Third Annual Underwater Needlepoint Championship. There are nine cities in the running: Atlanta, Boston, Charlotte, Denver, East Hampton, Fresno, Grand Rapids, Harrisburg, and Iglooville, Alaska. (a) How many combinations of cities are possible? (b) How many combinations include Iglooville? (c) How many combinations exclude Iglooville?

SOLUTION

(a) The first part is easy. The order doesn't matter, so use combinations:

$$_9C_4 = 126$$

(b) If Iglooville is definitely included, then there are three positions left to be chosen from the remaining eight cities:

$$_8C_3 = 56$$

(c) If Iglooville is definitely excluded (and who would want to do underwater needlepoint in Alaska, anyway?), there are still four slots to fill but only eight cities are eligible:

$$_8C_4 = 70$$

When you think about it, either a combination includes Iglooville, or it excludes it. There's no third option. Therefore, the number of combinations with Iglooville plus those without Iglooville should equal the total number of possibilities:

$$56 + 70 = 126. \text{ Bingo!}$$

CHOOSING FROM MORE THAN ONE GROUP

If the elements you're choosing from are divided into two or more groups, then you have to multiply the results you get.

EXAMPLE 8

The Yardville High chess team needs to send four representatives to Moscow for the International Chess Expo. If the team consists of seven girls and six boys, how many combinations are there if (a) there are no restrictions (b) the group is all girls, or (c) two boys and two girls go?

SOLUTION

(a) The first part is easy. There are 13 students, and four get to go. All you do is calculate $_{13}C_4$, which is **715**.

(b) If the group is all girls, then four girls are chosen from the group of seven. Now the calculation becomes $_7C_4$, or **35**.

(c) In this part of the problem, two out of seven girls and two out of six boys must be chosen. Figure out the number of combinations of each:

$$\text{Girls: } _7C_2 = 21$$

$$\text{Boys: } _6C_2 = 15$$

Now multiply those numbers together:

21 × 15 = **315** possible combinations

AT LEAST OR AT MOST

Combinations problems get more complicated when they involve a minimum or a maximum. (These are especially prevalent in probability questions, which we discuss in the next chapter.) In these cases, you have to find the number of combinations that exist in each case and then add them.

EXAMPLE 9

In Example 8, how many combinations of students that go to Moscow include *at least* one boy?

SOLUTION

There are four possible scenarios in which there is at least one boy in the four-person group:

1. one boy and three girls

2. two boys and two girls

3. three boys and one girl

4. four boys

Find the number of combinations in each scenario first. If one of six boys ($_6C_1$) and three of seven girls ($_7C_3$) are chosen, there are $_6C_1 \times _7C_3$ combinations:

$$_6C_1 = 6$$
$$_7C_3 = 35$$

There are 6 × 35, or 210 combinations involving exactly one boy.

Figure out the other scenarios in the same way:

two boys: $(_6C_2) \times (_7C_2) = 15 \times 21 \quad = 315$
three boys: $(_6C_3) \times (_7C_1) = 20 \times 7 \quad = 140$
four boys: $(_6C_4) \qquad\qquad\qquad\quad = 15$

Add these four numbers up: 210 + 315 + 140 + 15 = **680** combinations involving at least one boy.

Note: Here's where a slick math person can save some time. Look at Example 8 more closely; there are 715 possible combinations of students, right? There are also 35 possible groups in which there are only girls (i.e., no boys). Either a group has a boy, or it doesn't. Therefore, if 35 groups contain no boys, then the other 680 (715 − 35) must have at least one boy!

EXERCISES, SET 14B

Try these exercises! The answers are in chapter 16! I'm glad this chapter is over! I can stop yelling now!

1. Calculate the following:
    (a) $_4C_2$
    (b) $_6C_3$
    (c) $_8C_5$
    (d) $_8C_3$
    (e) $_9C_9$
    (f) $_9C_1$
    (g) $_9C_0$
    (h) $_nC_{(n-1)}$

2. Solve for x:
    (a) $_7C_x = 1$
    (b) $_xC_2 = 28$
    (c) $_7C_x = 35$
    (d) $_xC_3 = {}_xC_5$
    (e) $_xC_2 = 2x$
    (f) $_{(x+1)}C_3 = {}_xC_3 + 45$
    (g) $_nC_x = n$

3. Which of the following is not equal to the expression $_9C_4$?
    (a) $_9C_5$

    (b) $\dfrac{9!}{4!}$

    (c) $\dfrac{_9P_4}{4!}$

    (d) $\dfrac{3024}{24}$

4. Snow White must choose three of the Seven Dwarves to accompany her on her interview at WW Apple Orchards, Inc. Determine the number of different combinations that exist if:

   (a) there are no restrictions.

   (b) Doc goes along with Snow White.

   (c) Doc stays home.

   (d) Grumpy and Sneezy stay home.

   (e) Happy goes along, and Bashful and Sleepy stay home.

   (f) Dopey and Doc go along.

   (g) Sleepy and Sneezy are together, whether they go or not.

5. There are seven freshmen, nine sophomores, eleven juniors and eight seniors in a school bus when it breaks down. If five students are to be chosen to walk ahead for help, how many combinations exist if the group consists of:

   (a) five freshmen?

   (b) five sophomores?

   (c) five juniors?

   (d) five seniors?

   (e) four seniors and a freshman?

   (f) two sophomores and three juniors?

   (g) three freshmen, one junior, and one senior?

   (h) one senior, one junior, two sophomores, and a freshman?

6. When Mrs. Hobbie prepares a bowl of candy for Halloween, she puts in nine watermelon lollipops and eight sour apple lollipops. If her son thrusts his hand in and pulls out three lollipops, how many combinations involve *at least* one sour apple lollipop?

7. Solve for x: $_xC_x + {_xC_1} = 12$.

15

Probability

This chapter is devoted to figuring out the chance that something will happen. Become an expert in this stuff, and you'll make a fortune in Vegas.

You'll also use a lot of the work we discussed in chapter 14 about permutations and combinations, because much of your work here involves calculating the number of possible outcomes of a situation.

THE DEFINITION

If something that you want to happen does happen, that's known as a **favorable outcome**. The number of **possible outcomes** is the total of all things that could possibly happen. Your job is to figure out the chance that the outcome will be favorable.

> Therefore, **probability** relies upon this simple concept:
>
> $$\frac{\text{the number of favorable outcomes}}{\text{the number of possible outcomes}}$$
>
> The probability that event E will happen is commonly denoted as $P(E)$.

EXAMPLE 1

What is the probability that a member of the Brady Bunch household chosen at random is female?

SOLUTION

There are nine members of the household: the parents, Mike and Carol; three boys, Greg, Peter, and Bobby; three very lovely girls, Marcia, Jan, and Cindy; and the maid, Alice. (She's not technically a Brady, but we'll call her one here for the heck of it.) There are nine people (possible outcomes) and five females (favorable outcomes).

The probability that the chosen Brady is female is $\frac{5}{9}$.

OTHER BASIC FACTS

There are four basic truths in simple probability that you should know.

1. If a favorable outcome is impossible, then $P(E) = 0$.

    There's no chance that any member of the Brady family is 11 feet tall. Thus, the probability that a Brady chosen at random is 11 feet tall is **zero**.

2. If a favorable outcome is a certainty, then **P(E) = 1**.

   Everyone in the Brady home has two ears. Therefore, the probability that a Brady chosen at random has two ears is **one**.

3. The probability that something *will* happen plus the probability that it *won't* happen equals 1. That is, **P(E) + P(not E) = 1**.

   This makes sense. You're certain that every Brady is either female or *not* female. Since the chance that a Brady chosen at random is female is $\frac{5}{9}$, the probability that the person is *not* female is $1 - \frac{5}{9}$, or $\frac{4}{9}$.

4. The **higher** the probability, the **greater** the chance that the favorable outcome will occur.

Since the probability of choosing a female is $\frac{5}{9}$ and that of choosing a male is $\frac{4}{9}$, you have a greater chance of choosing a female.

We know what you're thinking: "Enough about the Bradys, already." More complex work with probabilities involves two or more events. Let's look at a standard deck of playing cards.

"AND" STATEMENTS
When you're considering the probability that two events will happen, you have to **multiply** the separate probabilities together.

Given events A and B, the probability that both will happen is the product of the two individual probabilities:

$$P(A \text{ and } B) = P(A) \times P(B)$$

This works for **simultaneous events** (things that happen at the same time) and **subsequent events** (things that happen one after the other).

Here's an example of two simultaneous events:

EXAMPLE 2

What is the probability that you'll choose the jack of diamonds at random from a standard deck of cards?

SOLUTION

There are two criteria at work here—the card must be both a jack *and* a diamond. The probability that you'll choose a jack from a deck of 52 cards is $\frac{4}{52}$, or $\frac{1}{13}$, because there are four jacks in the deck. The probability that you'll choose a diamond is $\frac{13}{52}$, or $\frac{1}{4}$, because there are 13 diamonds in the deck. Therefore, the probability that you'll choose the jack of diamonds at random is $\frac{1}{13} \times \frac{1}{4}$, or $\frac{1}{52}$.

When you think about it, this answer makes sense; there are 52 cards and only one jack of diamonds. Therefore, you have 1 chance in 52 of selecting it at random.

Working with **subsequent** events is very similar, and there are two possible scenarios: **with replacement** and **without replacement**.

EXAMPLE 3

You draw one card from a standard deck, then replace it. Then, you draw a second card from that same deck. What is the probability that you'll choose two face cards?

SOLUTION

Even though the two events didn't happen at the same time, the concept is the same. In a deck of 52 cards, there are 12 face cards (three in each suit). The probability that you'll draw a face card the first time is $\frac{12}{52}$, or $\frac{3}{13}$. Since you put the card back, the probability that you'll draw a face card the second time is still $\frac{3}{13}$. Therefore, the probability that you'll choose two face cards is $\frac{3}{13} \times \frac{3}{13}$, or $\frac{9}{169}$.

Basically, you have roughly a 1-in-18 chance of getting two subsequent face cards. Let's see how the odds change when the first card is *not* replaced in the deck.

EXAMPLE 4

You draw one card from a standard deck and put it aside. Then you draw a second card from the same deck. What is the probability that you'll choose two face cards?

SOLUTION

The idea is a bit different here. When you draw the first card, the probability that it's a face card is $\frac{3}{13}$. Once that card is removed, the probability of drawing a second face card is different. There are 11 face cards left out of a possible 51, and the probability is $\frac{11}{51}$.

The probability that you'll draw two face cards is $\frac{3}{13} \times \frac{11}{51}$, or $\frac{11}{221}$.

The odds here are roughly 1 in 20, which also makes sense. Since you took a face card out, the probability of drawing two in a row got a little smaller.

The bottom line of all this is that "and" statements run on multiplication, and the number of possible outcomes increases exponentially with each event.

For example, if you flip a coin once, there are two possible outcomes: heads or tails. If you flip it twice, there are 2^2, or 4 outcomes, and if you flip it three times, there are 2^3, or 8 possible outcomes:

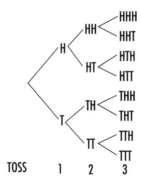

"OR" STATEMENTS

Knowing the number of possible outcomes is just as important for "or" statements. With these, you **add** probabilities. Most problems you'll encounter will involve probabilities in which there is **no overlap**.

> Given events A and B (which *cannot* occur at the same time), the probability that one or the other will happen is the sum of the two individual probabilities:
>
> $$P(A \text{ or } B) = P(A) + P(B)$$

EXAMPLE 5

If two fair dice are thrown, what is the probability that either (*a*) the sum will be 7 or (*b*) the sum will be 10?

SOLUTION

The first step is figuring out how many possible outcomes exist. When you throw one die, there are 6 possible rolls; when you throw two dice, there are 6^2, or 36 possible rolls.

Count up all the possible rolls that add up to 7. Contrary to what you might think based on all the work in chapter 14, the best way to do this is list them: 1 and 6; 2 and 5; 3 and 4; 4 and 3; 5 and 2; and 6 and 1 (remember that a 1 on the first die and a 6 on the second is a different roll from a 6 on the first and a 1 on the second).

There are six possible favorable outcomes, so the probability that you'll roll a seven is $\frac{6}{36}$.

Now repeat the technique for rolls of 10. The three favorable outcomes are: 4 and 6; 5 and 5; and 6 and 4. The probability is thus $\frac{3}{36}$.

To find the combined probability, add the two individual values: $\frac{6}{36} + \frac{3}{36} = \frac{9}{36}$

The combined probability is $\frac{9}{36}$, or $\frac{1}{4}$.

The issue changes a little when the two events **can overlap**.

Given events A and B (which *can* occur at the same time), the probability that one or the other will happen is the sum of the two individual probabilities, minus the probability that they'll both happen:

$$P(A \text{ or } B) = P(A) + P(B) - P(A \text{ and } B)$$

EXAMPLE 6

If two fair dice are thrown, what is the probability that either (*a*) you'll throw doubles or (*b*) the sum will be 10?

SOLUTION

Figure out the probabilities as you normally would. Since there are 6 ways to throw doubles, the probability is $\frac{6}{36}$. There are also 3 ways to throw a 10, so the probability of that happening is $\frac{3}{36}$.

The added factor is the probability that you roll a 10 **and** roll doubles. There's only one way you can do that (by throwing two 5's) so the probability is $\frac{1}{36}$.

Now put it all together: $\frac{6}{36} + \frac{3}{36} - \frac{1}{36} = \frac{8}{36}$

The combined probability is $\frac{8}{36}$, or $\frac{2}{9}$.

MORE ADDING

You also add probabilities if there's more than one way to have a favorable outcome.

EXAMPLE 7

Your sock drawer contains four red socks, three yellow socks, and five black socks only. If you reach in and grab two socks one at a time, without replacement, what is the probability that you'll choose a matched pair?

SOLUTION

There are three ways to fulfill the favored outcome; you can get a pair of red, a pair of yellow, or a pair of black socks. You have to calculate the probability that you'll get a pair of each color, then add them.

There are four red socks out of the 12 in the drawer. The probability that you'll get a red one the first time is $\frac{4}{12}$. After you remove a red sock, there are three left out of 11. The chance that you'll get a second red sock is $\frac{3}{11}$. The combined probability is $\frac{4}{12} \times \frac{3}{11}$, or $\frac{12}{132}$. (Resist reducing the fraction now. It'll be easier to add them later.)

The probability that both socks will be yellow is $\frac{3}{12} \times \frac{2}{11}$, or $\frac{6}{132}$.

The probability that both socks will be black is $\frac{5}{12} \times \frac{4}{11}$, or $\frac{20}{132}$. Add them up, and you're finished: $\frac{12}{132} + \frac{6}{132} + \frac{20}{132} = \frac{38}{132}$

The probability that you'll get a matching pair is $\frac{38}{132}$, which reduces to $\frac{19}{66}$.

USING PERMUTATIONS AND COMBINATIONS

You can also express a probability in terms of permutations and combinations, especially if the number of possible outcomes is very large.

EXAMPLE 8

If the letters *A, R, S,* and *T* are arranged in a row, what is the probability that a proper English word will be formed?

SOLUTION

Remember the formula: the number of favorable outcomes over the number of possible outcomes. The number of ways to arrange four distinct letters is $_4P_4$, or 16. Furthermore, you can form 5 proper English words: *ARTS, RATS, STAR, TARS,* and *TSAR.* (Any "Boggle" fans out there?)

The probability is $\frac{5}{16}$.

Your textbook might rely a lot more on combinations terminology than we have so far. Let's do Example 7 again, using combinations.

EXAMPLE 7 (AGAIN)

Your sock drawer contains four red socks, three yellow socks, and five black socks only. If you reach in and grab two socks one at a time, without replacement, what is the probability that you'll get a matched pair?

SOLUTION

The number of ways to choose two socks out of 12 is $_{12}C_2$, or 66. (See chapter 14 if you're scratching your head about this.) Calculate the ways you can choose two socks; the number of ways you can choose two red socks out of four is $_4C_2$, or 6. Yellow socks: $_3C_2 = 3$. Black socks: $_5C_2 = 10$.

The terminology looks like this:

$$P(\text{pair}) = \frac{_4C_2 + _3C_2 + _6C_2}{_{12}C_2} = \frac{6+3+10}{66} = \frac{19}{66}$$

Some people prefer to use permutations, and others don't. If your math teacher is like most, you'll have to learn both.

EXERCISES, SET 15A

Try these exercises to see if it's possible that your college education will be financed by the good people at the Nevada State Gaming Authority. The answers are in chapter 16.

1. Fred has three dimes, two nickels and four quarters in his pocket. If he reaches in and picks two coins one at a time, without replacement, what is the probability that he'll select **(a)** two dimes? **(b)** two nickels? **(c)** no quarters? **(d)** a matched pair?

2. The federal budget stipulates that one face on the front of Mount Rushmore be chosen at random and cleaned. What is the probability that the chosen president has facial hair?

3. Harry the Horse throws two fair dice. What is the probability that the combined roll will be **(a)** an eight? **(b)** a twelve? **(c)** a fourteen? **(d)** an integer? **(e)** a prime number? **(f)** greater than eight? **(g)** a prime number or greater than eight?

4. A dog breeder has four terriers, six Labradors and two dachshunds in her kennel, and she wants to send three dogs to the State Dog Fair. **(a)** How many possible combinations are there? What is the probability that **(b)** exactly two Labradors will be included? **(c)** all three dogs are the same breed?

5. On the president's desk, there is a jar that contains seven lemon, eight cherry, five lime and 10 licorice jellybeans. If the president reaches in and grabs four jellybeans, what is the probability that she'll get **(a)** four lemons? **(b)** two limes and two cherries? **(c)** three licorice and no lemons? **(d)** one of each flavor?

6. A bookshelf contains only dictionaries and novels. If the probability of choosing a dictionary at random is $\frac{3}{5}$, and there are four more dictionaries than novels on the shelf, how many books are on the shelf?

7. While playing Twister, Bernice notices that one out of every four slots on the spinner is colored green. If she spins the arrow on the spinner, what is the probability that the arrow will land on green (a) once? (b) twice in a row? (c) three times in a row?

8. Madeleine selects cards one at a time from an ordinary deck of playing cards and does not replace them. What is the probability that she'll select (a) a red card? (b) three black cards in a row? (c) a red face card, then a black seven? (d) the ace of clubs, two of spades, and ten of diamonds (in that order)?

16

Answers

CHAPTER 1: LOGIC

SET 1A, P. 7

1. **(a)** Law of *Modus Tollens*
   (b) De Morgan's Laws
   (c) Law of Contrapositive Inference
   (d) Law of Disjunctive Inference
   (e) Chain Rule
2. (2) De Morgan's Laws
3. (1) Law of Disjunctive Inference
4. (2) Law of *Modus Tollens*
5. (1) Law of Contrapositive Inference
6. (4) Contrapositive and Chain Rule
7. (1) Law of *Modus Tollens*
8. (3) Contrapositive, De Morgan's Laws

9. (a) (4)

    (b) (1) Contrapositive, De Morgan's Laws

    (c) (3)

    (d) (1)

10. (a) Nope.

    (b) ~C; Law of Disjunctive Inference

    (c) *E*; *Modus Tollens*

    (d) Nope.

    (e) *J*; Detachment

    (f) Nope.

    (g) Nope.

    (h) Nope.

    (i) $R \rightarrow T$; Chain Rule

    (j) ~X; De Morgan's Law, Disjunctive Inference

SET 1B, P. 12

1.

Statement	Reasons
1. $L \rightarrow N$; L	1. Given
2. N	2. Law of Detachment (1)
3. M $\vee$ ~N	3. Given
4. M	4. Law of Disjunctive Inference (2,3)

2.

Statements	Reasons
1. $E \rightarrow F$; E	1. Given
2. F	2. Law of Detachment (1)
3. ~G $\rightarrow$ ~F	3. Given
4. G	4. Law of *Modus Tollens* (2,3)

3.

Statement	Reasons
1. c ∨ e; ~c	1. Given
2. e	2. Law of Disjunctive Inference (1)
3. d → ~e	3. Given
4. e → ~d	4. Law of Contapositive Inference (2)
5. ~d	5. Law of Detachment (2,4)

Note: An extra step was added to include the contrapositive and the law of detachment. You can also combine steps 4 and 5 and state the law of *Modus Tollens*.

4.

Statement	Reasons
1. A ∨ B; ~B	1. Given
2. A	2. Law of Disjunctive Inference (1)
3. A → ~C	3. Given
4. D → ~D	4. Given
5. ~C → ~D	5. Law of Contapositive Inference (2)
6. A → ~D	6. Law of Syllogism (3,5)
7. ~D	7. Law of Detachment (2,6)

5.

Statement	Reasons
1. ~D → ~C; ~D	1. Given
2. ~C	2. Law of Detachment (1)
3. B → C	3. Given
4. ~B	4. Law of *Modus Tollens* (2,3)
5. A ∨ B	5. Given
6. A	6. Law of Disjunctive Inference (4,5)

6.

Statement	Reasons
1. (A ∧ ~B) → C	1. Given
2. ~C → ~(A ∧ ~B)	2. Law of Contrapositive Inference (1)
3. ~C	3. Given
4. ~(A ∧ ~B)	4. Law of Detachment (2,3)
5. ~A ∨ B	5. De Morgan's Law (4)
6. A	6. Given
7. B	7. Law of Disjunctive Inference (5,6)
8. B → F	8. Given
9. F	9. Law of Detachment (7,8)

7. Symbolize the clues first:

If Jerome goes to Florida, then he'll get a sunburn.	$F \rightarrow S$
Jerome will either go to Maine, or he will go to Florida.	$M \vee F$
If Jerome gets a sunburn, he will not enter the back-slapping contest.	$S \rightarrow {\sim}B$
Jerome entered the back-slapping contest.	B

Statement	Reasons
1. S → ~B; B	1. Given
2. ~S	2. Law *Modus Tollens* (1)
3. F → S	3. Given
4. ~F	4. Law *Modus Tollens* (2,3)
5. M ∨ F	5. Given
6. M	6. Law of Disjunctive Inference (4,5)

8.

Statements	Reasons
1. ~(B ∧ F)	1. Given
2. ~B ∨ ~F	2. De Morgan's Law (1)
3. B	3. Given
4. ~F	4. Law of Disjunctive Inference (2, 3)
5. ~F → R	5. Given
6. R → ~C	6. Given
7. ~F → ~C	7. Chain Rule (5, 6)
8. ~C	8. Law of Detachment (4, 7)

9.

Statement	Reasons
1. S → T, ~T	1. Given
2. ~S	2. Law of *Modus Tollens* (1)
3. ~S → M	3. Given
4. M	4. Law of Detachment (2,3)
5. P ∨ ~M	5. Given
6. P	6. Law of Disjunctive Inference (4,5)

10.

Statements	Reasons
1. W ∧ ~V; V	1. Given
2. ~W	2. Law of *Modus Tollens* (1)
3. (S ∧ C) → W	3. Given
4. ~W → ~(S ∧ C)	4. Law of Contrapositive Inference (3)
5. ~(S ∧ C)	5. Law of Detachment (2,4)
6. ~S ∨ ~C	6. De Morgan's Law
7. C	7. Given
8. ~S	8. Law of Disjunctive Inference (6,7)

CHAPTER 2: MATHEMATICAL SYSTEMS

SET 2A, P. 20

1. **(a)** 6
   (b) 5 ("between" means that 5 and 17 are not included)
   (c) infinite
   (d) 1
   (e) 0 (that we know of)
   (f) 2
   (g) 11
   (h) 3
   (i) 3
   (j) 1

2. (a), (d), and (f) are subsets of (c); (j) is a subset of (h) and (i)

3. **(a)** –3   **(b)** $-\dfrac{11}{9}$
   (c) –2   **(d)** ∞
   (e) $-\dfrac{1}{m}$

4. **(a)** 2   **(b)** 3
   (c) 6   **(d)** 4
   (e) 4   **(f)** Nope.

5. **(a)** S **(b)** R
   (c) R **(d)** C
   (e) R **(f)** B
   (g) Yes.

SET 2B, P. 25

1. **(a)** 0   **(b)** –2
   (c) Yes   **(d)** Yes
   (e) No

2. **(a)** 1   **(b)** 3
   (c) No   **(d)** 2
   (e) 3   **(f)** No
   (g) Yes

3. **(a)** b **(b)** b
   (c) c **(d)** d
   (e) Yes   **(f)** $x = d$
   (g) $x = \{a, d\}$

4. (a)

Δ	S	P	A	N	K
S	P	S	**N**	A	S
P	**S**	A	K	P	P
A	N	**K**	P	N	A
N	A	P	N	K	**N**
K	**S**	P	**A**	N	K

   (b) K

   (c) A

   (d) S

5. (a) 3   **(b)** 7

   (c) 7   **(d)** 3

   (e) 5   **(f)** 4

CHAPTER 3: ALGEBRA AND POLYNOMIALS

SET 3A, P. 34

1. (a) $8a$ **(b)** $9b$

   (c) $9c^2 + 10c + 3$ **(d)** $d^3 + 2d^2 + 2d$

2. (a) $4a$ **(b)** $-6b$

   (c) $5c - 1$ **(d)** $-9d^3 + 7d^2 + 7d$

3. (a) a^3 **(b)** $400b^{16}$

   (c) $2c^6d + 6c^4d^2$ **(d)** $6m^7n^5p^4$

   (e) $\dfrac{5}{2x^5}$, or $\dfrac{5}{2}x^{-5}$

4. (a) a^6 **(b)** b^{-2}, or $\dfrac{1}{b^2}$

   (c) $\dfrac{-2d^2}{7c^3e^4}$ **(d)** $\dfrac{1}{9p^2}$

5. (a) $x^2 - 3x + 2$ **(b)** $x^2 - 4x - 21$

   (c) $6x^2 - 5x - 4$ **(d)** $x^4 - 1$

   (e) $25x^2 - 4$

SET 3B, P. 44

1. **(a)** $2(x + 2)(x - 2)$ **(b)** $2y(6 + y - 4y^3)$
   (c) $(x + 7)(x - 5)$ **(d)** $(2x + 3)(x + 1)$
   (e) $3m^2n(n + 5)(n - 5)$ **(f)** $3y^3(x + 2)^2$
   (g) $2(3p + 5q)(3p - 5q)$

2. **(a)** $n^2 - 4n + 4$ **(b)** $p^2 + p + \dfrac{1}{4}$
   (c) $9y^2 - 12yz + 4z^2$ **(d)** $0.49s^2 + 2.1st + 2.25t^2$
   (e) $4d^6 - 12d^3e^4 + 9e^8$

3. **(2)**

4. **(a)** $x^2 - 1$ **(b)** $9x^2 - 16y^2$

   (c) $0.25m^2 - 0.04n^2$ **(d)** $\dfrac{d^2}{9} - \dfrac{1}{e^2}$

   (e) $9h^4 - 49k^{10}$

5. $\dfrac{x + 4}{2(x + 1)}$

6. -1

7. $\dfrac{2y^2(y + 1)}{y + 3}$

8. $\dfrac{2b + c}{b(b + 2c)}$

9. **(a)** Yes **(b)** No
   (c) Yes **(d)** Yes
   (e) No **(f)** Yes

10. **(a)** $\dfrac{2a + 9}{6a^2}$ **(b)** $\dfrac{2c^3 + 7c^2 + 7c + 28}{7c^2}$

    (c) $\dfrac{(d - 3)(d - 1)}{2d(d + 1)}$ **(d)** $\dfrac{2m^2 - 4mn + 3m + 4n}{4m^2}$

    (e) $\dfrac{-v^2 + 16v - 24}{5v - 15}$

CHAPTER 4: ALGEBRAIC EQUATIONS

SET 4A, P. 51

1. **(a)** $a = 7$ **(b)** $a = -4$
   (c) $a = -3$ **(d)** $a = 8$

2. **(a)** $b = -1$ **(b)** $b = 2$
   (c) $b = 10$ **(d)** $b = 2$

3. **(a)** $c = 5$ **(b)** $c = 8$
   (c) $c = -3$ **(d)** $c = 10$

4. **(a)** $d = 4$ **(b)** $d = 3$
   (c) $d = -\dfrac{47}{5}$ **(d)** $d = \dfrac{3}{2}$

5. **(a)** $e = 8$ **(b)** $e = 3$
   (c) $e = 6$ **(d)** $e = 5$
   (e) $e = -7$ **(f)** $e = -\dfrac{20}{3}$

SET 4B, P. 56

1. **(a)** $a = \pm 2$ **(b)** $a = \pm\dfrac{3}{2}$
   (c) $a = \pm 10$ **(d)** $a = \pm\dfrac{5}{12}$
   (e) $a = \pm\dfrac{\sqrt{5}}{2}$

2. **(a)** $b = \{0, -5\}$ **(b)** $b = \{0, 7\}$
   (c) $b = \{0, 3\}$ **(d)** $b = \{-x, x\}$

3. **(a)** $c = \{-1\}$ **(b)** $c = \{-5, 2\}$
   (c) $c = \{6, -5\}$ **(d)** $c = \{-6, 2\}$
   (e) $c = \{11, 7\}$

4. **(a)** $d = \left\{1, -\dfrac{5}{2}\right\}$ **(b)** $d = \left\{\dfrac{4}{3}, -2\right\}$
   (c) $d = \left\{-\dfrac{1}{2}, -\dfrac{5}{3}\right\}$ **(d)** $d = \left\{\dfrac{7}{5}, -\dfrac{3}{2}\right\}$
   (e) $d = \left\{0, -\dfrac{1}{6}, \dfrac{3}{2}\right\}$

5. **(a)** 11 meters by 18 meters
   (b) 5 and 8
   (c) 2 feet
   (d) $\frac{5}{2}$ inches by 8 inches
   (e) 2.5 feet

SET 4C, P. 63

3. **(a)** $2\sqrt{3}$ **(b)** $3\sqrt{5}$
   (c) $2\sqrt{15}$ **(d)** $5\sqrt{3}$
   (e) $9\sqrt{3}$ **(f)** $15\sqrt{2}$
   (g) 32   **(h)** $20\sqrt{10}$

4. **(a)** $x = 1 \pm \sqrt{3}$ **(b)** $x = \dfrac{-5 \pm \sqrt{5}}{2}$

   (c) $x = \dfrac{3 \pm \sqrt{41}}{4}$ **(d)** $x = \dfrac{3 \pm \sqrt{7}}{2}$

   (e) $x = 5$ **(f)** $x = \dfrac{3 \pm 2\sqrt{3}}{3}$

5. **(a)** $x = \{1.3, -2.3\}$ **(b)** $x = \{6.1, -1.1\}$
   (c) $x = \{2.9, -2.4\}$ **(d)** $x = \{4, -1.7\}$
   (e) $x = \{1.8, -4.5\}$ **(f)** $x = \{1.1, -0.6\}$
   (g) (d)

6. **(a)** two, imaginary   **(b)** two, real, irrational
   (c) one, real, rational   **(d)** two, imaginary
   (e) two, real, rational   **(f)** two, imaginary
   (g) two, real, irrational

7. **(a)** sum: 2; product: −15
   (b) sum: −6; product: 9
   (c) sum: $-\frac{7}{2}$; product: −2
   (d) sum: $\frac{m}{3}$; product: $-\frac{n}{3}$

8. (a) $x^2 + x - 6 = 0$ **(b)** $x^2 - 16 = 0$
(c) $x^2 - 10x + 25 = 0$ **(d)** $2x^2 + 5x - 25 = 0$
(e) $12x^2 + 31x + 20 = 0$

9. (a) $x^2 + 6x + 9 = (x + 3)^2$

(b) $x^2 - 8x + 16 = (x - 4)^2$

(c) $x^2 + 5x + \dfrac{25}{4} = \left(x + \dfrac{5}{2}\right)^2$

(d) $x^2 - x + \dfrac{1}{4} = \left(x - \dfrac{1}{2}\right)^2$

CHAPTER 5: GRAPHING AND GRAPHIC SOLUTIONS

SET 5A, P. 73
1. (2)
2.

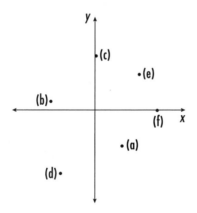

3. (a) II   **(b)** IV
   (c) III   **(d)** None
   (e) I

4. (a)

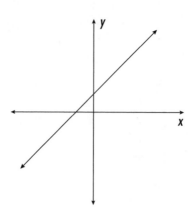

(b)

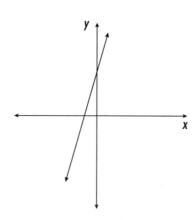

(c)

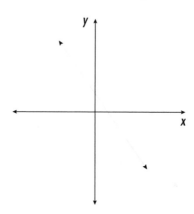

(d)

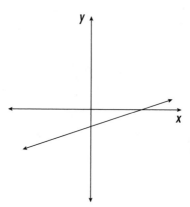

(e)

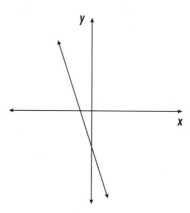

5. (a)

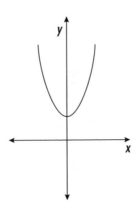

(b)

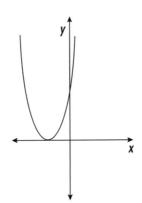

(c)

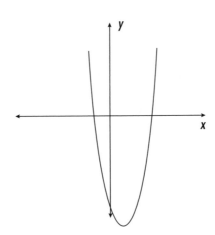

(d)

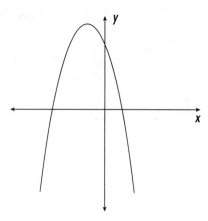

(e)

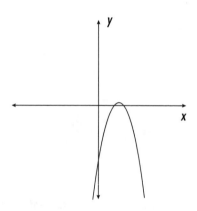

(f)

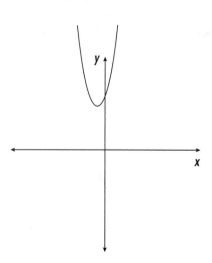

(g)

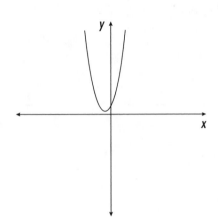

6. **(a)** $x = 0$, or the y-axis **(b)** $x = 2$

   (c) $x = -\dfrac{5}{4}$ **(d)** $x = 1$

   (e) $x = -\dfrac{1}{2}$

7. **(a)** $(0, 0)$ **(b)** $(3, -4)$

   (c) $\left(\dfrac{3}{2}, -\dfrac{15}{4}\right)$ **(d)** $\left(-\dfrac{2}{3}, -\dfrac{16}{3}\right)$

   (e) $(-1, -25)$

8. **(a)** $x = \{7. -2\}$
   (b) *first root*: between 3 and 4; *second root*: between −1 and −2
   (c) *first root*: between 5 and 6; *second root*: between 0 and −1
   (d) no real roots
   (e) *first root*: between 2 and 3; *second root*: −2
   (f) *first root*: between 4 and 5; *second root*: between −3 and −4

1. (2, 5) and (−2, 5)

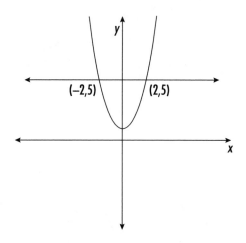

$$x^2 + 1 = 5$$
$$x^2 = 4$$
$$x = \{2, -2\}$$

$$y = (2)^2 + 1 \qquad\qquad y = (-2)^2 + 1$$
$$= 4 + 1 \qquad\qquad\quad = 4 + 1$$
$$= 5 \qquad\qquad\qquad\quad = 5$$

2. (4, 13) and (−2, 1)

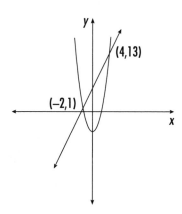

$$x^2 - 3 = 2x + 5$$
$$x^2 - 2x - 8 = 0$$
$$(x - 4)(x + 2) = 0$$
$$x = \{4, -2\}$$

$$y = (4)^2 - 3 \qquad\qquad y = (-2)^2 - 3$$
$$= 16 - 3 \qquad\qquad\qquad = 4 - 3$$
$$= 13 \qquad\qquad\qquad\qquad = 1$$

3. No solution; the graphs do not intersect.

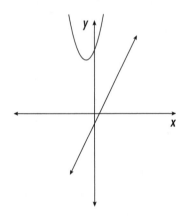

$$x^2 + 2x + 7 = 3x - 1$$
$$x^2 - x + 8 = 0$$

There are no real roots; $b^2 - 4ac = -31$

4. (1, −3) and (6, 2)

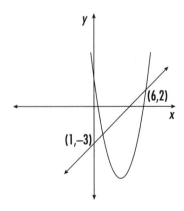

$$x^2 - 6x + 2 = x - 4$$
$$x^2 - 7x + 6 = 0$$
$$(x - 1)(x - 6) = 0$$
$$x = \{1,\ 6\}$$

$y = (1)^2 - 6(1) + 2 \qquad y = (6)^2 - 6(6) + 2$

$\qquad = 1 - 6 + 2 \qquad\qquad = 36 - 36 + 2$

$\qquad = -3 \qquad\qquad\qquad\quad = 2$

5. $(-3, 2)$ and $(-1, -2)$

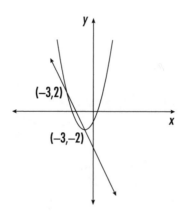

6. $\left(\dfrac{1}{2}, \dfrac{9}{2}\right)$ and $(2, 9)$

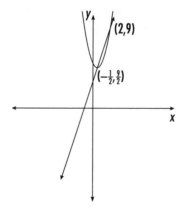

7. (2, –1) and (4, –3)

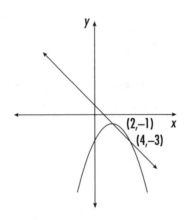

CHAPTER 6: TRANSFORMATIONS

SET 6A, P. 89

1. **(a)** (4, 2)   **(b)** (–4, –2)
   (c) (–2, 4)   **(d)** (–4, 2)
   (e) (–10, 6)

2. (–4, 3)

3. $y = -x$

4. **(a)** (–1, –3)   **(b)** (6, –15)
   (c) (–10, 21)   **(d)** (–5, 25)

5.

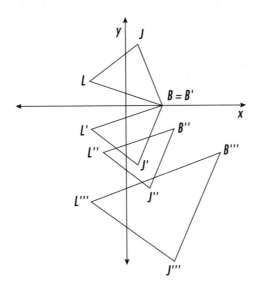

6. (0, −10)

7. (3, −12)

8. (3, 5)

9. (a) reflection in the *y*-axis
   (b) reflection in the line $y = x$
   (c) translation $(x + 2, y − 6)$, or reflection in $(−1, 3)$
   (d) dilation of $\dfrac{1}{3}$, or reflection in $(−4, 4)$

10. It's a parallelogram.

11. 4:1

CHAPTER 7: MORE COORDINATE GEOMETRY

SET 7A, P. 100

1. **(a)** undefined   **(b)** positive
   (c) negative   **(d)** zero

2. **(a)** (3)   **(b)** (1)

3. **(a)** $y = -2x + 3$ **(b)** $y = 3x + 7$

   (c) $y = \dfrac{1}{2}x + 9$ **(d)** $y = 0.4x - 1$

   (e) $y = -\dfrac{2}{3}x - \dfrac{14}{3}$, or $3y = -2x - 14$

   (f) $y = px + q$

4. **(a)** $y = x + 1$ **(b)** $y = 2x + 9$

   (c) $y = -\dfrac{2}{3}x - 2$ **(d)** $x = 6$

   (e) $y = \dfrac{1}{5}x + \dfrac{29}{10}$, or $10y = 2x + 29$

   (f) $y = 2$

5. (3)

6. (2)

7. **(a)** $y = 4x + 3$

   (b) $y = \dfrac{5}{4}x + 7$

   (c) $y = \dfrac{1}{2}x - \dfrac{1}{2}$, or $2y = x - 1$
   (d) $y = -7x + 4$

SET 7B, P. 109

1. **(a)** 5   **(b)** 7
   (c) 13   **(d)** $2\sqrt{17}$
   (e) 3   **(f)** $\sqrt{37}$
   (g) $4\sqrt{2}$ **(h)** $3\sqrt{34}$

2. (a) (5, 6) **(b)** (−5, 3)

(c) (4, 2) **(d)** $\left(-7, \dfrac{9}{2}\right)$

(e) $\left(\dfrac{13}{2}, -\dfrac{3}{2}\right)$ **(f)** $(a, 3b)$

(g) $\left(\dfrac{a+c}{2}, \dfrac{b+d}{2}\right)$

3. (a) $(x - 3)^2 + (y - 2)^2 = 16$
(b) $(x + 2)^2 + (y + 6)^2 = 5$
(c) $(x - 5)^2 + (y + 2)^2 = 12.25$

(d) $\left(x - \dfrac{1}{2}\right)^2 + \left(y + \dfrac{4}{3}\right)^2 = \dfrac{4}{81}$

(e) $(x - \clubsuit)^2 + (y - \blacklozenge)^2 = \heartsuit^2$

4. (a)

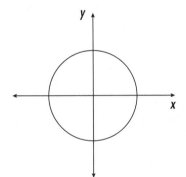

(b)

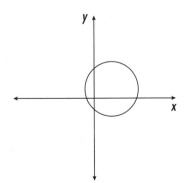

(c)

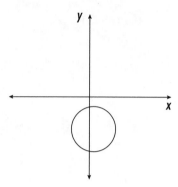

(d)

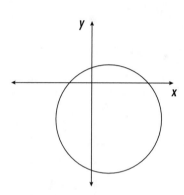

(e)

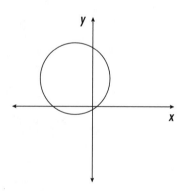

(f)

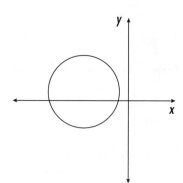

5. (a)

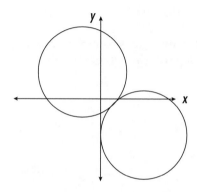

(b) The circles are tangent at the point (2, 0).

6. (a) 24   **(b)** 41

     (c) 54   **(d)** 42

     (e) 52   **(f)** 92

7. (a) $y = -\dfrac{1}{2}x + 4$

(b)

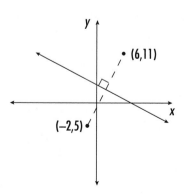

SET 7C, P. 118

1. Use the distance formula to show that two sides have equal measure.
2. Use the distance formula to show that all three sides do not have equal measure.
3. Use the slope formula to show that both pairs of opposite sides are parallel, or use the slope and distance formulas to show that one pair of opposite sides are both parallel and congruent.
4. Use the slope formula to show that one of the four angles is not a right angle (slopes are not negative reciprocals).
5. Use the slope formula to show that the slopes of two adjacent sides are negative reciprocals.
6. Use the distance formula to show that all four sides of the quadrilateral have the same length.
7. Use the slope formula to show that the slopes of two adjacent sides are not negative reciprocals.
8.

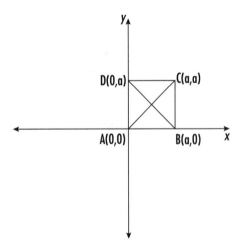

Use the midpoint formula to show that the midpoint of $\overline{AC}$ is also the midpoint of $\overline{BD}$.

9.

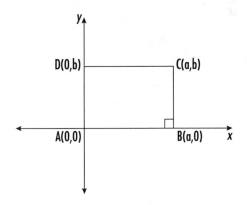

Use the slope formula to find the slopes of all four sides and to show that $\overline{AB}$ and $\overline{BC}$ are perpendicular.

10.

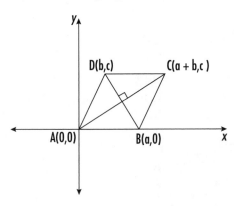

Use the slope formula to show that $\overline{AC}$ is perpendicular to $\overline{BD}$ because their slopes are negative reciprocals.

CHAPTER 8: GEOMETRIC CONCEPTS

SET 8A, P. 129

1. (3)
2. $x = 5$
3. **(a)** 25   **(b)** 19
   (c) 38   **(d)** 40 **(e)** 25
4. (4)
5. **(a)** 60   **(b)** 45
   (c) 36   **(d)** 30
   (e) 40   **(f)** 54
   (g) 48   **(h)** 50
6. **(a)** $x = 23$ **(b)** $x = 20$
   (c) $x = 34$ **(d)** $x = 43$
   (e) $x = \dfrac{m + 30}{4}$
7. **(a)** (1)   **(b)** 40
8. **(a)** 45   **(b)** 60
   (c) 67.5   **(d)** 30
   (e) 36

SET 8B, P. 136

1. **(a)** 22   **(b)** 7
   (c) 32   **(d)** 20
2.

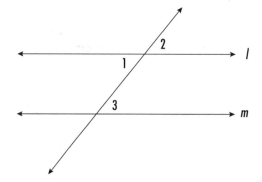

Given: Line *l* is parallel to line *m*.
Prove: ∠1 ≅ ∠3

Statements	Reasons
1. Line *l* is parallel to line *m*	1. Given
2. ∠2 ≅ ∠3	2. Corresponding angles are congruent.
3. ∠1 ≅ ∠2	3. Vertical angles are congruent.
4. ∠1 ≅ ∠3	4. Transitive Property of Equality

3. Lines 1 and 4 are parallel.

4. $q = 21$

5. (3)

6.

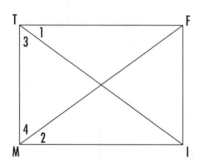

Statements	Reasons
1. *MIFT* is a rectangle	1. Given
2. ∠FTM and ∠TMI are right angles	2. A rectangle has four right angles.
3. m∠FTM = m∠1 + m∠3; m∠TMI = m∠2 + m∠4	3. Angle Addition Postulate
4. ∠1 and ∠3 are complementary; ∠2 and ∠4 are complementary	4. Definition of complementary
5. ∠1 ≅ ∠2	5. Given
6. ∠3 ≅ ∠4	6. Angles that are complementary to congruent angles are congruent.

7.

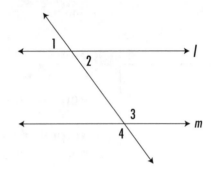

Statements	Reasons
1. $\angle 1$ and $\angle 4$ are supplementary	1. Given
2. $m\angle 1 + m\angle 4 = 180$	2. Definition of supplementary angles
3. $m\angle 1 \cong m\angle 2$; $m\angle 3 = m\angle 4$	3. Vertical angles are congruent.
4. $m\angle 2 + m\angle 3 = 180$	4. Substitution Property
5. $\angle 2$ and $\angle 3$ are supplementary	5. Definition of supplementary angles
6. l is parallel to m	6. If two lines are cut by a transversal, and interior angles on the same side of the transversal are congruent, then the lines are parallel.

8.

Statements	Reasons
1. l is parallel to m	1. Given
2. $\angle 2$ and $\angle 3$ are supplementary	2. If two parallel lines are cut by a transversal, then interior angles on the same side of the transversal are supplementary.
3. $\angle 1 \cong \angle 2$	3. Vertical angles are congruent.
4. $\angle 1$ and $\angle 3$ are supplementary	4. Substitution Property

CHAPTER 9: TRIANGLES

SET 9A, P. 146

1. **(a)** $x = 25$ **(b)** $x = 51$
   (c) $x = 12$ **(d)** $x = 53$
   (e) $x = 11$

2. $44°$

3. **(a)** $d = 122$ **(b)** $d = 92$

4. $58°$

5. $\overline{FG}$

6. (3)

7. $36 <$ perimeter < 56

8. (3)

9. **(a)** Yes   **(b)** No
   (c) No   **(d)** Yes
   (e) Yes   **(f)** Impossible to tell

10. **(a)** {13}   **(b)** $P = 32$

11. $\overline{KL}$

12. (4)

SET 9B, P. 152

1. (4)

2. **(a)** 10   **(b)** 12
   (c) 4   **(d)** $2\sqrt{14}$
   (e) 6   **(f)** $\sqrt{x^2 - y^2}$

3. $7\sqrt{2}$

4. $3\sqrt{10}$

5. **(a)** 20   **(b)** $10\sqrt{3} + 10$
   (c) $50\sqrt{3} + 50$

6. **(a)** $2x + x\sqrt{2}$ **(b)** $\dfrac{x^2}{2}$

7. $12 + 12\sqrt{3}$

8. (a) $4\sqrt{3}$ **(b)** $\dfrac{100\sqrt{3}}{9}$

   (c) $\dfrac{s^2\sqrt{3}}{4}$

9. (a) perimeter = 54

   (b) area = $85\sqrt{3}$

10. $5\sqrt{5}$

SET 9C, P. 168

1. 44

2. (a) $OL = 8$; $GF = 2\sqrt{5}$; $FL = 4\sqrt{5}$

   (b) $GF = 3\sqrt{10}$; $GO = 3$; $FL = 9\sqrt{10}$; $OL = 27$

   (c) $GO = 9$; $OL = 16$; $GF = 15$; $FL = 20$

3. $m\angle Z = 96$ (angle measures are the same in similar triangles!)

4. (a) 10   **(b)** 2

   (c) 4   **(d)** 8

5. (a) Hypotenuse-Leg   **(b)** Angle-Side-Angle

   (c) Side-Side-Side   **(d)** Angle-Angle-Side

   (e) Angle-Side-Angle

6. 135

7. (a) The plan: Prove that $\triangle ADC$ and $\triangle BDC$ are congruent through Side-Angle-Side, then use CPCTC.

Statements	Reasons
1. $\angle 1 \cong \angle 2$	1. Given
2. $\overline{AD} \cong \overline{BD}$	2. If two angles of a triangle are congruent, then the sides opposite are congruent.
3. $\angle ADC \cong \angle BDC$	3. Given
4. $\overline{DC} \cong \overline{DC}$	4. Reflexive Property of Equality
5. $\triangle ADC \cong \triangle BDC$	5. SAS $\cong$ SAS
6. $\angle 3 \cong \angle 4$	6. CPCTC

   (b) The plan: Use the Angle Addition Postulate and the Subtraction Property of Equality.

Statements	Reasons
1. $\overline{AC} \cong \overline{BC}$	1. Given
2. m$\angle CAB$ = m$\angle CBA$	2. If two sides of a triangle are congruent, then the angles opposite are congruent
3. m$\angle CAB$ = m$\angle 3$ + m$\angle 1$; m$\angle CBA$ = m$\angle 4$ + m$\angle 2$	3. Angle Addition Postulate
4. m$\angle 3$ + m$\angle 1$ = m$\angle 4$ + m$\angle 2$	4. Substitution Principle
5. m$\angle 3$ = m$\angle 4$	5. Given
6. m$\angle 1$ = m$\angle 2$	6. Subtraction Property of Equality

8. (a) The plan: Prove that $\triangle FHI$ and $\triangle GHI$ are congruent, then use CPCTC and the Transitive Property.

Statements	Reasons
1. $\overline{HI} \perp \overline{FG}$	1. Given
2. $\angle FIH$ and $\angle GIH$ are right angles	2. Definition of perpendicular lines
3. $\angle FIH \cong \angle GIH$	3. All right angles are congruent.
4. $\overline{HI} \cong \overline{HI}$	4. Reflexive Property of Equality
5. $\overline{HI}$ bisects $\angle FHG$	5. Given
6. $\angle 1 \cong \angle 2$	6. Definition of angle bisector
7. $\triangle FHI \cong \triangle GHI$	7. ASA $\cong$ ASA
8. $\angle 4 \cong \angle 3$	8. CPCTC
9. $\angle 3 \cong \angle 5$	9. Vertical angles are congruent.
10. $\angle 4 \cong \angle 5$	10. Transitive Property or Equality

(b) The plan: Use the Exterior Angle Theorem and the Substitution Principle.

Statements	Reasons
1. $\overline{FH} \cong \overline{GH}$	1. Given
2. m$\angle 3$ = m$\angle 4$	2. If two sides of a triangle are congruent, then the angles opposite have equal measure.
3. $\angle 6$ is an exterior angle	3. Definition of an exterior angle
4. m$\angle 6$ = m$\angle FHG$ + m$\angle 4$	4. The measure of an exterior angle of a triangle is equal to the sum of the measures of the two non-adjacent interior angles.
5. m$\angle FHG$ = m$\angle 1$ + m–2	5. Angle Addition Postulate
6. m$\angle 6$ = m$\angle 1$ + m$\angle 2$ + m$\angle 4$	6. Substitution Principle (4, 5)
7. m$\angle 6$ = m$\angle 1$ + m$\angle 2$ + m$\angle 3$	7. Substitution Principle (2, 6)

9. The plan: This one can be a little sneaky, because there are two congruent overlapping triangles: $\triangle SOE$ and $\triangle RFE$. Use Side-Angle-Side twice, then use CPCTC (a very powerful tool) to show that $\overline{FE} \cong \overline{OE}$.

Statements	Reasons
1. $\overline{ST} \cong \overline{TR}$; $\angle STE \cong \angle RTE$	1. Given
2. $\overline{TE} \cong \overline{TE}$	2. Reflexive Property of Equality
3. $\triangle STE \cong \triangle RTE$	3. SAS $\cong$ SAS
4. $\overline{SE} \cong \overline{RE}$	4. CPCTC
5. $\angle SER \cong \angle SER$	5. Reflexive Property of Equality
6. $\angle 1$ is supplemental to $\angle 3$, $\angle 2$ is supplemental to $\angle 4$	6. Definition of supplementary angles
7. $\angle 1 \cong \angle 2$	7. Given
8. $\angle 3 \cong \angle 4$	8. Supplements of congruent angles are congruent.
9. $\triangle SOE \cong \triangle RFE$	9. ASA $\cong$ ASA
10. $\overline{FE} \cong \overline{OE}$	10. CPCTC
11. $\triangle EFO$ is isosceles	11. Definition of an isosceles triangle

(b)

(b)

12. m $\angle EFO$ = m $\angle EOF$

12. Definition of an isosceles triangle

13. m $\angle EFT$ = m $\angle EOT$

13. CPCTC (9)

14. m $\angle EFO$ – m $\angle EFT$
= m $\angle EOF$ – m $\angle EOT$

14. Subtraction Property of Equality

15. m $\angle TFO$ = m $\angle TOF$

15. Substitution Property

16. $\triangle TFO$ is isosceles

16. Definition of an isosceles triangle

Note: As an alternate plan for part **(b)**, you can prove that $\triangle FTS$ is congruent to $\triangle OTR$ through Angle-Side-Angle, then use CPCTC.

CHAPTER 10: QUADRILATERALS AND OTHER POLYGONS

SET 10A, P. 191

1. **(a)** m $\angle M$ = 160; m $\angle I$ = 80; m $\angle L$ = 38; m $\angle K$ = 82
   (b) m $\angle D$ = 95; m $\angle R$ = 85; m $\angle U$ = 95; m $\angle M$ = 85

2. **(a)** $q = 7$ **(b)** $q = 8$
   (c) $q = 9$

3. (2)

4. **(a)** 60   **(b)** 42
   (c) 54   **(d)** 32

5. (4)

6. an isosceles trapezoid

7. **(a)** 720°   **(b)** 1,180°
   (c) 5,940°

8. **(a)** 15 sides   **(b)** 20 sides
   (c) 12 sides   **(d)** 30 sides
   (e) 60 sides

9. The plan: Show that the two right triangles ONL and JKM are congruent using Hypotenuse-Leg, then use CPCTC to show that the base angles of $\triangle PML$ are congruent.

Statements	Reasons
1. $JKNO$ is a rectangle	1. Given
2. $\angle ONL$ and $\angle JKM$ are right angles	2. Definition of a rectangle
3. $\overline{JM} \cong \overline{OL}$	3. Given
4. $\overline{JK} \cong \overline{ON}$	4. Opposite sides of a rectangle are congruent.
5. $\triangle ONL \cong \triangle JKM$	5. HL $\cong$ HL
6. $\angle JMK \cong \angle OLN$	6. CPCTC
7. $\triangle PML$ is isosceles	7. Definition of an isosceles triangle
(b)	**(b)**
8. $\overline{JO}$ is parallel to $\overline{KN}$	8. Opposite sides of a rectangle are parallel.
9. $\angle OLN \cong \angle JOP$; $\angle JMK \cong \angle OJP$	9. Alternate interior angles are congruent.
10. $\angle JOP \cong \angle OJP$	10. Transitive Property of Equality (6, 9)
11. $\triangle JPO$ is isosceles	11. Definition of an isosceles triangle

10. The plan: Prove that $\triangle MQN$ is congruent to $\triangle MSN$, then use CPCTC to prove that $\triangle MRN$ is isosceles.

Statements	Reasons
1. $MNOP$ is an isosceles trapezoid	1. Given
2. $\overline{MP} \cong \overline{ON}$	2. Legs of an isosceles trapezoid are congruent.
3. Q is the midpoint of $\overline{PM}$; S is the midpoint of $\overline{ON}$	3. Given
4. $QM = \frac{1}{2}PM$; $SN = \frac{1}{2}ON$	4. Definition of midpoint
5. $\overline{QM} \cong \overline{SN}$	5. Halves of congruent segments are congruent.

6. $\overline{QN} \perp \overline{MP}$; $\overline{MS} \perp \overline{ON}$	6. Given
7. $\angle MQN$ and $\angle MSN$ are right angles	7. Definition of perpendicular lines
8. $\overline{MN} \cong \overline{MN}$	8. Reflexive Property of Equality
9. $\triangle MQN \cong \triangle MSN$	9. HL $\cong$ HL
10. $\angle RMN \cong \angle RNM$	10. CPCTC
11. $\overline{RM} \cong \overline{RN}$	11. If two angles in a triangle are congruent, the sides opposite them are congruent.

11. The plan: Show that $\triangle COP$ is congruent to $\triangle QRN$ using Side-Side-Side, then use CPCTC.

Statements	Reasons
1. $PNQC$ is a parallelogram	1. Given
2. $\overline{CP} \cong \overline{QN}$	2. Opposite sides of a parallelogram are congruent.
3. $PRQO$ is a parallelogram	3. Given
4. $\overline{OP} \cong \overline{QR}$	4. Opposite sides of a parallelogram are congruent.
5. $CR = ON$	5. Given
6. $OR = OR$	6. Reflexive Property of Equality
7. $CR - OR = ON - OR$	7. Subtraction Property of Equality
8. $CO = RN$	8. Substitution Property
9. $\overline{CO} \cong \overline{RN}$	9. Definition of congruent
10. $\triangle COP \cong \triangle QRN$	10. SSS $\cong$ SSS
11. $\angle COP \cong \angle QRN$	11. CPCTC

CHAPTER 11: GEOMETRIC PROOFS

SET 11A, P. 202

1. The plan: Since $\overline{AE}$ and $\overline{FC}$ are corresponding parts of $\triangle ADE$ and $\triangle BCF$, prove that the triangles are congruent using Angle-Angle-Side and then use CPCTC.

Statements	Reasons
1. $\overline{DE} \perp \overline{AC}$; $\overline{FB} \perp \overline{AC}$	1. Given
2. $\angle DEA$ and $\angle AFB$ are right angles	2. Definition of perpendicular lines
3. $\angle DEA \cong \angle AFB$	3. All right angles are congruent.
4. $ABCD$ is a parallelogram	4. Given
5. $\overline{AD}$ is parallel to $\overline{BC}$	5. Definition of a parallelogram
6. $\angle DAE \cong \angle FCB$	6. Alternate interior angles are congruent.
7. $\overline{AD} \cong \overline{BC}$	7. Opposite sides of a parallelogram are congruent.
8. $\triangle ADE \cong \triangle BCF$	8. AAS $\cong$ AAS
9. $\overline{AE} \cong \overline{FC}$	9. CPCTC

2. The plan: Show that $\overline{AD}$ and $\overline{CF}$ are both and parallel (because of the converse of the Alternate Interior Angles theorem) and congruent.

Statements	Reasons
1. $\angle CFB \cong \angle CBF$	1. Given
2. $\overline{CF} \cong \overline{CB}$	2. If two angles of a triangle are congruent, then the sides opposite those angles are congruent.
3. $ABCD$ is an isosceles trapezoid	3. Given
4. $\overline{AD} \cong \overline{CB}$	4. Definition of an isosceles trapezoid
5. $\overline{AD} \cong \overline{CF}$	5. Substitution Property
6. $\angle DAC \cong \angle ACF$	6. Given

7. $\overline{AD}$ is parallel to $\overline{CF}$	7. If alternate interior angles are congruent, then the lines are parallel.
8. $AFCD$ is a parallelogram	8. If two sides of a quadrilateral are parallel and congruent, it is a parallelogram.

3. The plan: Use the fact that all rectangles are parallelograms to show that $\angle AIO$ is congruent to $\angle LOI$ (because $\overline{IO}$ is a transversal), then use Side-Angle-Side.

Statements	Reasons
1. $LRAN$ is a rectangle	1. Given
2. $NA = LR$	2. Opposite sides of a rectangle have the same length.
3. $\overline{NI} \cong \overline{OR}$	3. Given
4. $NI = OR$	4. Definition of congruent
5. $NA - NI = LR - OR$	5. Subtraction Property of Equality
6. $IA = LO$	6. Substitution Principle
7. $\overline{IA} \cong \overline{LO}$	7. Definition of congruent
8. $\overline{NA}$ is parallel to $\overline{LR}$	8. Opposite sides of a rectangle are parallel.
9. $\angle AIO \cong \angle LOI$	9. Alternate interior angles are congruent.
10. $\overline{IO} \cong \overline{IO}$	10. Reflexive Property of Equality
11. $\triangle LOI \cong \triangle AIO$	11. SAS $\cong$ SAS

4. The plan: Determine that $ACDF$ is also a parallelogram because $\overline{FD}$ and $\overline{AC}$ are parallel and congruent. (**Note:** you can also prove that $\triangle AFC$ is congruent to $\triangle DCF$ because of Side-Angle-Side.)

Statements	Reasons
1. $BCEF$ is a parallelogram	1. Given
2. $\overline{FD}$ is parallel to $\overline{AC}$	2. Definition of a parallelogram
3. E is the midpoint of $\overline{FD}$; B is the midpoint of $\overline{AC}$	3. Given
4. $FE = ED$; $AB = BC$	4. Definition of midpoint
5. $FE = BC$	5. Opposite sides of a parallelogram have the same length.
6. $ED = AB$	6. Transitive Property of Equality
7. $FD = AC$	7. Addition Property of Equality
8. $ACDF$ is a parallelogram	8. If two sides of a quadrilateral are congruent and parallel, it is a parallelogram.
9. $\overline{AF} \cong \overline{CD}$	9. Opposite sides of a parallelogram are congruent.

5. The plan: Prove that $\triangle KRD$ is congruent to $\triangle EKR$, then use CPCTC (do you see a pattern here?) to prove that $\triangle ARK$ is isosceles.

Statements	Reasons
1. $FORK$ is an isosceles trapezoid	1. Given
2. $FK = RO$	2. Definition of an isosceles trapezoid
3. $FE = OD$	3. Given
4. $FE + FK = RO + OD$	4. Additive Property of Equality
5. $EK = RD$	5. Segment Addition Postulate
6. $\overline{EK} \cong \overline{RD}$	6. Definition of congruence
7. $\angle EKR \cong \angle KRD$	7. Base angles of an isosceles trapezoid are congruent.
8. $\overline{KR} \cong \overline{KR}$	8. Reflexive Property of Equality
9. $\triangle EKR \cong \triangle KRD$	9. SAS $\cong$ SAS
10. $\angle RKA \cong \angle KRA$	10. CPCTC
11. $\triangle ARK$ is isosceles	11. Definition of an isosceles triangle

6. The plan: Prove that $\triangle SAG$ is congruent to $\triangle OUG$ through Side-Angle-Side, then use CPCTC to prove that $\triangle SAL$ is congruent to $\triangle OUD$. Then use CPCTC again.

Statements	Reasons
1. $\overline{OA}$ and $\overline{US}$ bisect each other	1. Given
2. $\overline{OG} \cong \overline{GA}$; $\overline{SG} \cong \overline{GU}$	2. Definition of angle bisector
3. $\angle SGA \cong \angle UGO$	3. Vertical angles are congruent.
4. $\triangle SAG \cong \triangle OUG$	4. SAS $\cong$ SAS
5. $\overline{SA} \cong \overline{OU}$; $\angle A \cong \angle O$	5. CPCTC
6. $\overline{AL} \cong \overline{OD}$	6. Given
7. $\triangle SAL \cong \triangle OUD$	7. SAS $\cong$ SAS
8. $\overline{SL} \cong \overline{DU}$	8. CPCTC

The proof for part **(b)** is left for you.

7. The plan for **(a)**: Prove that $\triangle GLR$ and $\triangle ELR$ are congruent through Side-Angle-Side, then use the Angle Subtraction Postulate.

Statements	Reasons
1. $\angle G \cong \angle E$	1. Given
2. $\overline{RL}$ bisects $\angle DRN$	2. Given
3. $\angle GRL \cong \angle ERL$	3. Definition of angle bisector
4. $\overline{RL} \cong \overline{RL}$	4. Reflexive Property of Equality
5. $\triangle GLR \cong \triangle ELR$	5. AAS $\cong$ AAS
6. $\angle GLR \cong \angle ELR$	6. CPCTC
7. $\overline{RL} \perp \overline{DN}$	7. Given
8. $\angle DLR$ and $\angle NLR$ are right angles	8. Definition of perpendicular lines
9. $\angle DLR \cong \angle NLR$	9. All right angles are congruent.
10. $\angle 2 \cong \angle 3$	10. Angle Subtraction Postulate

The proofs for parts **(b)** and **(c)** are left for you.

SET 11B, P. 208

1.

Statements	Reasons
1. *CODA* is a square	1. Assumed
2. m∠*ACO* = 90	2. Each angle of a square measures 90°
3. $\overline{CD}$ bisects ∠*ACO*	3. Diagonals of a square bisect the vertex angles.
4. m∠*SCO* = 45	4. Definition of bisector

2.

Statements	Reasons
1. $\overline{YK}$ is parallel to $\overline{JE}$	1. Assumed
2. ∠*Y* ≅ ∠*E*	2. If two parallel lines are cut by a transversal, alternate interior angles are congruent.
3. $\overline{JK}$ bisects $\overline{YE}$	3. Given
4. $\overline{YR} \cong \overline{RE}$	4. Definition of bisector
5. ∠*YRK* ≅ ∠*JRE*	5. Vertical angles are congruent.
6. △*YRK* ≅ △*JRE*	6. ASA ≅ ASA
7. $\overline{JR} \cong \overline{RK}$	7. CPCTC

3.

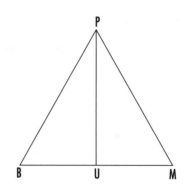

Statements	Reasons
1. $\overline{PU}$ is a median of $\triangle BMP$	1. Assumed
2. $\overline{BU} \cong \overline{UM}$	2. Definition of a median
3. $\triangle BMP$ is equilateral	3. Given
4. $\overline{BP} \cong \overline{MP}$	4. Definition of an equilateral triangle
5. $\overline{PU} \cong \overline{PU}$	5. Reflexive Property of Equality
6. $\triangle BUP \cong \triangle MUP$	6. SSS $\cong$ SSS
7. $\angle BUP \cong \angle MUP$	7. CPCTC
8. $\angle BUP$ and $\angle MUP$ are supplementary	8. Definition of supplementary angles
9. $\angle BUP$ and $\angle MUP$ are right angles	9. If two triangles are both congruent and supplementary then they are right angles.
10. $\overline{PU} \cong \overline{BM}$	10. Definition of perpendicular lines
11. $\overline{PU}$ is an altitude of $\triangle BMP$	11. Definition of an altitude

CHAPTER 12: INTRODUCTION TO TRIGONOMETRY

SET 12A, P. 216

1. **(a)** 0.3584 **(b)** 0.9659
   (c) 3.2709 **(d)** 34.0°
   (e) 40.9° **(f)** 59.0°

2. **(a)** $\tan q = \dfrac{a}{b}$ **(b)** $\cos q = \dfrac{d}{c}$

   (c) $\sin q = \dfrac{d}{c}$

3. (2)

4. **(a)** 8.9 **(b)** 14.3
   (c) 5.5 **(d)** 10

5. **(a)** 58.2° **(b)** 45°
   (c) 33.6° **(d)** 90°
   (e) 66.4°

6. **(a)** $x = 49$ **(b)** $x = 45$
    (c) $x = 60$ **(d)** $x = 18$
    (e) $x = 9$

7.

	0°	30°	45°	60°	90°
sin	0	$\frac{1}{2}$	$\frac{\sqrt{2}}{2}$	$\frac{\sqrt{3}}{2}$	1
cos	1	$\frac{\sqrt{3}}{2}$	$\frac{\sqrt{2}}{2}$	$\frac{1}{2}$	0
tan	0	$\frac{\sqrt{3}}{3}$	1	$\sqrt{3}$	∞

SET 12B, P. 225

1. perimeter = 53.3; area = 182.6
2. perimeter = 25.5; area = 38.7
3. **(a)** m $\angle A = 26.6°$; m $\angle B = 63.4°$
   (b) m $\angle EAB = 68.0°$
   (c) m $\angle QPO = 100.3°$
4. perimeter = 39.0; area = 82.8
5. **(a)** $MO = 46.2$ **(b)** $MP = 27.5$ **(c)** perimeter = 110.2
6. m $\angle GLA = 25.0°$; perimeter = 66.2
7. 92.9 feet
8. **(a)** 13.1 feet   **(b)** 117.9 square feet
9. 73.0 feet
10. 1,690.4 feet

CHAPTER 13: LOCUS AND CONSTRUCTIONS

SET 13A, P. 242

1. (a)

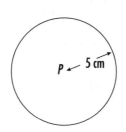

(b)

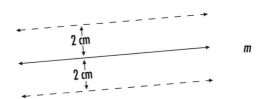

(c)

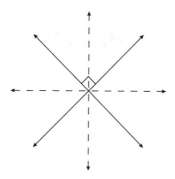

(d)

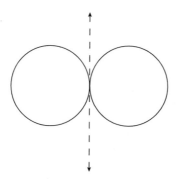

2. (a) $x = 1$

(b) $y = -1$

(c) $y = -3x + 1$

(d) $(x - 2)^2 + (y + 5)^2 = 16$

3. (a) $y = 2x$

(b) $y = \dfrac{1}{2}x + 3$

(c) $x = 1$

(d) $x = 7$, $x = -1$

(e) $y = x$

(f) $x^2 + y^2 = 16$

4. (a) 4

(b) 4

(c) 0

(d) 2

(e) 1

(f) 4

(g) 2

5. (a) 2

(b) 1

(c) 0

6. 2

7. 1

8. (−5, −3)

9. infinite (they're the same line)

10. 6

CHAPTER 14: PERMUTATIONS AND COMBINATIONS

SET 14A, P. 250

1. (a) 24

(b) 720

(c) 336

(d) 5,040

(e) 151,200

(f) 5!, or 120

(g) 1

2. (a) 24

(b) 120

(c) 5,040

(d) 2,520

(e) 1,814,400

(f) 120

(g) 1,260

(h) 3,360

(i) 15,120

(j) 34,650

3. (a) 5,040

(b) 720

(c) 720

(d) 240

(e) 144

(f) 144

(g) 120

(h) 24

4. **(a)** 3,125 **(b)** 120

   (c) 72 **(d)** 24

   (e) 72

5. **(a)** $x = 5$ **(b)** $x = 3$
   (c) $x = 4$ **(d)** $x = 5$

6. 48

7. **(a)** 1,260 **(b)** 35

8. 28,800

9. **(a)** 86,400
   (b) 241,920
   (c) 518,400

10. $n(n - 1)$

SET 14B, P. 258

1. **(a)** 6 **(b)** 20
   (c) 56 **(d)** 56
   (e) 1 **(f)** 9
   (g) 1 **(h)** n

2. **(a)** $x = 7$ **(b)** $x = 8$

   (c) $x = 3$ **(d)** $x = 8$

   (e) $x = 5$ **(f)** $x = 10$

   (g) $x = n - 1$

3. (b)

4. **(a)** 35 **(b)** 15
   (c) 20 **(d)** 10
   (e) 6 **(f)** 5
   (g) 15

5. **(a)** 21 **(b)** 126
   (c) 462 **(d)** 56
   (e) 490 **(f)** 5,940
   (g) 3,080 **(h)** 22,176

6. 596

7. $x = 11$

CHAPTER 15: PROBABILITY

SET 15A, P. 270

1. (a) $\dfrac{6}{72}$ (b) $\dfrac{2}{72}$

   (c) $\dfrac{20}{72}$ (d) $\dfrac{20}{72}$

2. $\dfrac{1}{2}$

3. (a) $\dfrac{5}{36}$ (b) $\dfrac{1}{36}$

   (c) 0   (d) 1

   (e) $\dfrac{15}{36}$ (f) $\dfrac{10}{36}$

   (g) $\dfrac{23}{36}$

4. (a) 220

   (b) $\dfrac{15}{220}$

   (c) $\dfrac{24}{220}$

5. (a) $\dfrac{35}{27,405}$ (b) $\dfrac{28}{27,405}$

   (c) $\dfrac{9,360}{27,405}$ (d) $\dfrac{2,800}{27,405}$

6. 20

7. (a) $\dfrac{1}{4}$

   (b) $\dfrac{1}{16}$

   (c) $\dfrac{1}{64}$

8. (a) $\dfrac{1}{2}$ (b) $\dfrac{3}{17}$

   (c) $\dfrac{1}{221}$ (d) $\dfrac{1}{132,600}$

PRACTICE TEST ONE

Part I

Answer 30 questions from this part. Each correct answer will receive 2 credits. No partial credit will be allowed. Write your answers in the spaces provided on the separate answer sheet. Where applicable, answers may be left in terms of π or in radical form.

1 Using the accompanying table, solve for x if $x \circ b = a$.

$\odot$	a	b	c
a	a	b	c
b	b	a	c
c	c	c	b

2 In the accompanying table, $\triangle ABC$ is similar to $\triangle A'B'C'$, $AB=14.4$, $BC = 8$, $CA = 12$, $A'B' = x$, and $B'C' = 4$. Find the value of x.

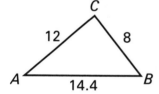 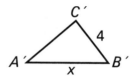

3 In the accompanying diagram, parallel lines $\overleftrightarrow{AB}$ and are intersected by $\overleftrightarrow{GH}$ at E and F, respectively. If m $\angle BEF$ = $5x - 10$ and m $\angle CFE = 4x + 20$, find x.

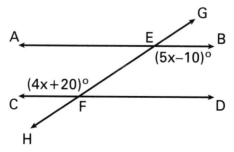

4 If tan A = 0.5400, find the measure of $\angle A$ to the *nearest degree*.

5 Find the length of a side of a square if two consecutive vertices have coordinates $(-2,6)$ and $(6,6)$.

6 In the accompanying diagram of isosceles triangle ABC, $CA = CB$ and $\angle CBD$ is an exterior angle formed by extending $\overline{AB}$ to point D. If m $\angle CBD$ = 130, find m $\angle C$.

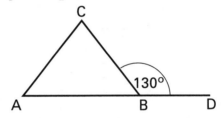

7 If $\overleftrightarrow{AB}$ intersect $\overleftrightarrow{CD}$ at E, m $\angle AEC$ = 3x, and m $\angle AED$ = 5x – 60, find the value of x.

8 Point (x,y) is the image of $(2,4)$ after a reflection in point $(5,6)$. In which quadrant does (x,y) lie?

9 In the accompanying diagram, $ABCD$ is a parallelogram, $\overline{EC} \perp \overline{DC}$, $\angle B \cong E$, and m $\angle A$ = 100. Find m $\angle CDE$.

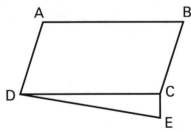

10 The lengths of the sides of $\triangle DEF$ are 6, 8, and 10. Find the perimeter of the triangle formed by connecting the midpoints of the sides of $\triangle DEF$.

11 The coordinates of the midpoint of line segment $\overline{AB}$ are $(1,2)$. If the coordinates of point A are $(1,0)$, find the coordinates of point B.

12 In $\triangle PQR$, $\angle Q \cong \angle R$. If $PQ = 10x - 14$, $PR = 2x + 50$, and $RQ = 4x - 30$, find the value of x.

13 What is the image of $(-2,4)$ after a reflection in the x-axis?

14 In rectangle $ABCD$, $\overline{AC}$ and $\overline{BD}$ are diagonals. If m $\angle 1$ = 55, find m $\angle ABD$.

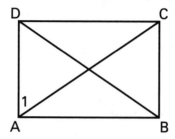

15 What is the slope of the line that passes through points $(-1,5)$ and $(2,3)$?

16 The coordinates of the turning point of the graph of the equation $y = x^2 - 2x - 8$ are $(1,k)$. What is the value of k?

Directions (17-35): For *each* question chosen, write the *numeral* preceding the word or expression that best completes the statement or answers the question.

17 Which equation represents the line that has a slope of $\frac{1}{2}$ and contains the point $(0,3)$?

(1) $y = x\frac{1}{3} + \frac{1}{2}$ (3) $y = \frac{3}{2}x$

(2) $y = 3x + \frac{1}{2}$ (4) $y = \frac{1}{2}x + 3$

18 If the measures of the angles in a triangle are in the ratio 3:4:5, the measure of an exterior angle of the triangle can *not* be

(1) 165° (3) 120°
(2) 135° (4) 105°

19 According to De Morgan's laws, which statement is logically equivalent to $\sim(p \wedge q)$?

(1) $\sim(p \vee \sim q)$ (3) $\sim(p \wedge q)$
(2) $\sim(p \vee q)$ (4) $\sim(p \wedge \sim q)$

20 One angle of the triangle measures 30°. If the measures of the other two angles are in the ratio 3:7, the measure of the largest angle of the triangle is

(1) 15° (3) 126°
(2) 105° (4) 147°

21 In the accompanying diagram, $ABCD$ is a rectangle, E is a point on $\overline{CD}$, m $\angle DAE = 30$, and m $\angle CBE = 20$.

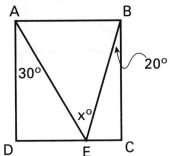

What is m $\angle x$?

(1) 25   **(3)** 60

(2) 50   **(4)** 70

22 The graph of the equation $y = ax^2 + bx + c$, a $\neq$ 0, forms

(1) a circle   **(3)** a straight line

(2) a parabola   **(4)** an ellipse

23 Which set of numbers can represent the lengths of the sides of a triangle?

(1) {4,4,8}   **(3)** {3,5,7}

(2) {3,9,14}   **(4)** {1,2,3}

24 Which is an equation of the line that passes through point (3,5) and is parallel to the x-axis?

(1) $x = 3$ **(3)** $y = 5$

(2) $x = 5$ **(4)** $y = 3$

25 What are the factors of $y^3 - 4y$?

(1) $y(y - 2)(y - 2)$ **(3)** $y(y^2 + 1)(y - 4)$

(2) $y(y + 4)(y - 4)$ **(4)** $y(y + 2)(y - 2)$

26 In the accompanying diagram of right triangle ABC, $AB = 4$ and $BC = 7$.

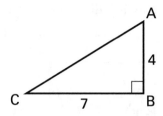

What is the length of $\overline{AC}$ to the *nearest hundredth*?

(1) 5.74   (3) 8.06

(2) 5.75   (4) 8.08

27 Which is the converse of the statement "If today is President's Day, then there is no school"?

(1) If there is school, then today is not President's Day.

(2) If there is no school, then today is President's Day.

(3) If today is President's Day, then there is school.

(4) If today is not President's Day, then there is school.

28 How many different eight-letter permutations can be formed from the letters in the word "PARALLEL"?

(1) $\dfrac{8!}{3! \, 2!}$ (3) 360

(2) $8!$ (4) $\dfrac{8!}{3!}$

29 Which equation describes the locus of points equidistant from $A(-3,2)$ and $B(-3,8)$?

(1) $x = -3$ (3) $x = 5$

(2) $y = -3$ (4) $y = 5$

30 A translation maps $A(1,2)$ onto $A'(-1,3)$. What are the coordinates of the image of the origin under the same translation?

(1) $(0,0)$ (3) $(-2,1)$

(2) $(2,-1)$ (4) $(-1,2)$

31 The solution set of the equation $x^2 + 5x = 0$ is

(1) {0} (3) {−5}
(2) {5} (4) {0,−5}

32 In the accompanying diagram of parallelogram $MATH$, $m \angle T = 100$ and $\overline{SH}$ bisects $\angle MHT$.

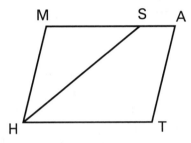

What is $m \angle HSA$?

(1) 80 (3) 120
(2) 100 (4) 140

33 What are the roots of the equation $x^2 + 9x + 12 = 0$?

(1) $\dfrac{-9 \pm \sqrt{33}}{2}$ (3) $\dfrac{-9 \pm \sqrt{129}}{2}$

(2) $\dfrac{9 \pm \sqrt{33}}{2}$ (4) $\dfrac{9 \pm \sqrt{129}}{2}$

34 The vertices of trapezoid $ABCD$ are $A(-3,0)$, $B(-3,4)$, $C(2,4)$, and $D(4,0)$. What is the area of trapezoid $ABCD$?

(1) 6 (3) 28
(2) 24 (4) 48

35 The accompanying diagram shows how $\triangle A'B'C'$ is constructed similar to $\triangle ABC$.

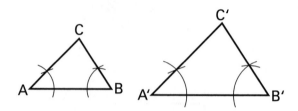

Which statement proves the construction?

(1) If two triangles are congruent, they are similar.

(2) If two triangles are similar, the angles of one triangle are congruent to the corresponding angles of the other triangle.

(3) Two triangles are similar if two angles of one triangle are congruent to two angles of the other triangle.

(4) The corresponding sides of two similar triangles are proportional.

Part II

Answer *three* questions from this part. Clearly indicate the necessary steps, including appropriate formula substitutions, diagrams, graphs, charts, etc. Calculations that may be obtained by mental arithmetic or the calculator do not need to be shown.

36 Answer both (a) and (b) for all values of y for which these expressions are defined.

  (a) Express as a single fraction in lowest terms:

$$\frac{y - 4}{2y} + \frac{3y - 5}{5y}$$

  (b) Simplify:

$$\frac{y^2 - 7y + 10}{5y - y^2} \div \frac{y^2 - 4}{25y^3}$$

37 In the accompanying diagram of isosceles triangle KLC, $\overline{LK} \cong \overline{LC}$, m $\angle K = 53$, altiutde $\overline{CA}$ is drawn to leg $\overline{LK}$, and $LA = 3$. Find the perimeter of $\triangle KLC$ to the *nearest integer*.

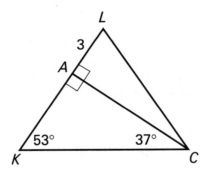

38 *(a)* On graph paper, draw the graph of the equation $y = -x^2 + 6x - 8$ for all values of x in the interval $0 \le x \le 6$.

(b) What is the maximum value of y in the equation $y = -x^2 + 6x - 8$?

(c) Write an equation of the line that passes through the turning point and is parallel to the x-axis.

39 At a video rental store, Elyssa has only enough money to rent three videos. She has chosen four comedies, six dramas, and one mystery movie to consider.

(a) How many different selections of three videos may she rent from the movies she has chosen?

(b) How many selections of three videos will consist of one comedy and two dramas?

(c) What is the probability that a selection of three videos will consist of one of each type of video?

(d) Elyssa decides to rent one comedy, one drama, and one mystery movie. In how many different orders may she view these videos?

40 In the accompanying diagram of right triangle ABC, altitude is drawn to hypotenuse $\overline{BD}$, $AC = 20$, $AD <$ DC, and $BD = 6$.

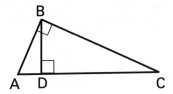

(*a*) If $AD = x$, express DC in terms of x.

(*b*) Solve for x.

(*c*) Find AB in simplest radical form.

Part III

Answer *one* question from this part. Clearly indicate the necessary steps, including appropriate formula substitutions, diagrams, graphs, charts, etc. Calculations that may be obtained by   mental arithmetic or the calculator do not need to be shown.

41 Given: $\triangle ABC$; $\overline{BD}$ is both the median and the altitude to $\overline{AC}$.

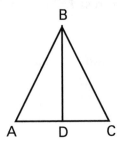

Prove: $\overline{BA} \cong \overline{BC}$

42 Quadrilateral $ABCD$ has vertices $A(-6,3)$, $B(-3,6)$, $C(9,6)$, and $D(-5,-8)$. Prove that quadrilateral $ABCD$ is

(a) a trapezoid

(b) *not* an isosceles trapezoid

ANSWER KEY

Part I

1. b

2. 7.2

3. 30

4. 28

5. 8

6. 80

7. 30

8. Quadrant I

9. 10

10. 12

11. (1,4)

12. 8

13. (−2,−4)

14. 35

15. $-\dfrac{2}{3}$

16. −9

17. (4)

18. (1)

19. (1)

20. (2)

21. (2)

22. (2)

23. (3)

24. (3)

25. (4)

26. (3)

27. (2)

28. (1)

29. (4)

30. (3)

31. (4)

32. (4)

33. (1)

34. (2)

35. construction

PRACTICE TEST TWO

Part I

Answer 30 questions from this part. Each correct answer will receive 2 credits. No partial credit will be allowed. Write your answers in the spaces provided on the separate answer sheet. Where applicable, answers may be left in terms of π or in radical form.

1 Using the table below, compute $(1 \star 5) \star (2 \star 7)$.

$\star$	1	2	5	7
1	2	7	1	5
2	7	5	2	1
5	1	2	5	7
7	5	1	7	2

2 In the accompanying diagram, line l is parallel to line k, line $m \perp$ line k, and m $\angle x$ = m $\angle y$. Find m $\angle x$.

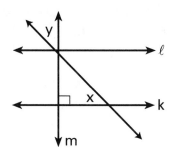

3 If ♥ is a binary operation defined as $a ♥ b = \sqrt{a^2 + b^2}$, find the value of $12 ♥ 5$.

4 In the accompanying diagram of similar triangles ABE and ACD, $\overline{ABC}$, $\overline{AED}$, $AB = 6$, $BC = 3$, and $ED = 4$. Find the length of $\overline{AE}$.

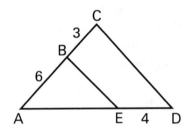

5 How many different 5-letter arrangements can be formed from the letters in the word "DANNY"?

6 Evaluate: $\dfrac{9!}{3!\,5!}$

7 In the accompanying diagram of $\triangle ABC$, $\overline{AB}$ is extended to E and D, exterior angle CBD measures 130°, and m $\angle C = 75$. Find m $\angle CAE$.

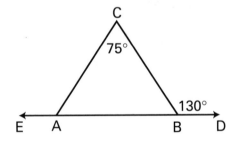

8 In right triangle ABC, $\angle C$ is a right triangle and m $\angle B$ = 60. What is the ratio of m $\angle A$ to m $\angle B$?

9 In $\triangle ABC$, m $\angle A = 3x + 40$, m $\angle B = 8x + 35$, and m $\angle C = 10x$. Which is the longest side of the triangle?

10 A bookshelf contains seven math textbooks and three science textbooks. If two textbooks are drawn at random without replacement, what is the probability both books are science textbooks?

11 Express the product in lowest terms:

$$\frac{x^2 - x - 6}{3x - 9} \cdot \frac{2}{x + 2}$$

12 In rhombus $ABCD$, the measure of $\angle A$ is 30°, more than twice the measure of $\angle B$. Find m $\angle B$.

13 The endpoints of the diameter of a circle are $(-6,2)$ and $(10,-2)$. What·are the coordinates of the center of the circle?

14 Find the area of a triangle whose vertices are $(1,2)$, $(8,2)$, and $(1,6)$.

15 Find the distance between points $(-1,1)$ and $(2,-5)$.

16 In the accompanying diagram, the bisectors of $\angle A$ and $\angle B$ in acute triangle ABC meet at D, and m $\angle ADB$ = 130. Find m $\angle C$.

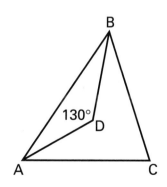

17 Point P is on line m. What is the total number of points 3 centimeters from line m and 5 centimeters from point P?

18 The diagonals of a rhombus are 8 and 10. Find the measure of a side of the rhombus to the *nearest tenth*.

Directions (19-34): For *each* question chosen, write the *numeral* preceding the word or expression that best completes the statement or answers the question.

19 In isosceles triangle ABC, $\overline{AB} \cong \overline{BC}$, point D lies on $\overline{AC}$, and $\overline{BD}$ is drawn. Which inequality is true?

20 If the statements m, $m \to p$, and $r \to \sim p$ are true, which statement must also be true?
(1) $\sim r$ (3) $r \wedge \sim p$
(2) $\sim p$ (4) $\sim p \vee \sim m$

21 If a point in Quadrant IV is reflected in the y-axis, its image will lie in Quadrant
(1) I   (3) III
(2) II   (4) IV

22 In right triangle ABC, m $\angle C$ = 90, m $\angle A$ = 63, and AB = 10. If BC is represented by a, then which equation can be used to find a?

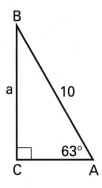

(1) $\sin 63° = \dfrac{a}{10}$ **(3)** $\tan 63° = \dfrac{a}{10}$

(2) $a = 10 \cos 63°$ **(4)** $a = \tan 27°$

23 If point $R'(6,3)$ is the image of point $R(2,1)$ under a dilation with respect to the origin, what is the constant of the dilation?

(1) 1   **(3)** 3

(2) 2   **(4)** 6

24 What is an equation of a line that passes through the point (0,3) and is perpendicular to the line whose equation is $y = 2x - 1$?

(1) $y = -2x + 3$ **(3)** $y = -\dfrac{1}{2}x + 3$

(2) $y = 2x + 3$ **(4)** $y = \dfrac{1}{2}x + 3$

25 What is an equation of the function shown in the accompanying diagram?

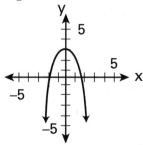

(1) $y = x^2 + 3$ (3) $y = -x^2 - 3$
(2) $y = -x^2 + 3$ (4) $y = (x^2 - 3)^2$

26 What is an equation of the line that is parallel to the y-axis and passes through the point $(2,4)$?

(1) $x = 2$ (3) $x = 4$
(2) $y = 2$ (4) $y = 4$

27 In the accompanying diagram, the altitude to the hypotenuse of right triangle ABC is 8.

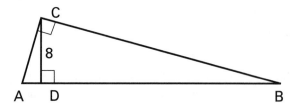

The altitude divides the hypotenuse into segments whose measures may be

(1) 8 and 12   (3) 6 and 10
(2) 3 and 24   (4) 2 and 32

28 If the coordinates of the center of a circle are $(-3,1)$ and the radius is 4, what is an equation of the circle?

(1) $(x - 3)^2 + (y + 1)^2 = 4$
(2) $(x + 3)^2 + (y - 1)^2 = 16$
(3) $(x + 3)^2 + (y - 1)^2 = 4$
(4) $(x - 3)^2 + (y + 1)^2 = 16$

29 Which expression is a solution for the equation $2x^2 - x = 7$?

(1) $\dfrac{-1 \pm \sqrt{57}}{2}$

(3) $\dfrac{-1 \pm \sqrt{57}}{4}$

(2) $\dfrac{1 \pm \sqrt{57}}{2}$

(4) $\dfrac{1 \pm \sqrt{57}}{4}$

30 If the complement of $\angle A$ is greater than the supplement of $\angle B$, which statement *must* be true?

(1) $m\angle A + m\angle B = 180$

(2) $m\angle A + m\angle B = 90$

(3) $m\angle A < m\angle B$

(4) $m\angle A > m\angle B$

31 How many different four-person committees can be formed from a group of six boys and four girls?

(1) $\dfrac{10!}{4!}$

(3) $_6C_2 \cdot {}_4C_2$

(2) $_{10}P_4$

(4) $_{10}C_4$

32 Which equation represents the axis of symmetry of the graph of the eqaution $y = x^2 - 4x - 12$?

(1) $y = 4$

(3) $y = -2$

(2) $x = 2$

(4) $x = -4$

33 What is $\dfrac{1}{x} + \dfrac{1}{1-x}$, $x \neq 1, 0$, expressed as a single fraction?

(1) $\dfrac{1}{x(1-x)}$

(3) $\dfrac{2}{-x}$

(2) $\dfrac{-1}{x(x+1)}$

(4) $\dfrac{1}{x(x-1)}$

34 In the accompanying diagram, $\overline{RL} \perp \overline{LP}$, $\overline{LR} \perp \overline{RT}$, and M is the midpoint of $\overline{TP}$.

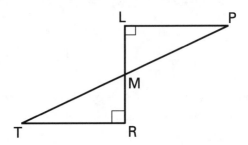

Which method could be used to prove $\triangle TMR \cong \triangle PML$?

(1) SAS $\cong$ SAS   **(3)** HL $\cong$ HL

(2) AAS $\cong$ AAS   **(4)** SSS $\cong$ SSS

Directions (35): Leave all construction lines on the answer sheet.

35 On the answer sheet, construct an equilateral triangle in which $\overline{AB}$ is one of the sides.

Part Two

Answer *three* questions from this part. Clearly indicate the necessary steps, including appropriate formula substitutions, diagrams, graphs, charts, etc. Calculations that may be obtained by mental arithmetic or the calculator do not need to be shown.

36 **(a)** On graph paper, draw the graph of the equation $y = x^2 - 8x + 2$, including all values of x in the interval $0 \leq x \leq 8$.

(b) Find the roots of the equation $x^2 - 8x + 2 = 0$ to the *nearest hundredth*. [*Only an algebraic solution will be accepted.*]

37 The coordinates of the endpoints of $\overline{AB}$ a re $A(-2,4)$ and $B(4,1)$.

(a) On a set of axes, graph $\overline{AB}$.

(b) On the same set of axes, graph and state the coordinates of

(1) $\overline{A'B'}$, the image of $\overline{AB}$ after a reflection in the x-axis

(2) $\overline{A''B''}$, the image of $\overline{A'B'}$ after a translation that shifts (x,y) to $(x + 2,y)$

(c) Using coordinate geometry, determine if $\overline{A'B'} \cong \overline{A''B''}$. Justify your answer.

38 Answer both *(a)* and *(b)* for all values for which these expressions are defined.

(a) Solve for x: $-\dfrac{2}{5} + \dfrac{x + 4}{x} = 1$

(b) Express the difference in simplest form:

$$\frac{3y}{y^2 - 4} - \frac{2}{y + 2}$$

39 Solve the following system of equations algebraically and check:

$$y = 2x^2 - 4x - 5$$
$$2x + y + 1 = 0$$

40 In the accompanying diagram of $\triangle ABC$, altitude $AD = 13$, $\overline{AB} \cong \overline{AC}$, and m $\angle BAC = 70$.

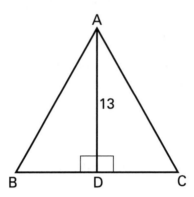

(a) Find BC to the *nearest tenth*.

(b) Using the answer from part *(a)*, find, to the *nearest tenth*, the
   (1) area of $\triangle ABC$
   (2) perimeter of $\triangle ABC$

Part III

Answer *one* question from this part. Clearly indicate the necessary steps, including appropriate formula substitutions, diagrams, graphs, charts, etc. Calculations that may be obtained by mental arithmetic or the calculator do not need to be shown.

41 Given: If Sue goes out on Friday night and not on Saturday night, then she does not study.

If Sue does not fail mathematics, then she studies.

Sue does not fail mathematics.

If Sue does not go out on friday night, then she watches a movie.

Sue does not watch a movie.

Let A represent: "Sue fails mathematics."
Let B represent: "Sue studies."
Let C represent: "Sue watches a movie."
Let D represent: "Sue goes out on Friday night."
Let E represent: "Sue goes out on Saturday night."

Prove: Sue goes out on Saturday night.

42 Given:parallelogram $ABCD$, $\overline{DFC}$, $\overline{AEB}$, $\overline{ED}$ bisects $\angle ADC$, and $\overline{FB}$ bisects $\angle ABC$.

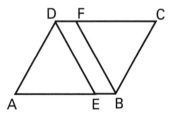

Prove: $\overline{EB} \cong \overline{DF}$

ANSWER KEY

Part I

1. 2

2. 45

3. 13

4. 8

5. 60

6. 504

7. 125

8. $\dfrac{1}{2}$

9. $\overline{AC}$

10. $\dfrac{1}{15}$

11. $\dfrac{2}{3}$

12. 50

13. (2,0)

14. 14

15. 5

16. 80

17. 4

18. 6.4

19. (4)

20. (1)

21. (3)

22. (1)

23. (3)

24. (3)

25. (2)

26. (1)

27. (4)

28. (2)

29. (4)

30. (3)

31. (4)

32. (2)

33. (1)

34. (2)

35. construction

Glossary

If a term you're looking for doesn't appear here, it may be defined in the Stuff You Should Know chapter. Otherwise, consult your math textbook.

A

abscissa   Another name for the *x*-coordinate of a point.

acute angle   An angle that measures less than 90°.

acute triangle   A triangle with three acute angles.

additive inverse   The opposite value of a number (which, when added to that number, yields zero). For example, the additive inverse of *a* is –*a*, because *a* + (–*a*) = 0.

alternate interior angles   Two interior angles that are on opposite sides of a transversal that intersects with two parallel lines.

altitude   A segment drawn from a vertex of a polygon (usually a triangle) that is perpendicular to the opposite side of that polygon.

associative property   Mathematical rule that states: $a + (b + c) = (a + b) + c$ and $a \times (b \times c) = (a \times b) \times c$.

axis of symmetry   The line that contains the vertex of a parabola and cuts the parabola exactly in half.

B

backsolving   The practice of plugging the answers provided on a multiple-choice test into the question to see which one works.

base angle   An angle that includes the base of a polygon (usually a triangle).

bisect   To cut exactly in half.

C

collinear   Located in the same line.

combinations   The number of ways you can choose a specific number of items in no particular order from a group.

commutative property   Mathematical rule that states: $a + b = b + a$ and $a \times b = b \times a$.

complementary angles Two angles whose sum is 90°.

congruent The same size and shape (symbolized by ≅).

corresponding angles Two angles that appear in the same position when two lines are cut by a transversal.

D

denominator The bottom number of a fraction.

diameter The greatest distance within the circumference of a circle.

dilation The process under which the coordinates of each point in a figure are multiplied by a constant.

distributive property Mathematical property that states: $a(b + c) = ab + ac$.

E

equidistant The same distance away from a point or series of points.

equilateral triangle A triangle with three congruent sides and three angles that measure 60°.

exterior angle An angle that is formed when a side of a triangle is extended beyond the vertex of the triangle and is supplementary to its adjacent interior angle. (It also equals the sum of the triangle's other two non-adjacent interior angles.)

F

FOIL An acronym for First, Outer, Inner, Last, a process by which you multiply algebraic terms.

H

hypotenuse The longest side of a right triangle.

I

identity element An element within an operation.

image The result after a point or series of points undergoes a transformation.

intercept The point at which a graph intersects one of the coordinate axes.

internal angle   An angle that lies in the interior of a triangle.

isosceles trapezoid   A trapezoid with two non-parallel sides that are congruent.

isosceles triangle   A triangle with at least two congruent sides.

L

leg   One of the two perpendicular sides of a right triangle.

locus   A set of points.

M

median of a triangle   A segment drawn from the vertex of a triangle to the midpoint of the opposite side of that triangle.

midpoint   The point equidistant from the endpoints of a line segment.

multiplicative inverse   The reciprocal of a number that is not equal to zero. For example, $\frac{1}{a}$ is the multiplicative inverse of a, because $a \times \frac{1}{a} = 1$.

N

negation   Asserting that a statement is false (A becomes $\sim A$).

negative reciprocals   Two numbers whose product is –1.

numerator   The top number in a fraction.

O

obtuse angle   An angle that measures greater than 90°.

obtuse triangle   A triangle that contains an obtuse angle.

operation   A process, such as addition or multiplication, by which numbers or variables are combined.

ordered pair   Two numbers written in a specific order (usually involving the coordinates of a point).

ordinate   Another name for the y-coordinate of a point.

origin   The point (0, 0) on the coordinate axes.

P

parallel lines   Lines within the same plane that have the same slope and will never intersect

parallelogram   A quadrilateral with two pairs of opposite sides that are parallel.

perfect square   A number or term with a square root that is rational.

perimeter   The sum of the lengths of all the sides of a polygon.

permutations   The number of ways in which a certain number of items can be displayed or arranged.

perpendicular lines   Two lines that intersect in a right angle.

plugging in   The process of replacing variables with numbers to turn an algebraic problem into an arithmetic problem.

process of elimination (POE)   Arriving at the right answer by eliminating all the other answer choices that you know are incorrect.

proportion   An equation you set up when the relationship between two pairs of numbers is the same.

Q

quadrilateral   A polygon with four sides.

R

radical sign   Another word for the root of a number (in this book, it means the square root and is denoted by the $\sqrt{\ }$ sign).

radicand   The number that appears beneath the radical sign.

radius   The distance from the center of a circle to the circumference of that circle.

rational number   A number that can be expressed as the quotient of two integers.

reflection   A transformation in which a point is "reflected" in a line, usually the x- or y-axis.

regular polygon   A polygon in which the sides and angles are congruent.

rhombus   A quadrilateral with four congruent sides.

right angle   An angle formed by two perpendicular lines that measures 90°.

right triangle   A triangle that contains a right angle.

root   A number that makes an equation true. For example, 2 and –2 are the roots of the equation $x^2 - 4 = 0$.

Rule of 180   The sum of the three angles in a triangle is 180°.

S

scalene triangle   A triangle with three unequal sides.

segment   A finite linear connection between two points.

similar triangles   Two triangles that have the same shape but not the same size (corresponding angles are congruent and corresponding sides are proportional).

SOHCAHTOA   Abbreviation for the relationships of the three main trigonometric ratios.

supplementary angles   Two angles whose sum is 180°.

system of equations   Two or more equations involving the same variables.

T

T-chart   A list of coordinates of a particular graph.

translation   A transformation in which you add to or subtract from the coordinates of a point, thus mapping it onto its image, which is a specific distance away.

transversal   A line that cuts through two parallel lines, thus creating several pairs of congruent angles.

trapezoid   A quadrilateral with exactly two parallel sides.

turning point   The point at which the graph of a parabola changes direction (also known as a vertex).

V

vertex   (1) The point at which the graph of a parabola changes direction (also known as the turning point); (2) the point of a polygon; (3) the center point of an angle.

vertex angle   The angle in an isosceles triangle that is not equal to either of the other two angles.

vertical angles   Two opposite angles formed by two intersecting angles.

Index

I

identity element 22
indirect proofs 206
infinite 15
inverse 4, 22
inverse trigonometry 215
irrational numbers 16

L

Law of Conjunctive Simplification 6
Law of Contrapositive Inference 5
Law of Detachment 6
Law of Disjunctive Inference 5
Law of the Syllogism 6
legs 211
like terms 30
line 120
linear equation 47

M

measure of each interior angle 189
median 139
midpoint 103, 123
midpoint formula 113
midpoint of a line segment 234
Modus Ponens 6
monomial 29
multiplication property of equality 121

N

nCr 252
negation 2
negative exponent 30
nPr 249

O

operation 16
operations table 17
opposite 212
"or" Statements 266

P

Q

R

S

ABOUT THE AUTHOR

Doug French graduated from the University of Virginia and has been working as a teacher, writer, editor, and course developer with The Princeton Review since 1991. He has taught classes for the PSAT, SAT, LSAT, GMAT, and GRE in the U.S., Europe, and Asia, and he has tutored math students in everything from fifth-grade arithmetic to BC calculus.

Doug also works as a freelance writer, draws cartoons, and does voice-overs. (He sounds a lot like that MovieFone guy.) His mom, however, has more talent in her little finger than he has in his little finger.

NOTES

NOTES

NOTES

NOTES

NOTES

NOTES

NOTES

NOTES

NOTES

NOTES

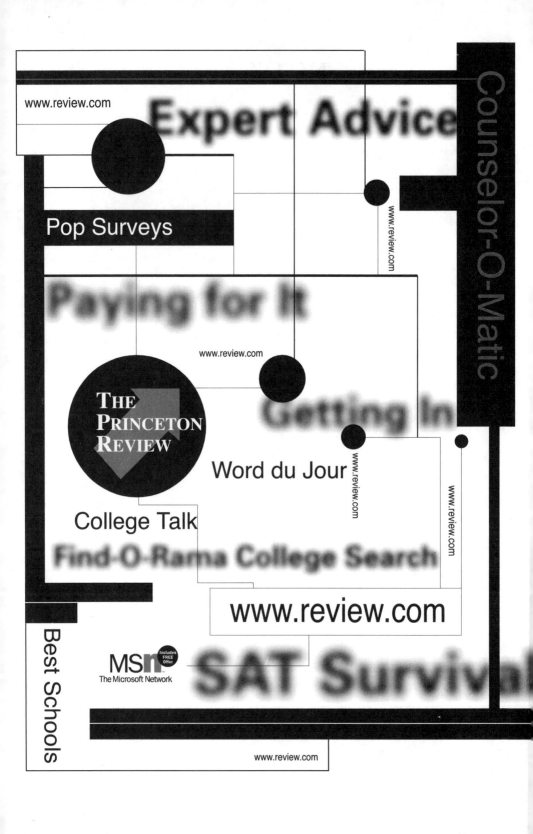

Free!

Did you know that The Microsoft Network gives you one free month?

Call us at 1-800-FREE MSN. We'll send you a free CD to get you going.

Then, you can explore the World Wide Web for one month, free. Exchange e-mail with your family and friends. Play games, book airline tickets, handle finances, go car shopping, explore old hobbies and discover new ones. There's one big, useful online world out there. And for one month, it's a free world.

Call **1-800-FREE MSN,** Dept. 3197, for offer details or visit us at **www.msn.com**. Some restrictions apply.

Microsoft Where do you want to go today?®   The Microsoft Network

©1997 Microsoft Corporation. All rights reserved. Microsoft, MSN, and Where do you want to go today? are either registered trademarks or trademarks of Microsoft Corporation in the United States and/or other countries.

FIND US...

International

Hong Kong
4/F. Sun Hung Kai Centre
30 Harbour Road, Wan Chai,
Hong Kong
Tel: (011)85-2-517-3016

Japan
Fuji Building 40, 15-14
Sakuragaokacho, Shibuya Ku,
Tokyo 150, Japan
Tel: (011)81-3-3463-1343

Korea
Tae Young Bldg, 944-24,
Daechi- Dong, Kangnam-Ku
The Princeton Review- ANC
Seoul, Korea 135-280,
South Korea
Tel: (011)82-2-554-7763

Mexico City
PR Mex S De RL De Cv
Guanajuato 228 Col. Roma
06700 Mexico D.F., Mexico
Tel: 525-564-9468

Montreal
666 Sherbrooke St.
West, Suite 202
Montreal, QC H3A 1E7 Canada
Tel: (514) 499-0870

Pakistan
1 Bawa Park - 90 Upper Mall
Lahore, Pakistan
Tel: (011)92-42-571-2315

Spain
Pza. Castilla, 3 - 5° A, 28046
Madrid, Spain
Tel: (011)341-323-4212

Taiwan
155 Chung Hsiao East Road
Section 4 - 4th Floor,
Taipei R.O.C., Taiwan
Tel: (011)886-2-751-1243

Thailand
Building One, 99 Wireless Road
Bangkok, Thailand 10330
Tel: (662) 256-7080

Toronto
1240 Bay Street, Suite 300
Toronto M5R 2A7 Canada
Tel: (800) 495-7737
Tel: (716) 839-4391

Vancouver
4212 University Way NE,
Suite 204
Seattle, WA 98105
Tel: (206) 548-1100

National (U.S.)

We have over 60 offices around the U.S. and
run courses in over 400 sites. For courses and locations
within the U.S. call 1 (800) 2/Review and you will be
routed to the nearest office.